THE FOUR
AGREEMENTS

A Practical Guide to Personal Freedom

A

Toltec

THE FOUR
AGREEMENTS

Wisdom

Book

DON MIGUEL RUIZ

WITH JANET MILLS

AMBER-ALLEN PUBLISHING
SAN RAFAEL, CALIFORNIA

Published by Amber-Allen Publishing, Inc.
P. O. Box 6657
San Rafael, California 94903

Cover Illustration: Nicholas Wilton
Cover Design: Michele Wetherbee
Author Photo: Ellen Denuto

Note: The term "black magic" is not meant to convey racial connotation; it is merely used to describe the use of magic for adverse or harmful purposes.

Library of Congress Cataloging-in-Publication Data
Ruiz, Miguel, 1952– The four agreements : a practical guide to personal freedom / Miguel Ruiz.   p. cm. — (A Toltec wisdom book) (alk. paper)
I. Conduct of life.   2. Toltec philosophy — Miscellanea. I. Title.
II. Series: Ruiz, Miguel, 1952 –   Toltec wisdom book.
BJ1581. 2. R85 1997   299'.792 — dc21   97-18256 CIP

ISBN 978-1-878424-31-0
Printed in China
Distributed by Hay House, Inc.

18 17 16 15 14 13 12 11 10

To the *Circle of Fire;*
those who have gone before,
those who are present,
and those who have yet to come.

Contents

Acknowledgments

I WOULD LIKE TO HUMBLY ACKNOWLEDGE MY mother Sarita, who taught me unconditional love; my father Jose Luis, who taught me discipline; my grandfather Leonardo Macias, who gave me the key to unlock the Toltec mysteries; and my sons Miguel, Jose Luis, and Leonardo.

I wish to express my deep affection and appreciation to the dedication of Gaya Jenkins and Trey Jenkins.

I would like to extend my profound gratitude to Janet Mills — publisher, editor, believer. I am also abidingly grateful to Ray Chambers for lighting the way.

I would like to honor my dear friend Gini Gentry, an amazing "brain" whose faith touched my heart.

I would like to pay tribute to the many people who have given freely of their time, hearts, and resources to support the teachings. A partial list includes: Gae Buckley, Ted and Peggy Raess, Christinea Johnson, Judy "Red" Fruhbauer, Vicki Molinar, David and Linda Dibble, Bernadette Vigil, Cynthia Wootton, Alan Clark, Rita Rivera, Catherine Chase, Stephanie Bureau, Todd Kaprielian, Glenna Quigley, Allan and Randi Hardman, Cindee Pascoe, Terry and Chuck Cowgill, Roberto and Diane Paez, Siri Gian Singh Khalsa, Heather Ash, Larry Andrews, Judy Silver, Carolyn Hipp, Kim Hofer, Mersedeh Kheradmand, Diana and Sky Ferguson, Keri Kropidlowski, Steve Hasenburg, Dara Salour, Joaquin Galvan, Woodie Bobb, Rachel Guerrero, Mark Gershon, Collette Michaan, Brandt Morgan, Katherine Kilgore (Kitty Kaur), Michael Gilardy, Laura Haney, Marc Cloptin, Wendy Bobb, Ed Fox, Yari Jaeda, Mary

Acknowledgments

Carroll Nelson, Amari Magdelana, JaneAnn Dow, Russ Venable, Gu and Maya Khalsa, Mataji Rosita, Fred and Marion Vatinelli, Diane Laurent, V.J. Polich, Gail Dawn Price, Barbara Simon, Patti Torres, Kaye Thompson, Ramin Yazdani, Linda Lightfoot, Terry Gorton, Dorothy Lee, J.J. Frank, Jennifer and Jeanne Jenkins, George Gorton, Tita Weems, Shelley Wolf, Gigi Boyce, Morgan Drasmin, Eddie Von Sonn, Sydney de Jong, Peg Hackett Cancienne, Germaine Bautista, Pilar Mendoza, Debbie Rund Caldwell, Bea La Scalla, Eduardo Rabasa, and The Cowboy.

The Toltec

THOUSANDS OF YEARS AGO, THE TOLTEC WERE known throughout southern Mexico as "women and men of knowledge." Anthropologists have spoken of the Toltec as a nation or a race, but, in fact, the Toltec were scientists and artists who formed a society to explore and conserve the spiritual knowledge and practices of the ancient ones. They came together as masters *(naguals)* and students at Teotihuacan, the ancient city of pyramids outside Mexico City known as the place where "Man Becomes God."

Over the millennia, the *naguals* were forced to conceal the ancestral wisdom and maintain its existence in obscurity. European conquest, coupled with rampant misuse of personal power by a few of the apprentices, made it necessary to shield the knowledge from those who were not prepared to use it wisely or who might intentionally misuse it for personal gain.

Fortunately, the esoteric Toltec knowledge was embodied and passed on through generations by different lineages of *naguals*. Though it remained veiled in secrecy for hundreds of years, ancient prophecies foretold the coming of an age when it would be necessary to return the wisdom to the people. Now, don Miguel Ruiz, a *nagual* from the Eagle Knight lineage, has been guided to share with us the powerful teachings of the Toltec.

Toltec knowledge arises from the same essential unity of truth as all the sacred esoteric traditions found around the world. Though it is not a religion, it honors all the spiritual masters who have taught on the earth. While it does embrace spirit, it is most accurately described as a way of life, distinguished by the ready accessibility of happiness and love.

The Smokey Mirror

THREE THOUSAND YEARS AGO, THERE WAS A HUMAN just like you and me who lived near a city surrounded by mountains. The human was studying to become a medicine man, to learn the knowledge of his ancestors, but he didn't completely agree with everything he was learning. In his heart, he felt there must be something more.

One day, as he slept in a cave, he dreamed that he saw his own body sleeping. He came out of the cave on the night of a new moon. The sky was clear, and he could see millions of stars. Then something happened inside of him that transformed his life forever. He looked at his hands, he felt his body, and he heard his own voice say, "I am made of light; I am made of stars."

He looked at the stars again, and he realized that it's not the stars that create light, but rather light that creates the stars. "Everything is made of light," he said, "and the space in-between isn't empty." And he knew that everything that exists is one living being, and that light is the messenger of life, because it is alive and contains all information.

Then he realized that although he was made of stars, he was not those stars. "I am in-between the stars," he thought. So he called the stars the *tonal* and the light between the stars the *nagual,* and he knew that what created the harmony and space between the two is Life or Intent. Without Life, the *tonal* and the *nagual* could not exist. Life is the force of the absolute, the supreme, the Creator who creates everything.

This is what he discovered: Everything in existence is a manifestation of the one living being we call God. Everything is God. And he came to the conclusion that human perception is merely light perceiving light. He also saw that matter is a mirror — everything is a mirror that reflects light and creates images of that light — and the world of illusion, the *Dream,* is just like smoke which doesn't allow us to see what we really are. "The real us is pure love, pure light," he said.

This realization changed his life. Once he knew what he really was, he looked around at other humans and the rest of nature, and he was amazed at what he saw. He saw himself in everything — in every human, in every animal, in every tree, in the water, in the rain, in the clouds, in the earth. And he saw that Life mixed the *tonal* and the *nagual* in different ways to create billions of manifestations of Life.

In those few moments he comprehended everything. He was very excited, and his heart was filled with peace. He could hardly wait to tell his people what he had discovered. But there were no words to explain it. He tried to tell the others, but they could not understand. They could see that he had changed, that something beautiful was radiating from his eyes and his voice. They noticed that he no longer had judgment about anything or anyone. He was no longer like anyone else.

He could understand everyone very well, but no one could understand him. They believed that he was an incarnation of God, and he smiled when he heard this and he said, "It is true. I am God. But you are also God. We are the same, you and I. We are images of light. We are God." But still the people didn't understand him.

He had discovered that he was a mirror for the rest of the people, a mirror in which he could see himself. "Everyone is a mirror," he said. He saw himself in everyone, but nobody saw him as themselves.

And he realized that everyone was dreaming, but without awareness, without knowing what they really are. They couldn't see him as themselves because there was a wall of fog or smoke between the mirrors. And that wall of fog was made by the interpretation of images of light — the *Dream* of humans.

Then he knew that he would soon forget all that he had learned. He wanted to remember all the visions he had had, so he decided to call himself the Smokey Mirror so that he would always know that matter is a mirror and the smoke in-between is what keeps us from knowing what we are. He said, "I am the Smokey Mirror, because I am looking at myself in all of you, but we don't recognize each other because of the smoke in-between us. That smoke is the *Dream*, and the mirror is you, the dreamer."

Living is easy with eyes closed,
misunderstanding all you see. . . .
— John Lennon

1

Domestication and the Dream of the Planet

WHAT YOU ARE SEEING AND HEARING RIGHT NOW IS
nothing but a dream. You are dreaming right now in
this moment. You are dreaming with the brain awake.

Dreaming is the main function of the mind, and
the mind dreams twenty-four hours a day. It dreams
when the brain is awake, and it also dreams when
the brain is asleep. The difference is that when the

brain is awake, there is a material frame that makes us perceive things in a linear way. When we go to sleep we do not have the frame, and the dream has the tendency to change constantly.

Humans are dreaming all the time. Before we were born the humans before us created a big outside dream that we will call society's dream or *the dream of the planet.* The dream of the planet is the collective dream of billions of smaller, personal dreams, which together create a dream of a family, a dream of a community, a dream of a city, a dream of a country, and finally a dream of the whole humanity. The dream of the planet includes all of society's rules, its beliefs, its laws, its religions, its different cultures and ways to be, its governments, schools, social events, and holidays.

We are born with the capacity to learn how to dream, and the humans who live before us teach us how to dream the way society dreams. The outside dream has so many rules that when a new human is born, we hook the child's attention and introduce these rules into his or her mind. The outside dream uses Mom and Dad, the schools, and religion to teach us how to dream.

Attention is the ability we have to discriminate and to focus only on that which we want to perceive. We can perceive millions of things simultaneously, but using our attention, we can hold whatever we want to perceive in the foreground of our mind. The adults around us hooked our attention and put information into our minds through repetition. That is the way we learned everything we know.

By using our attention we learned a whole reality, a whole dream. We learned how to behave in society: what to believe and what not to believe; what is acceptable and what is not acceptable; what is good and what is bad; what is beautiful and what is ugly; what is right and what is wrong. It was all there already — all that knowledge, all those rules and concepts about how to behave in the world.

When you were in school, you sat in a little chair and put your attention on what the teacher was teaching you. When you went to church, you put your attention on what the priest or minister was telling you. It is the same dynamic with Mom and Dad, brothers and sisters: They were all trying to hook your attention. We also learn to hook the attention of other humans, and we develop a need for attention which can become very competitive. Children compete for the attention of their parents, their teachers, their friends. "Look at me! Look at what I'm doing! Hey, I'm here." The need for attention becomes very strong and continues into adulthood.

The outside dream hooks our attention and teaches us what to believe, beginning with the language that we speak. Language is the code for understanding and communication between humans. Every letter, every word in each language is an agreement. We call this a page in a book; the word *page* is an agreement that we understand. Once we understand the code, our attention is hooked and the energy is transferred from one person to another.

It was not your choice to speak English. You

didn't choose your religion or your moral values — they were already there before you were born. We never had the opportunity to choose what to believe or what not to believe. We never chose even the smallest of these agreements. We didn't even choose our own name.

As children, we didn't have the opportunity to choose our beliefs, but we *agreed* with the information that was passed to us from the dream of the planet via other humans. The only way to store information is by agreement. The outside dream may hook our attention, but if we don't agree, we don't store that information. As soon as we agree, we *believe* it, and this is called faith. To have faith is to believe unconditionally.

That's how we learn as children. Children believe everything adults say. We agree with them, and our faith is so strong that the belief system controls our whole dream of life. We didn't choose these beliefs, and we may have rebelled against them, but we were not strong enough to win the rebellion.

The result is surrender to the beliefs with our *agreement*.

I call this process *the domestication of humans.* And through this domestication we learn how to live and how to dream. In human domestication, the information from the outside dream is conveyed to the inside dream, creating our whole belief system. First the child is taught the names of things: Mom, Dad, milk, bottle. Day by day, at home, at school, at church, and from television, we are told how to live, what kind of behavior is acceptable. The outside dream teaches us how to be a human. We have a whole concept of what a "woman" is and what a "man" is. And we also learn to judge: We judge ourselves, judge other people, judge the neighbors.

Children are domesticated the same way that we domesticate a dog, a cat, or any other animal. In order to teach a dog we punish the dog and we give it rewards. We train our children whom we love so much the same way that we train any domesticated animal: with a system of punishment and reward.

We are told, "You're a good boy," or "You're a good girl," when we do what Mom and Dad want us to do. When we don't, we are "a bad girl" or "a bad boy."

When we went against the rules we were punished; when we went along with the rules we got a reward. We were punished many times a day, and we were also rewarded many times a day. Soon we became afraid of being punished and also afraid of not receiving the reward. The reward is the attention that we got from our parents or from other people like siblings, teachers, and friends. We soon develop a need to hook other people's attention in order to get the reward.

The reward feels good, and we keep doing what others want us to do in order to get the reward. With that fear of being punished and that fear of not getting the reward, we start pretending to be what we are not, just to please others, just to be good enough for someone else. We try to please Mom and Dad, we try to please the teachers at school, we try to please the church, and so we start acting. We pretend to be what we are not because we are afraid of being rejected. The fear of being rejected becomes the fear of not being good enough. Eventually we become someone that we are not. We become a copy of Mamma's beliefs, Daddy's beliefs, society's beliefs, and religion's beliefs.

All our normal tendencies are lost in the process of domestication. And when we are old enough for our mind to understand, we learn the word *no.* The adults say, "Don't do this and don't do that." We rebel and say, "No!" We rebel because we are defending our freedom. We want to be ourselves, but we are very little, and the adults are big and strong. After a certain time we are afraid because we know that every time we do something wrong we are going to be punished.

The domestication is so strong that at a certain point in our lives we no longer need anyone to domesticate us. We don't need Mom or Dad, the school or the church to domesticate us. We are so well trained that we are our own domesticator.

We are an autodomesticated animal. We can now domesticate ourselves according to the same belief system we were given, and using the same system of punishment and reward. We punish ourselves when we don't follow the rules according to our belief system; we reward ourselves when we are the "good boy" or "good girl."

The belief system is like a Book of Law that rules our mind. Without question, whatever is in that Book of Law, is our truth. We base all of our judgments according to the Book of Law, even if these judgments go against our own inner nature. Even moral laws like the Ten Commandments are programmed into our mind in the process of domestication. One by one, all these agreements go into the Book of Law, and these agreements rule our dream.

There is something in our minds that judges everybody and everything, including the weather, the dog, the cat — everything. The inner Judge uses what is in our Book of Law to judge everything we do and don't do, everything we think and don't think, and everything we feel and don't feel. Everything lives under the tyranny of this Judge. Every time we do something that goes against the Book of Law, the Judge says we are guilty, we need to be punished, we should be ashamed. This happens many times a day, day after day, for all the years of our lives.

There is another part of us that receives the judgments, and this part is called the Victim. The Victim carries the blame, the guilt, and the shame. It is the part of us that says, "Poor me, I'm not good enough, I'm not intelligent enough, I'm not attractive enough, I'm not worthy of love, poor me." The big Judge agrees and says, "Yes, you are not good enough." And this is all based on a belief system that we never chose to believe. These beliefs are so strong, that even years later when we are exposed to new concepts and try to make our own decisions, we find that these beliefs still control our lives.

Whatever goes against the Book of Law will make you feel a funny sensation in your solar plexus, and it's called fear. Breaking the rules in the Book of Law opens your emotional wounds, and your reaction is to create emotional poison. Because everything that is in the Book of Law has to be true, anything that challenges what you believe is going to make you feel unsafe. Even if the Book of Law is wrong, it makes you *feel safe.*

That is why we need a great deal of courage to challenge our own beliefs. Because even if we know we didn't choose all these beliefs, it is also true that we agreed to all of them. The agreement is so strong that even if we understand the concept of it not being true, we feel the blame, the guilt, and the shame that occur if we go against these rules.

Just as the government has a book of laws that rule the society's dream, our belief system is the Book of Laws that rules our personal dream. All these laws exist in our mind, we believe them, and the Judge inside us bases everything on these rules. The Judge decrees, and the Victim suffers the guilt and punishment. But who says there is justice in this dream? True justice is paying only once for each mistake. True *injustice* is paying more than once for each mistake.

How many times do we pay for one mistake? The answer is thousands of times. The human is the only animal on earth that pays a thousand times for the same mistake. The rest of the animals pay once for every mistake they make. But not us. We have a powerful memory. We make a mistake, we judge ourselves, we find ourselves guilty, and we punish ourselves. If justice exists, then that was enough; we don't need to do it again. But every time we remember, we judge ourselves again, we are guilty again, and we punish ourselves again, and again, and again. If we have a wife or husband he or she also reminds us of the mistake, so we can judge ourselves again, punish ourselves again, and find ourselves guilty again. Is this fair?

How many times do we make our spouse, our children, or our parents pay for the same mistake? Every time we remember the mistake, we blame them again and send them all the emotional poison we feel at the injustice, and then we make them pay again for the same mistake. Is that justice? The Judge in the mind is wrong because the belief system, the Book of Law, is wrong. The whole dream is based on false law. Ninety-five percent of the beliefs we have stored in our minds are nothing but lies, and we suffer because we believe all these lies.

In the dream of the planet it is normal for humans to suffer, to live in fear, and to create emotional dramas. The outside dream is not a pleasant dream; it is a dream of violence, a dream of fear, a dream of war, a dream of injustice. The personal dream of humans will vary, but globally it is mostly a nightmare. If we look at human society we see a place so difficult to live in because it is ruled by fear. Throughout the world we see human suffering, anger, revenge, addictions, violence in the street, and tremendous injustice. It may exist at different levels in different countries around the world, but fear is controlling the outside dream.

If we compare the dream of human society with the description of hell that religions all around the world have promulgated, we find they are exactly the same. Religions say that hell is a place of punishment, a place of fear, pain, and suffering, a place where the fire burns you. Fire is generated by emotions that come from fear. Whenever we feel the emotions of anger, jealousy, envy, or hate, we experience a fire burning within us. We are living in a dream of hell.

If you consider hell as a state of mind, then hell is all around us. Others may warn us that if we don't do what they say we should do, we will go to hell. Bad news! We are already in hell, including the people who tell us that. No human can condemn another to hell because we are already there. Others can put us into a deeper hell, true. But only if we allow this to happen.

Every human has his or her own personal dream, and just like the society dream, it is often ruled by fear. We learn to dream hell in our own life, in our personal dream. The same fears manifest in different ways for each person, of course, but we experience anger, jealousy, hate, envy, and other negative emotions. Our personal dream can also become an ongoing nightmare where we suffer and live in a state of fear. But we don't need to dream a nightmare. It is possible to enjoy a pleasant dream.

All of humanity is searching for truth, justice, and beauty. We are on an eternal search for the truth because we only believe in the lies we have stored in our mind. We are searching for justice because in the belief system we have, there is no justice. We search for beauty because it doesn't matter how beautiful a person is, we don't believe that person has beauty. We keep searching and searching, when everything is already within us. There is no truth to find. Wherever we turn our heads, all we see is the truth, but with the agreements and beliefs we have stored in our mind, we have no eyes for this truth.

We don't see the truth because we are blind. What blinds us are all those false beliefs we have in our mind. We have the need to be right and to make others wrong. We trust what we believe, and our beliefs set us up for suffering. It is as if we live in the middle of a fog that doesn't let us see any further than our own nose. We live in a fog that is not even real. This fog is a dream, your personal dream of life — what you believe, all the concepts you have about what you are, all the agreements you have made with others, with yourself, and even with God.

Your whole mind is a fog which the Toltecs called a *mitote* (pronounced MIH-TOE´-TAY). Your mind is a dream where a thousand people talk at the same time, and nobody understands each other. This is the condition of the human mind — a big *mitote,* and with that big *mitote* you cannot see what you really are. In India they call the *mitote maya,* which means illusion. It is the personality's notion of "I am." Everything you believe about yourself and the world, all the concepts and programming you have in your mind, are all the *mitote.* We cannot see who we truly are; we cannot see that we are not free.

That is why humans resist life. To be alive is the biggest fear humans have. Death is not the biggest fear we have; our biggest fear is taking the risk to be alive — the risk to be alive and express what we really are. Just being ourselves is the biggest fear of humans. We have learned to live our lives trying to satisfy other people's demands. We have learned to live by other people's points of view because of the fear of not being accepted and of not being good enough for someone else.

During the process of domestication, we form an image of what perfection is in order to try to be good enough. We create an image of how we should be in order to be accepted by everybody. We especially try to please the ones who love us, like Mom and Dad, big brothers and sisters, the priests and the teacher. Trying to be good enough for them, we create an image of perfection, but we don't fit this image. We create this image, but this image is not real. We are never going to be perfect from this point of view. Never!

Not being perfect, we reject ourselves. And the level of self-rejection depends upon how effective the adults were in breaking our integrity. After domestication it is no longer about being good enough for anybody else. We are not good enough for ourselves because we don't fit with our own image of perfection. We cannot forgive ourselves for not being what we wish to be, or rather what we *believe* we should be. We cannot forgive ourselves for not being perfect.

We know we are not what we believe we are supposed to be and so we feel false, frustrated, and dishonest. We try to hide ourselves, and we pretend to be what we are not. The result is that we feel unauthentic and wear social masks to keep others from noticing this. We are so afraid that somebody else will notice that we are not what we pretend to be. We judge others according to our image of perfection as well, and naturally they fall short of our expectations.

We dishonor ourselves just to please other people. We even do harm to our physical bodies just to be accepted by others. You see teenagers taking drugs just to avoid being rejected by other teenagers. They are not aware that the problem is that they don't accept themselves. They reject themselves because they are not what they pretend to be. They wish to be a certain way, but they are not, and for this they carry shame and guilt. Humans punish themselves endlessly for not being what they believe they should be. They become very self-abusive, and they use other people to abuse themselves as well.

But nobody abuses us more than we abuse ourselves, and it is the Judge, the Victim, and the belief system that make us do this. True, we find people who say their husband or wife, or mother or father, abused them, but you know that we abuse ourselves much more than that. The way we judge ourselves is the worst judge that ever existed. If we make a mistake in front of people, we try to deny the mistake and cover it up. But as soon as we are alone, the Judge becomes so strong, the guilt is so strong, and we feel so stupid, or so bad, or so unworthy.

THE FOUR AGREEMENTS

In your whole life nobody has ever abused you more than you have abused yourself. And the limit of your self-abuse is exactly the limit that you will tolerate from someone else. If someone abuses you a little more than you abuse yourself, you will probably walk away from that person. But if someone abuses you a little less than you abuse yourself, you will probably stay in the relationship and tolerate it endlessly.

If you abuse yourself very badly, you can even tolerate someone who beats you up, humiliates you, and treats you like dirt. Why? Because in your belief system you say, "I deserve it. This person is doing me a favor by being with me. I'm not worthy of love and respect. I'm not good enough."

We have the need to be accepted and to be loved by others, but we cannot accept and love ourselves. The more self-love we have, the less we will experience self-abuse. Self-abuse comes from self-rejection, and self-rejection comes from having an image of what it means to be perfect and never measuring up to that ideal. Our image of perfection is the reason we reject ourselves; it is why we don't accept ourselves the way we are, and why we don't accept others the way they are.

PRELUDE TO A NEW DREAM

There are thousands of agreements you have made with yourself, with other people, with your dream of life, with God, with society, with your parents, with your spouse, with your children. But the most important agreements are the ones you made with yourself. In these agreements you tell yourself who you are, what you feel, what you believe, and how to behave. The result is what you call your personality. In these agreements you say, "This is what I am. This is what I believe. I can do certain things, and some things I cannot do. This is reality, that is fantasy; this is possible, that is impossible."

One single agreement is not such a problem, but we have many agreements that make us suffer, that make us fail in life. If you want to live a life of joy and fulfillment, you have to find the courage to break those agreements that are fear-based and claim your personal power. The agreements that come from fear require us to expend a lot of energy, but the agreements that come from love help us to conserve energy and even gain extra energy.

Each of us is born with a certain amount of personal power that we rebuild every day after we rest. Unfortunately, we spend all our personal power first to create all these agreements and then to keep these agreements. Our personal power is dissipated by all the agreements we have created, and the result is that we feel powerless. We have just enough power to survive each day, because most of it is used to keep the agreements that trap us in the dream of the planet. How can we change the entire dream of our life when we have no power to change even the smallest agreement?

If we can see it is our agreements that rule our own life, and we don't like the dream of our life, we need to change the agreements. When we are finally ready to change our agreements, there are four very powerful agreements that will help us to break those agreements that come from fear and deplete our energy.

Each time you break an agreement, all the power you used to create it returns to you. If you adopt these four new agreements, they will create enough personal power for you to change the entire system of your old agreements.

You need a very strong will in order to adopt The Four Agreements — but if you can begin to live your life with these agreements, the transformation in your life will be amazing. You will see the drama of hell disappear right before your very eyes. Instead of living in a dream of hell, you will be creating a new dream — your personal dream of heaven.

2

THE FIRST AGREEMENT

Be Impeccable with Your Word

THE FIRST AGREEMENT IS THE MOST IMPORTANT ONE and also the most difficult one to honor. It is so important that with just this first agreement you will be able to transcend to the level of existence I call heaven on earth.

The first agreement is to *be impeccable with your word.* It sounds very simple, but it is very, very powerful.

Why your word? Your word is the power that you have to create. Your word is the gift that comes directly from God. The Gospel of John in the Bible, speaking of the creation of the universe, says, "In the beginning was the word, and the word was with God, and the word is God." Through the word you express your creative power. It is through the word that you manifest everything. Regardless of what language you speak, your intent manifests through the word. What you dream, what you feel, and what you really are, will all be manifested through the word.

The word is not just a sound or a written symbol. The word is a force; it is the power you have to express and communicate, to think, and thereby to create the events in your life. You can speak. What other animal on the planet can speak? The word is the most powerful tool you have as a human; it is the tool of magic. But like a sword with two edges, your word can create the most beautiful dream, or your word can destroy everything around you. One edge is the misuse of the word, which creates a living hell. The other edge is the impeccability of the word, which will only create beauty, love, and heaven on earth. Depending upon how it is used, the word can set you free, or it can enslave you even more than you know. All the magic you possess is based on your word. Your word is pure magic, and misuse of your word is black magic.

The word is so powerful that one word can change a life or destroy the lives of millions of people. Some years ago one man in Germany, by the use of the word, manipulated a whole country of the most intelligent people. He led them into a world war with just the power of his word. He convinced others to commit the most atrocious acts of violence. He activated people's fear with the word, and like a big explosion, there was killing and war all around the world. All over the world humans destroyed other humans because they were afraid of each other. Hitler's word, based on fear-generated beliefs and agreements, will be remembered for centuries.

The human mind is like a fertile ground where seeds are continually being planted. The seeds are opinions, ideas, and concepts. You plant a seed, a thought, and it grows. The word is like a seed, and the human mind is so fertile! The only problem is that too often it is fertile for the seeds of fear. Every human mind is fertile, but only for those kinds of seeds it is prepared for. What is important is to see which kind of seeds our mind is fertile for, and to prepare it to receive the seeds of love.

Take the example of Hitler: He sent out all those seeds of fear, and they grew very strong and beautifully achieved massive destruction. Seeing the awesome power of the word, we must understand what power comes out of our mouths. One fear or doubt planted in our mind can create an endless drama of events. One word is like a spell, and humans use the word like black magicians, thoughtlessly putting spells on each other.

Every human is a magician, and we can either put a spell on someone with our word or we can release someone from a spell. We cast spells all the time with our opinions. An example: I see a friend and give him an opinion that just popped into my mind. I say, "Hmmm! I see that kind of color in your face in people who are going to get cancer." If he listens to the word, and if he agrees, he will have cancer in less than one year. That is the power of the word.

During our domestication, our parents and siblings gave their opinions about us without even thinking. We believed these opinions and we lived in fear over these opinions, like not being good at swimming, or sports, or writing. Someone gives an opinion and says, "Look, this girl is ugly!" The girl listens, believes she is ugly, and grows up with the idea that she is ugly. It doesn't matter how beautiful she is; as long as she has that agreement, she will believe that she is ugly. That is the spell she is under.

By hooking our attention, the word can enter our mind and change a whole belief for better or for worse. Another example: You may believe you are stupid, and you may have believed this for as long as you can remember. This agreement can be very tricky, causing you to do a lot of things just to ensure that you are stupid. You may do something and think to yourself, "I wish I were smart, but I must be stupid or I wouldn't have done that." The mind goes in hundreds of different directions, and we could spend days getting hooked by just that one belief in our own stupidity.

Then one day someone hooks your attention and using the word, lets you know that you are not stupid. You believe what the person says and make a new agreement. As a result, you no longer feel or act stupid. A whole spell is broken, just by the power of the word. Conversely, if you believe you are stupid, and someone hooks your attention and says, "Yes, you are really the most stupid person I have ever met," the agreement will be reinforced and become even stronger.

Now let us see what the word *impeccability* means. *Impeccability* means "without sin." *Impeccable* comes from the Latin *pecatus,* which means "sin." The *im* in impeccable means "without," so *impeccable* means "without sin." Religions talk about sin and sinners, but let's understand what it really means to sin. A sin is anything that you do which goes against yourself. Everything you feel or believe or say that goes against yourself is a sin. You go against yourself when you judge or blame yourself for anything. Being without sin is exactly the opposite. Being impeccable is not going against yourself. When you are impeccable, you take responsibility for your actions, but you do not judge or blame yourself.

From this point of view, the whole concept of sin changes from something moral or religious to something commonsense. Sin begins with rejection of yourself. Self-rejection is the biggest sin that you commit. In religious terms self-rejection is a "mortal sin," which leads to death. Impeccability, on the other hand, leads to life.

Being impeccable with your word is not using the word against yourself. If I see you in the street and I call you stupid, it appears that I'm using the word against you. But really I'm using my word against myself, because you're going to hate me for this, and your hating me is not good for me. Therefore, if I get angry and with my word send all that emotional poison to you, I'm using the word against myself.

If I love myself I will express that love in my interactions with you, and then I am being impeccable with the word, because that action will produce a like reaction. If I love you, then you will love me. If I insult you, you will insult me. If I have gratitude for you, you will have gratitude for me. If I'm selfish with you, you will be selfish with me. If I use the word to put a spell on you, you are going to put a spell on me.

Being impeccable with your word is the correct use of your energy; it means to use your energy in the direction of truth and love for yourself. If you make an agreement with yourself to be impeccable with your word, just with that intention, the truth will manifest through you and clean all the emotional poison that exists within you. But making this agreement is difficult because we have learned to do precisely the opposite. We have learned to lie as a habit of our communication with others and more importantly with ourselves. We are not impeccable with the word.

The power of the word is completely misused in hell. We use the word to curse, to blame, to find guilt, to destroy. Of course, we also use it in the right way, but not too often. Mostly we use the word to spread our personal poison — to express anger, jealousy, envy, and hate. The word is pure magic — the most powerful gift we have as humans — and we use it against ourselves. We plan revenge. We create chaos with the word. We use the word to create hate between different races, between different people, between families, between nations. We misuse the word so often, and this misuse is how we create and perpetuate the dream of hell. Misuse of the word is how we pull each other down and keep each other in a state of fear and doubt. Because the word is the magic that humans possess and misuse of the word is black magic, we are using black magic all the time without knowing that our word is magic at all.

There was a woman, for example, who was intelligent and had a very good heart. She had a daughter whom she adored and loved very much. One night she came home from a very bad day at work, tired, full of emotional tension, and with a terrible headache. She wanted peace and quiet, but her daughter was singing and jumping happily. The daughter was unaware of how her mother was feeling; she was in her own world, in her own dream. She felt so wonderful, and she was jumping and singing louder and louder, expressing her joy and her love. She was singing so loud that it made her mother's headache even worse, and at a certain moment, the mother lost control. Angrily she looked at her beautiful little girl and said, "Shut up! You have an ugly voice. Can you just shut up!"

The truth is that the mother's tolerance for any noise was nonexistent; it was not that the little girl's voice was ugly. But the daughter believed what her mother said, and in that moment she made an agreement with herself. After that she no longer sang, because she believed her voice was ugly and would bother anyone who heard it. She became shy at school, and if she was asked to sing, she refused. Even speaking to others became difficult for her. Everything changed in the little girl because of this new agreement: She believed she must repress her emotions in order to be accepted and loved.

Whenever we hear an opinion and believe it, we make an agreement, and it becomes part of our belief system. This little girl grew up, and even though she had a beautiful voice, she never sang again. She developed a whole complex from one spell. This spell was cast upon her by the one who loved her the most: her own mother. Her mother didn't notice what she did with her word. She didn't notice that she used black magic and put a spell on her daughter. She didn't know the power of her word, and therefore she isn't to blame. She did what her own mother, father, and others had done to her in many ways. They misused the word.

How many times do we do this with our own children? We give them these types of opinions and our children carry that black magic for years and years. People who love us do black magic on us, but they don't know what they do. That is why we must forgive them; they don't know what they do.

Another example: You awake in the morning feeling very happy. You feel so wonderful, you stay one or two hours in front of the mirror, making yourself beautiful. Well, one of your best friends says, "What has happened to you? You look so ugly. Look at the dress you are wearing; you look ridiculous." That's it; that is enough to put you all the way down in hell. Maybe this girlfriend just told you this to hurt you. And, she did. She gave you an opinion with all the power of her word behind it. If you accept the opinion, it becomes an agreement now, and you put all your power into that opinion. That opinion becomes black magic.

These types of spells are difficult to break. The only thing that can break a spell is to make a new agreement based on truth. The truth is the most important part of being impeccable with your word. On one side of the sword are the lies which create black magic, and on the other side of the sword is the truth which has the power to break the spell of black magic. Only the truth will set us free.

Looking at everyday human interactions, imagine how many times we cast spells on each other with our word. Over time this interaction has become the worst form of black magic, and we call it *gossip.*

Gossip is black magic at its very worst because it is pure poison. We learned how to gossip by agreement. When we were children, we heard the adults around us gossiping all the time, openly giving their opinions about other people. They even had opinions about people they didn't know. Emotional poison was transferred along with the opinions, and we learned this as the normal way to communicate.

Gossiping has become the main form of communication in human society. It has become the way we feel close to each other, because it makes us feel better to see someone else feel as badly as we do. There is an old expression that says, "Misery likes company," and people who are suffering in hell don't want to be all alone. Fear and suffering are an important part of the dream of the planet; they are how the dream of the planet keeps us down.

Using the analogy of the human mind as a computer, gossip can be compared to a computer virus. A computer virus is a piece of computer language written in the same language all the other codes are written in, but with a harmful intent. This code is inserted into the program of your computer when you least expect it and most of the time without your awareness. After this code has been introduced, your computer doesn't work quite right, or it doesn't function at all because the codes get so mixed up with so many conflicting messages that it stops producing good results.

Human gossip works exactly the same way. For example, you are beginning a new class with a new teacher and you have looked forward to it for a long time. On the first day of class, you run into someone who took the class before, who tells you, "Oh that instructor was such a pompous jerk! He didn't know what he was talking about, and he was a pervert too, so watch out!"

You are immediately imprinted with the word and the emotional code the person had when saying this, but what you are not aware of is his or her motivation in telling you. This person could be angry for failing the class or simply making an assumption based on fears and prejudices, but because you have learned to ingest information like a child, some part of you believes the gossip, and you go on to the class.

As the teacher speaks, you feel the poison come up inside you and you don't realize you see the teacher through the eyes of the person who gave you that gossip. Then you start talking to other people in the class about this, and they start to see the teacher in the same way: as a jerk and a pervert. You really hate the class, and soon you decide to drop out. You blame the teacher, but it is gossip that is to blame.

All of this mess can be caused by one little computer virus. One little piece of misinformation can break down communication between people, causing every person it touches to become infected and contagious to others. Imagine that every single time others gossip to you, they insert a computer virus into your mind, causing you to think a little less clearly every time. Then imagine that in an effort to clean up your own confusion and get some relief from the poison, you gossip and spread these viruses to someone else.

Now imagine this pattern going on in a never-ending chain between all the humans on earth. The result is a world full of humans who can only read information through circuits that are clogged with a poisonous, contagious virus. Once again, this poisonous virus is what the Toltecs called the *mitote*, the chaos of a thousand different voices all trying to talk at once in the mind.

Even worse are the black magicians or "computer hackers" who intentionally spread the virus. Think back to a time when you or someone you know was angry with someone else and desired revenge. In order to seek revenge you said something to or about that person with the intention of spreading poison and making that person feel bad about him- or herself. As children we do this quite thoughtlessly, but as we grow older we become much more calculated in our efforts to bring other people down. Then we lie to ourselves and say that person received a just punishment for their wrongdoing.

When we see the world through a computer virus, it is easy to justify the cruelest behavior. What we don't see is that misuse of our word is putting us deeper into hell.

❧

For years we have received the gossip and spells from the words of others, but also from the way we use our word with ourselves. We talk to ourselves constantly and most of the time we say things like, "Oh, I look fat, I look ugly. I'm getting old, I'm losing my hair. I'm stupid, I never understand anything. I will never be good enough, and I'm never going to be perfect." Do you see how we use the word against ourselves? We must begin to understand what the word *is* and what the word *does*. If you understand the first agreement, *be impeccable with your word*, you begin to see all the changes that can happen in your life. Changes first in the way you deal with yourself, and later in the way you deal with other people, especially those you love the most.

Consider how many times you have gossiped about the person you love the most to gain the support of others for your point of view. How many times have you hooked other people's attention, and spread poison about your loved one in order to make your opinion right? Your opinion is nothing but your point of view. It is not necessarily true. Your opinion comes from your beliefs, your own ego, and your own dream. We create all this poison and spread it to others just so we can feel right about our own point of view.

If we adopt the first agreement, and become impeccable with our word, any emotional poison will eventually be cleaned from our mind and from our communication in our personal relationships, including with our pet dog or cat.

Impeccability of the word will also give you immunity from anyone putting a negative spell on you. You will only receive a negative idea if your mind is fertile ground for that idea. When you become impeccable with your word, your mind is no longer fertile ground for words that come from black magic. Instead, it is fertile for the words that come from love. You can measure the impeccability of your word by your level of self-love. How much you love yourself and how you feel about yourself are directly proportionate to the quality and integrity of your word. When you are impeccable with your word, you feel good; you feel happy and at peace.

You can transcend the dream of hell just by making the agreement to be impeccable with your word. Right now I am planting that seed in your mind. Whether or not the seed grows depends upon how fertile your mind is for the seeds of love. It is up to you to make this agreement with yourself: *I am impeccable with my word.* Nurture this seed, and as it grows in your mind, it will generate more seeds of love to replace the seeds of fear. This first agreement will change the kind of seeds your mind is fertile for.

Be impeccable with your word. This is the first agreement that you should make if you want to be free, if you want to be happy, if you want to transcend the level of existence that is hell. It is very powerful. Use the word in the correct way. Use the word to share your love. Use white magic, beginning with yourself. Tell yourself how wonderful you are, how great you are. Tell yourself how much you love yourself. Use the word to break all those teeny, tiny agreements that make you suffer.

It is possible. It is possible because I did it, and I am no better than you. No, we are exactly the same. We have the same kind of brain, the same kind of bodies; we are humans. If I was able to break those agreements and create new agreements, then you can do the same. If I can be impeccable with my word, why not you? Just this one agreement can change your whole life. Impeccability of the word can lead you to personal freedom, to huge success and abundance; it can take away all fear and transform it into joy and love.

Just imagine what you can create with impeccability of the word. With the impeccability of the word you can transcend the dream of fear and live a different life. You can live in heaven in the middle of thousands of people living in hell because you are immune to that hell. You can attain the kingdom of heaven from this one agreement: *Be impeccable with your word.*

3

THE SECOND AGREEMENT

Don't Take Anything Personally

THE NEXT THREE AGREEMENTS ARE REALLY BORN from the first agreement. The second agreement is *don't take anything personally.*

Whatever happens around you, don't take it personally. Using an earlier example, if I see you on the street and I say, "Hey, you are so stupid," without knowing you, it's not about you; it's about me. If you take it personally, then perhaps you believe you are stupid. Maybe you think to yourself, "How does he know? Is he clairvoyant, or can everybody see how stupid I am?"

You take it personally because you agree with whatever was said. As soon as you agree, the poison goes through you, and you are trapped in the dream of hell. What causes you to be trapped is what we call *personal importance.* Personal importance, or taking things personally, is the maximum expression of selfishness because we make the assumption that everything is about "me." During the period of our education, or our domestication, we learn to take everything personally. We think we are responsible for everything. Me, me, me, always me!

Nothing other people do is because of you. It is because of themselves. All people live in their own dream, in their own mind; they are in a completely different world from the one we live in. When we take something personally, we make the assumption that they know what is in our world, and we try to impose our world on their world.

Even when a situation seems so personal, even if others insult you directly, it has nothing to do with you. What they say, what they do, and the opinions they give are according to the agreements they have in their own minds. Their point of view comes from all the programming they received during domestication.

If someone gives you an opinion and says, "Hey, you look so fat," don't take it personally, because the truth is that this person is dealing with his or her own feelings, beliefs, and opinions. That person tried to send poison to you and if you take it personally, then you take that poison and it becomes yours. Taking things personally makes you easy prey for these predators, the black magicians. They can hook you easily with one little opinion and feed you whatever poison they want, and because you take it personally, you eat it up.

You eat all their emotional garbage, and now it becomes your garbage. But if you do not take it personally, you are immune in the middle of hell.

Immunity to poison in the middle of hell is the gift of this agreement.

When you take things personally, then you feel offended, and your reaction is to defend your beliefs and create conflicts. You make something big out of something so little, because you have the need to be right and make everybody else wrong. You also try hard to be right by giving them your own opinions. In the same way, whatever you feel and do is just a projection of your own personal dream, a reflection of your own agreements. What you say, what you do, and the opinions you have are according to the agreements you have made — and these opinions have nothing to do with me.

It is not important to me what you think about me, and I don't take what you think personally. I don't take it personally when people say, "Miguel, you are the best," and I also don't take it personally when they say, "Miguel, you are the worst." I know that when you are happy you will tell me, "Miguel, you are such an angel!" But, when you are mad at me you will say, "Oh, Miguel, you are such a devil! You are so disgusting. How can you say those things?" Either way, it does not affect me because I know what I am. I don't have the need to be accepted. I don't have the need to have someone tell me, "Miguel, you are doing so good!" or "How dare you do that!"

No, I don't take it personally. Whatever you think, whatever you feel, I know is your problem and not my problem. It is the way you see the world. It is nothing personal, because you are dealing with yourself, not with me. Others are going to have their own opinion according to their belief system, so nothing they think about me is really about me, but it is about them.

You may even tell me, "Miguel, what you are saying is hurting me." But it is not what I am saying that is hurting you; it is that you have wounds that I touch by what I have said. You are hurting yourself. There is no way that I can take this personally. Not because I don't believe in you or don't trust you, but because I know that you see the world with different eyes, with your eyes. You create an entire picture or movie in your mind, and in that picture you are the director, you are the producer, you are the main actor or actress. Everyone else is a secondary actor or actress. It is your movie.

The way you see that movie is according to the agreements you have made with life. Your point of view is something personal to you. It is no one's truth but yours. Then, if you get mad at me, I know you are dealing with yourself. I am the excuse for you to get mad. And you get mad because you are afraid, because you are dealing with fear. If you are not afraid, there is no way you will get mad at me. If you are not afraid, there is no way you will hate me. If you are not afraid, there is no way you will be jealous or sad.

If you live without fear, if you love, there is no place for any of those emotions. If you don't feel any of those emotions, it is logical that you will feel good. When you feel good, everything around you is good. When everything around you is great, everything makes you happy. You are loving everything that is around you, because you are loving yourself. Because you like the way you are. Because you are content with you. Because you are happy with your life. You are happy with the movie that you are producing, happy with your agreements with life. You are at peace, and you are happy. You live in that state of bliss where everything is so wonderful, and everything is so beautiful. In that state of bliss you are making love all the time with everything that you perceive.

꘍

Whatever people do, feel, think, or say, *don't take it personally.* If they tell you how wonderful you are, they are not saying that because of you. You know you are wonderful. It is not necessary to believe other people who tell you that you are wonderful. Don't take *anything* personally. Even if someone got a gun and shot you in the head, it was nothing personal. Even at that extreme.

Even the opinions you have about yourself are not necessarily true; therefore, you don't need to take whatever you hear in your own mind personally. The mind has the ability to talk to itself, but it also has the ability to hear information that is available from other realms. Sometimes you hear a voice in your mind, and you may wonder where it came from. This voice may have come from another reality in which there are living beings very similar to the human mind. The Toltecs called these beings Allies. In Europe, Africa, and India they called them the Gods.

Our mind also exists in the level of the Gods. Our mind also lives in that reality and can perceive that reality. The mind sees with the eyes and perceives this waking reality. But the mind also sees and perceives without the eyes, although the reason is hardly aware of this perception. The mind lives in more than one dimension. There may be times when you have ideas that don't originate in your mind, but you are perceiving them with your mind. You have the right to believe or not believe these voices and the right not to take what they say personally. We have a choice whether or not to believe the voices we hear within our own minds, just as we have a choice of what to believe and agree with in the dream of the planet.

The mind can also talk and listen to itself. The mind is divided as your body is divided. Just as you can say, "I have one hand, and I can shake my other hand and feel the other hand," the mind can talk to itself. Part of the mind is speaking, and the other part is listening. It is a big problem when a thousand parts of your mind are all speaking at the same time. This is called a *mitote*, remember?

The *mitote* can be compared to a huge marketplace where thousands of people are talking and bartering at the same time. Each one has different thoughts and feelings; each one has a different point of view. The programming in the mind — all of those agreements we have made — are not necessarily compatible with each other. Every agreement is like a separate living being; it has its own personality and its own voice. There are conflicting agreements that go against other agreements and on and on until it becomes a big war in the mind. The *mitote* is the reason humans hardly know what they want, how they want it, or when they want it. They don't agree with themselves because there are parts of the mind that want one thing, and other parts that want exactly the opposite.

Some part of the mind has objections to certain thoughts and actions, and another part supports the actions of the opposing thoughts. All these little living beings create inner conflict because they are alive and they each have a voice. Only by making an inventory of our agreements will we uncover all of the conflicts in the mind and eventually make order out of the chaos of the *mitote*.

Don't take anything personally because by taking things personally you set yourself up to suffer for nothing. Humans are addicted to suffering at different levels and to different degrees, and we support each other in maintaining these addictions. Humans agree to help each other suffer. If you have the need to be abused, you will find it easy to be abused by others. Likewise, if you are with people who need to suffer, something in you makes you abuse them. It is as if they have a note on their back that says, "Please kick me." They are asking for justification for their suffering. Their addiction to suffering is nothing but an agreement that is reinforced every day.

Wherever you go you will find people lying to you, and as your awareness grows, you will notice that you also lie to yourself. Do not expect people to tell you the truth because they also lie to themselves. You have to trust yourself and choose to believe or not to believe what someone says to you.

When we really see other people as they are without taking it personally, we can never be hurt by what they say or do. Even if others lie to you, it is okay. They are lying to you because they are afraid. They are afraid you will discover that they are not perfect. It is painful to take that social mask off. If others say one thing, but do another, you are lying to yourself if you don't listen to their actions. But if you are truthful with yourself, you will save yourself a lot of emotional pain. Telling yourself the truth about it may hurt, but you don't need to be attached to the pain. Healing is on the way, and it's just a matter of time before things will be better for you.

If someone is not treating you with love and respect, it is a gift if they walk away from you. If that person doesn't walk away, you will surely endure many years of suffering with him or her. Walking away may hurt for a while, but your heart will eventually heal. Then you can choose what you really want. You will find that you don't need to trust others as much as you need to trust yourself to make the right choices.

When you make it a strong habit not to take anything personally, you avoid many upsets in your life. Your anger, jealousy, and envy will disappear, and even your sadness will simply disappear if you don't take things personally.

If you can make this second agreement a habit, you will find that nothing can put you back into hell. There is a huge amount of freedom that comes to you when you take nothing personally. You become immune to black magicians, and no spell can affect you regardless of how strong it may be. The whole world can gossip about you, and if you don't take it personally you are immune. Someone can intentionally send emotional poison, and if you don't take it personally, you will not eat it. When you don't take the emotional poison, it becomes even worse in the sender, but not in you.

You can see how important this agreement is. Taking nothing personally helps you to break many habits and routines that trap you in the dream of hell and cause needless suffering. Just by practicing this second agreement you begin to break dozens of teeny, tiny agreements that cause you to suffer. And if you practice the first two agreements, you will break seventy-five percent of the teeny, tiny agreements that keep you trapped in hell.

Write this agreement on paper, and put it on your refrigerator to remind you all the time: *Don't take anything personally.*

As you make a habit of not taking anything personally, you won't need to place your trust in what others do or say. You will only need to trust yourself to make responsible choices. You are never responsible for the actions of others; you are only responsible for you. When you truly understand this, and refuse to take things personally, you can hardly be hurt by the careless comments or actions of others.

If you keep this agreement, you can travel around the world with your heart completely open and no one can hurt you. You can say, "I love you," without fear of being ridiculed or rejected. You can ask for what you need. You can say yes, or you can say no — whatever you choose — without guilt or self-judgment. You can choose to follow your heart always. Then you can be in the middle of hell and still experience inner peace and happiness. You can stay in your state of bliss, and hell will not affect you at all.

4

THE THIRD AGREEMENT

Don't Make Assumptions

THE THIRD AGREEMENT IS *DON'T MAKE ASSUMPTIONS*.

We have the tendency to make assumptions about everything. The problem with making assumptions is that we *believe* they are the truth. We could swear they are real. We make assumptions about what others are doing or thinking — we take it personally — then we blame them and react by sending emotional poison with our word. That is why when-ever we make assumptions, we're asking for prob-lems. We make an assumption, we misunderstand, we take it personally, and we end up creating a whole big drama for nothing.

All the sadness and drama you have lived in your life was rooted in making assumptions and tak-ing things personally. Take a moment to consider the truth of this statement. The whole war of con-trol between humans is about making assumptions and taking things personally. Our whole dream of hell is based on that.

We create a lot of emotional poison just by mak-ing assumptions and taking it personally, because usually we start gossiping about our assumptions. Remember, gossiping is the way we communicate to each other in the dream of hell and transfer poison to one another. Because we are afraid to ask for clar-ification, we make assumptions, and believe we are right about the assumptions; then we defend our assumptions and try to make someone else wrong.

It is always better to ask questions than to make an assumption, because assumptions set us up for suffering.

The big *mitote* in the human mind creates a lot of chaos which causes us to misinterpret everything and misunderstand everything. We only see what we want to see, and hear what we want to hear. We don't perceive things the way they are. We have the habit of dreaming with no basis in reality. We literally dream things up in our imaginations. Because we don't understand something, we make an assumption about the meaning, and when the truth comes out, the bubble of our dream pops and we find out it was not what we thought it was at all.

An example: You are walking in the mall, and you see a person you like. That person turns to you and smiles, and then walks away. You can make a lot of assumptions just because of this one experience. With these assumptions you can create a whole fantasy. And you really want to believe this fantasy and make it real. A whole dream begins to form just from your assumptions, and you can believe, "Oh, this person really likes me." In your mind a whole relationship begins from that. Maybe you even get married in this fantasyland. But the fantasy is in *your* mind, in your personal dream.

Making assumptions in our relationships is really asking for problems. Often we make the assumption that our partners know what we think and that we don't have to say what we want. We assume they are going to do what we want, because they know us so well. If they don't do what we assume they should do, we feel so hurt and say, "You should have known."

Another example: You decide to get married, and you make the assumption that your partner sees marriage the same way that you do. Then you live together and you find out this is not true. This creates a lot of conflict, but you still don't try to clarify your feelings about marriage. The husband comes home from work and the wife is mad, and the husband doesn't know why. Maybe it's because the wife made an assumption. Without telling him what she wants, she makes an assumption that he knows her so well, that he knows what she wants, as if he can read her mind. She gets so upset because he fails to meet her expectations. Making assumptions in relationships leads to a lot of fights, a lot of difficulties, a lot of misunderstandings with people we supposedly love.

In any kind of relationship we can make the assumption that others know what we think, and we don't have to say what we want. They are going to do what we want because they know us so well. If they don't do what we want, what we assume they should do, we feel hurt and think, "How could you do that? You should know." Again, we make the assumption that the other person knows what we want. A whole drama is created because we make this assumption and then put more assumptions on top of it.

It is very interesting how the human mind works. We have the need to justify everything, to explain and understand everything, in order to feel safe. We have millions of questions that need answers because there are so many things that the reasoning mind cannot explain. It is not important if the answer is correct; just the answer itself makes us feel safe. This is why we make assumptions.

If others tell us something, we make assumptions, and if they don't tell us something we make assumptions to fulfill our need to know and to replace the need to communicate. Even if we hear something and we don't understand, we make assumptions about what it means and then believe the assumptions. We make all sorts of assumptions because we don't have the courage to ask questions.

These assumptions are made so fast and unconsciously most of the time because we have agreements to communicate this way. We have agreed that it is not safe to ask questions; we have agreed that if people love us, they should know what we want or how we feel. When we believe something, we assume we are right about it to the point that we will destroy relationships in order to defend our position.

We make the assumption that everyone sees life the way *we* do. We assume that others think the way we think, feel the way we feel, judge the way we judge, and abuse the way we abuse. This is the biggest assumption that humans make. And this is why we have a fear of being ourselves around others. Because we think everyone else will judge us, victimize us, abuse us, and blame us as we do ourselves. So even before others have a chance to reject us, we have already rejected ourselves. That is the way the human mind works.

We also make assumptions about ourselves, and this creates a lot of inner conflict. "I think I am able to do this." You make this assumption, for instance, then you discover you aren't able to do it. You overestimate or underestimate yourself because you haven't taken the time to ask yourself questions and to answer them. Perhaps you need to gather more facts about a particular situation. Or maybe you need to stop lying to yourself about what you truly want.

Often when you go into a relationship with someone you like, you have to justify why you like that person. You only see what you want to see and you deny there are things you don't like about that person. You lie to yourself just to make yourself right. Then you make assumptions, and one of the assumptions is "My love will change this person." But this is not true. Your love will not change any-body. If others change, it's because they want to change, not because you can change them. Then something happens between the two of you, and you get hurt. Suddenly you see what you didn't want to see before, only now it is amplified by your emotional poison. Now you have to justify your emotional pain and blame them for your choices.

We don't need to justify love; it is there or not there. Real love is accepting other people the way they are without trying to change them. If we try to change them, this means we don't really like them. Of course, if you decide to live with someone, if you make that agreement, it is always better to make that agreement with someone who is exactly the way you want him or her to be. Find someone whom you don't have to change at all. It is much easier to find someone who is already the way you want him or her to be, instead of trying to change that person. Also, that person must love you just the way you are, so he or she doesn't have to change you at all. If others feel they have to change you, that means they really don't love you just the way you are. So why be with someone if you're not the way he or she wants you to be?

We have to be what we are, so we don't have to present a false image. If you love me the way I am, "Okay, take me." If you don't love me the way I am, "Okay, bye-bye. Find someone else." It may sound harsh, but this kind of communication means the personal agreements we make with others are clear and impeccable.

Just imagine the day that you stop making assumptions with your partner and eventually with everyone else in your life. Your way of communicating will change completely, and your relationships will no longer suffer from conflicts created by mistaken assumptions.

The way to keep yourself from making assumptions is to ask questions. Make sure the communication is clear. If you don't understand, ask. Have the courage to ask questions until you are clear as you can be, and even then do not assume you know all there is to know about a given situation. Once you hear the answer, you will not have to make assumptions because you will know the truth.

Also, find your voice to ask for what you want. Everybody has the right to tell you no or yes, but you always have the right to ask. Likewise, everybody has the right to ask you, and you have the right to say yes or no.

If you don't understand something, it is better for you to ask and be clear, instead of making an assumption. The day you stop making assumptions you will communicate cleanly and clearly, free of emotional poison. Without making assumptions your word becomes impeccable.

With clear communication, all of your relationships will change, not only with your partner, but with everyone else. You won't need to make assumptions because everything becomes so clear. This is what I want; this is what you want. If we communicate in this way, our word becomes impeccable. If all humans could communicate in this way, with impeccability of the word, there would be no wars, no violence, no misunderstandings. All human problems would be resolved if we could just have good, clear communication.

This, then, is the Third Agreement: *Don't make assumptions.* Just saying this sounds easy, but I understand that it is difficult to do. It is difficult because we so often do exactly the opposite. We have all these habits and routines that we are not even aware of. Becoming aware of these habits and understanding the importance of this agreement is the first step. But understanding its importance is not enough. Information or an idea is merely the seed in your mind. What will really make the difference is action.

Taking the action over and over again strengthens your will, nurtures the seed, and establishes a solid foundation for the new habit to grow. After many repetitions these new agreements will become second nature, and you will see how the magic of your word transforms you from a black magician into a white magician.

A white magician uses the word for creation, giving, sharing, and loving. By making this one agreement a habit, your whole life will be completely transformed.

When you transform your whole dream, magic just happens in your life. What you need comes to you easily because spirit moves freely through you. This is the mastery of intent, the mastery of the spirit, the mastery of love, the mastery of gratitude, and the mastery of life. This is the goal of the Toltec. This is the path to personal freedom.

5

THE FOURTH AGREEMENT

Always Do Your Best

THERE IS JUST ONE MORE AGREEMENT, BUT IT'S THE one that allows the other three to become deeply ingrained habits. The fourth agreement is about the action of the first three: *Always do your best.*

Under any circumstance, always do your best, no more and no less. But keep in mind that your best is never going to be the same from one moment to the next. Everything is alive and changing all the time, so your best will sometimes be high quality, and other times it will not be as good. When you wake up refreshed and energized in the morning, your best will be better than when you are tired at night. Your best will be different when you are healthy as opposed to sick, or sober as opposed to drunk. Your best will depend on whether you are feeling wonderful and happy, or upset, angry, or jealous.

In your everyday moods your best can change from one moment to another, from one hour to the next, from one day to another. Your best will also change over time. As you build the habit of the four new agreements, your best will become better than it used to be.

Regardless of the quality, keep doing your best — no more and no less than your best. If you try too hard to do more than your best, you will spend more energy than is needed and in the end your best will not be enough. When you overdo, you deplete your body and go against yourself, and it will take you longer to accomplish your goal. But if you do less than your best, you subject yourself to frustrations, self-judgment, guilt, and regrets.

Just do your best — in any circumstance in your life. It doesn't matter if you are sick or tired, if you always do your best there is no way you can judge yourself. And if you don't judge yourself there is no way you are going to suffer from guilt, blame, and self-punishment. By always doing your best, you will break a big spell that you have been under.

There was a man who wanted to transcend his suffering so he went to a Buddhist temple to find a Master to help him. He went to the Master and asked, "Master, if I meditate four hours a day, how long will it take me to transcend?"

The Master looked at him and said, "If you meditate four hours a day, perhaps you will transcend in ten years."

Thinking he could do better, the man then said, "Oh, Master, what if I meditated eight hours a day, how long will it take me to transcend?"

The Master looked at him and said, "If you meditate eight hours a day, perhaps you will transcend in twenty years."

"But why will it take me longer if I meditate more?" the man asked.

The Master replied, "You are not here to sacrifice your joy or your life. You are here to live, to be happy, and to love. If you can do your best in two hours of meditation, but you spend eight hours instead, you will only grow tired, miss the point, and you won't enjoy your life. Do your best, and perhaps you will learn that no matter how long you meditate, you can live, love, and be happy."

Doing your best, you are going to live your life intensely. You are going to be productive, you are going to be good to yourself, because you will be giving yourself to your family, to your community, to everything. But it is the action that is going to make you feel intensely happy. When you always do your best, you take action. Doing your best is taking the action because you love it, not because you're expecting a reward. Most people do exactly the opposite: They only take action when they expect a reward, and they don't enjoy the action. And that's the reason why they don't do their best.

For example, most people go to work every day just thinking of payday, and the money they will get from the work they are doing. They can hardly wait for Friday or Saturday, whatever day they receive their money and can take time off. They are working for the reward, and as a result they resist work. They try to avoid the action and it becomes more difficult, and they don't do their best.

They work so hard all week long, suffering the work, suffering the action, not because they like to, but because they feel they have to. They have to work because they have to pay the rent, because they have to support their family. They have all that frustration, and when they do receive their money they are unhappy. They have two days to rest, to do what they want to do, and what do they do? They try to escape. They get drunk because they don't like themselves. They don't like their life. There are many ways that we hurt ourselves when we don't like who we are.

On the other hand, if you take action just for the sake of doing it, without expecting a reward, you will find that you enjoy every action you do. Rewards will come, but you are not attached to the reward. You can even get more than you would have imagined for yourself without expecting a reward. If we like what we do, if we always do our best, then we are really enjoying life. We are having fun, we don't get bored, we don't have frustrations.

When you do your best, you don't give the Judge the opportunity to find you guilty or to blame you. If you have done your best and the Judge tries to judge you according to your Book of Law, you've got the answer: "I did my best." There are no regrets. That is why we always do our best. It is not an easy agreement to keep, but this agreement is really going to set you free.

When you do your best you learn to accept yourself. But you have to be aware and learn from your mistakes. Learning from your mistakes means you practice, look honestly at the results, and keep practicing. This increases your awareness.

Doing your best really doesn't feel like work because you enjoy whatever you are doing. You know you're doing your best when you are enjoying the action or doing it in a way that will not have negative repercussions for you. You do your best because you want to do it, not because you have to do it, not because you are trying to please the Judge, and not because you are trying to please other people.

If you take action because you have to, then there is no way you are going to do your best. Then it is better not to do it. No, you do your best because doing your best all the time makes *you* so happy. When you are doing your best just for the pleasure of doing it, you are taking action because you enjoy the action.

Action is about living fully. Inaction is the way that we deny life. Inaction is sitting in front of the television every day for years because you are afraid to be alive and to take the risk of expressing what you are. Expressing what you are is taking action. You can have many great ideas in your head, but what makes the difference is the action. Without action upon an idea, there will be no manifestation, no results, and no reward.

A good example of this comes from the story about Forrest Gump. He didn't have great ideas, but he took action. He was happy because he always did his best at whatever he did. He was richly rewarded without expecting any reward at all. Taking action is being alive. It's taking the risk to go out and express your dream. This is different than imposing your dream on someone else, because everyone has the right to express his or her dream.

Doing your best is a great habit to have. I do my best in everything I do and feel. Doing my best has become a ritual in my life because I made the choice to make it a ritual. It's a belief like any other belief that I choose. I make everything a ritual, and I always do my best. Taking a shower is a ritual for me, and with that action I tell my body how much I love it. I feel and enjoy the water on my body. I do my best to fulfill the needs of my body. I do my best to give to my body and to receive what my body gives to me.

In India they perform a ritual called *puja*. In this ritual, they take idols that represent God in many different forms and bathe them, feed them, and give their love to them. They even chant mantras to these idols. The idol itself is not important. What is important is the way they perform the ritual, the way they say, "I love you, God."

God is life. God is life in action. The best way to say, "I love you, God," is to live your life doing your best. The best way to say, "Thank you, God," is by letting go of the past and living in the present moment, right here and now. Whatever life takes away from you, let it go. When you surrender and let go of the past, you allow yourself to be fully alive in the moment. Letting go of the past means you can enjoy the dream that is happening right now.

If you live in a past dream, you don't enjoy what is happening right now because you will always wish it to be different than it is. There is no time to miss anyone or anything because you are alive. Not enjoying what is happening right now is living in the past and being only half alive. This leads to self-pity, suffering, and tears.

You were born with the right to be happy. You were born with the right to love, to enjoy and to share your love. You are alive, so take your life and enjoy it. Don't resist life passing through you, because that is God passing through you. Just your existence proves the existence of God. Your existence proves the existence of life and energy.

We don't need to know or prove anything. Just to be, to take a risk and enjoy your life, is all that matters. Say no when you want to say no, and yes when you want to say yes. You have the right to be you. You can only be you when you do your best. When you don't do your best you are denying yourself the right to be you. That's a seed that you should really nurture in your mind. You don't need knowledge or great philosophical concepts. You don't need the acceptance of others. You express your own divinity by being alive and by loving yourself and others. It is an expression of God to say, "Hey, I love you."

The first three agreements will only work if you do your best. Don't expect that you will always be able to be impeccable with your word. Your routine habits are too strong and firmly rooted in your mind. But you can do your best. Don't expect that you will never take anything personally; just do your best. Don't expect that you will never make another assumption, but you can certainly do your best.

By doing your best, the habits of misusing your word, taking things personally, and making assumptions will become weaker and less frequent with time. You don't need to judge yourself, feel guilty, or punish yourself if you cannot keep these agreements. If you're doing your best, you will feel good about yourself even if you still make assumptions, still take things personally, and still are not impeccable with your word.

If you do your best always, over and over again, you will become a master of transformation. Practice makes the master. By doing your best *you* become a master. Everything you have ever learned, you learned through repetition. You learned to write, to drive, and even to walk by repetition. You are a master of speaking your language because you practiced. Action is what makes the difference.

If you do your best in the search for personal freedom, in the search for self-love, you will discover that it's just a matter of time before you find what you are looking for. It's not about daydreaming or sitting for hours dreaming in meditation. You have to stand up and be a human. You have to honor the man or woman that you are. Respect your body, enjoy your body, love your body, feed, clean, and heal your body. Exercise and do what makes your body feel good. This is a *puja* to your body, and that is a communion between you and God.

You don't need to worship idols of the Virgin Mary, the Christ, or the Buddha. You can if you want to; if it feels good, do it. Your own body is a manifestation of God, and if you honor your body everything will change for you. When you practice giving love to every part of your body, you plant seeds of love in your mind, and when they grow, you will love, honor, and respect your body immensely.

Every action then becomes a ritual in which you are honoring God. After that, the next step is honoring God with every thought, every emotion, every belief, even what is "right" or "wrong." Every thought becomes a communion with God, and you will live a dream without judgments, victimization, and free of the need to gossip and abuse yourself.

When you honor these four agreements together, there is no way that you will live in hell.

There is *no way*. If you are impeccable with your word, if you don't take anything personally, if you don't make assumptions, if you always do your best, then you are going to have a beautiful life. You are going to control your life one hundred percent.

The Four Agreements are a summary of the mastery of transformation, one of the masteries of the Toltec. You transform hell into heaven. The dream of the planet is transformed into your personal dream of heaven. The knowledge is there; it's just waiting for you to use it. The Four Agreements are there; you just need to adopt these agreements and respect their meaning and power.

Just do your best to honor these agreements. You can make this agreement today: I choose to honor The Four Agreements. It's so simple and logical that even a child can understand them. But, you must have a very strong will, a very strong will to keep these agreements. Why? Because wherever we go we find that our path is full of obstacles. Everyone tries to sabotage our commitment to these new agreements, and everything around us is a setup for us to break them. The problem is all the other agreements that are a part of the dream of the planet. They are alive, and they are very strong.

That's why you need to be a great hunter, a great warrior, who can defend these Four Agreements with your life. Your happiness, your freedom, your entire way of living depends on it. The warrior's goal is to transcend this world, to escape from this hell, and never come back. As the Toltecs teach us, the reward is to transcend the human experience of suffering, to become the embodiment of God. That is the reward.

We really need to use every bit of power we have to succeed in keeping these agreements. I didn't expect that I could do it at first. I have fallen many times, but I stood up and kept going. And I fell again, and I kept going. I didn't feel sorry for myself. There was no way that I felt sorry for myself. I said, "If I fall, I am strong enough, I'm intelligent enough, I can do it!" I stood up and kept going. I fell and I kept going and going, and each time it became easier and easier. Yet, in the beginning it was so hard, so difficult.

So if you fall, do not judge. Do not give your Judge the satisfaction of turning you into a victim. No, be tough with yourself. Stand up and make the agreement again. "Okay, I broke my agreement to be impeccable with my word. I will start all over again. I am going to keep The Four Agreements just for today. Today I will be impeccable with my word, I will not take anything personally, I will not make any assumptions, and I am going to do my best."

If you break an agreement, begin again tomorrow, and again the next day. It will be difficult at first, but each day will become easier and easier, until someday you will discover that you are ruling your life with these Four Agreements. And, you will be surprised at the way your life has been transformed.

You don't need to be religious or go to church every day. Your love and self-respect are growing and growing. You can do it. If I did it, you can do it also.

Do not be concerned about the future; keep your attention on today, and stay in the present moment. Just live one day at a time. *Always do your best* to keep these agreements, and soon it will be easy for you. Today is the beginning of a new dream.

6

THE TOLTEC PATH TO FREEDOM

Breaking Old Agreements

EVERYONE TALKS ABOUT FREEDOM. ALL AROUND the world different people, different races, different countries are fighting for freedom. But what is freedom? In America we speak of living in a free country. But are we really free? Are we free to be who we really are? The answer is no, we are not free. True freedom has to do with the human spirit — it is the freedom to be who we really are.

Who stops us from being free? We blame the government, we blame the weather, we blame our parents, we blame religion, we blame God. Who really stops us from being free? We stop ourselves. What does it really mean to be free? Sometimes we get married and we say that we lose our freedom, then we get divorced and we are still not free. What stops us? Why can't we be ourselves?

We have memories of long ago, when we used to be free and we loved being free, but we have forgotten what freedom really means.

If we see a child who is two or three, perhaps four years old, we find a free human. Why is this human free? Because this human does whatever he or she wants to do. The human is completely wild. Just like a flower, a tree, or an animal that has not been domesticated — wild! And if we observe humans who are two years old, we find that most of the time these humans have a big smile on their face and they're having fun. They are exploring the world. They are not afraid to play. They are afraid when they are hurt, when they are hungry, when some of their needs are not met, but they don't worry about the past, don't care about the future, and only live in the present moment.

Very young children are not afraid to express what they feel. They are so loving that if they perceive love, they melt into love. They are not afraid to love at all. That is the description of a normal human being. As children we are not afraid of the future or ashamed of the past. Our normal human tendency is to enjoy life, to play, to explore, to be happy, and to love.

But, what has happened with the adult human? Why are we so different? Why are we not wild? From the point of view of the Victim we can say that something sad happened to us, and from the point of view of the warrior we can say that what happened to us is normal. What has happened is that we have the Book of Law, the big Judge and the

Victim who rule our lives. We are no longer free because the Judge, the Victim, and the belief system don't allow us to be who we really are. Once our minds have been programmed with all that garbage, we are no longer happy.

This chain of training from human to human, from generation to generation, is perfectly normal in human society. You don't need to blame your parents for teaching you to be like them. What else could they teach you but what they know? They did the best they could, and if they abused you, it was due to their own domestication, their own fears, their own beliefs. They had no control over the programming they received, so they couldn't have behaved any differently.

There is no need to blame your parents or anyone who abused you in your life, including yourself. But it is time to stop the abuse. It is time to free yourself of the tyranny of the Judge by changing the foundation of your own agreements. It is time to be free from the role of the Victim.

The real you is still a little child who never grew up. Sometimes that little child comes out when you are having fun or playing, when you feel happy, when you are painting, or writing poetry, or playing the piano, or expressing yourself in some way. These are the happiest moments of your life — when the real you comes out, when you don't care about the past and you don't worry about the future. You are childlike.

But there is something that changes all that: We call them *responsibilities.* The Judge says, "Wait a second, you are responsible, you have things to do, you have to work, you have to go to school, you have to earn a living." All these responsibilities come to mind. Our face changes and becomes serious again. If you watch children when they are playing adults, you will see their little faces change. "Let's pretend I'm a lawyer," and right away their faces change; the adult face takes over. We go to court and that is the face we see — and that is what we are. We are still children, but we have lost our freedom.

The freedom we are looking for is the freedom to be ourselves, to express ourselves. But if we look at our lives we will see that most of the time we do things just to please others, just to be accepted by others, rather than living our lives to please ourselves. That is what has happened to our freedom. And we see in our society and all the societies around the world, that for every thousand people, nine hundred and ninety-nine are completely domesticated.

The worst part is that most of us are not even aware that we are not free. There is something inside that whispers to us that we are not free, but we do not understand what it is, and why we are not free.

The problem with most people is that they live their lives and never discover that the Judge and the Victim rule their mind, and therefore they don't have a chance to be free. The first step toward personal freedom is awareness. We need to be aware that we are not free in order to be free. We need to be aware of what the problem is in order to solve the problem.

Awareness is always the first step because if you are not aware, there is nothing you can change. If you are not aware that your mind is full of wounds and emotional poison, you cannot begin to clean and heal the wounds and you will continue to suffer.

There is no reason to suffer. With awareness you can rebel and say, "This is enough!" You can look for a way to heal and transform your personal dream. The dream of the planet is just a dream. It is not even real. If you go into the dream and start challenging your beliefs, you will find that most of the beliefs that guided you into the wounded mind are not even true. You will find that you suffered all those years of drama for nothing. Why? Because the belief system that was put inside your mind is based on lies.

That is why it is important for you to master your own dream; that is why the Toltecs became dream masters. Your life is the manifestation of your dream; it is an art. And you can change your life anytime if you aren't enjoying the dream. Dream masters create a masterpiece of life; they control the dream by making choices. Everything has consequences and a dream master is aware of the consequences.

To be Toltec is a way of life. It is a way of life where there are no leaders and no followers, where you have your own truth and live your own truth. A Toltec becomes wise, becomes wild, and becomes free again.

There are three masteries that lead people to become Toltecs. First is the Mastery of Awareness. This is to be aware of who we really are, with all the possibilities. The second is the Mastery of Transformation — how to change, how to be free of domestication. The third is the Mastery of Intent. Intent from the Toltec point of view is that part of life that makes transformation of energy possible; it is the one living being that seamlessly encompasses all energy, or what we call "God." Intent is life itself; it is unconditional love. The Mastery of Intent is therefore the Mastery of Love.

When we talk about the Toltec path to freedom, we find that they have an entire map for breaking free of domestication. They compare the Judge, the Victim, and the belief system to a parasite that invades the human mind. From the Toltec point of view, all humans who are domesticated are sick. They are sick because there is a parasite that controls the mind and controls the brain. The food for the parasite is the negative emotions that come from fear.

If we look at the description of a parasite, we find that a parasite is a living being who lives off of other living beings, sucking their energy without any useful contribution in return, and hurting their host little by little. The Judge, the Victim, and the belief system fit this description very well. Together they comprise a living being made of psychic or emotional energy, and that energy is alive. Of course it is not material energy, but neither are emotions material energy. Our dreams are not material energy either, but we know they exist.

One function of the brain is to transform material energy into emotional energy. Our brain is the factory of the emotions. And we have said that the main function of the mind is to dream. The Toltecs believe that the parasite — the Judge, the Victim, and the belief system — has control of your mind; it controls your personal dream. The parasite dreams through your mind and lives its life through your body. It survives on the emotions that come from fear, and thrives on drama and suffering.

The freedom we seek is to use our own mind and body, to live our own life, instead of the life of the belief system. When we discover that the mind is controlled by the Judge and the Victim and the real "us" is in the corner, we have just two choices. One choice is to keep living the way we are, to surrender to the Judge and the Victim, to keep living in the dream of the planet. The second choice is to do what we do as children when parents try to domesticate us. We can rebel and say "No!" We can declare a war against the parasite, a war against the Judge and the

Victim, a war for our independence, a war for the right to use our own mind and our own brain.

That is why in all the shamanic traditions in America, from Canada to Argentina, people call themselves *warriors*, because they are in a war against the parasite in the mind. That is the real meaning of a warrior. The warrior is one who rebels against the invasion of the parasite. The warrior rebels and declares a war. But to be a warrior doesn't mean we always win the war; we may win or we may lose, but we always do our best and at least we have a chance to be free again. Choosing this path gives us, at the very least, the dignity of rebellion, and ensures that we will not be the helpless victim of our own whimsical emotions or the poisonous emotions of others. Even if we succumb to the enemy — the parasite — we will not be among those victims who would not fight back.

At best, being a warrior gives us an opportunity to transcend the dream of the planet, and to change our personal dream to a dream that we call *heaven*. Just like hell, heaven is a place that exists within our mind. It is a place of joy, a place where we are happy, where we are free to love and to be who we really are. We can reach heaven while we are alive; we don't have to wait until we die. God is always present and the kingdom of heaven is everywhere, but first we need to have the eyes and ears to see and hear that truth. We need to be free of the parasite.

The parasite can be compared to a monster with a thousand heads. Every head of the parasite is one of the fears that we have. If we want to be free, we have to destroy the parasite. One solution is to attack the parasite head by head, which means we face each of our fears, one by one. This is a slow process, but it works. Every time we face one of the fears we are a little more free.

A second approach is to stop feeding the parasite. If we don't give the parasite any food, we kill the parasite by starvation. To do this we have to gain control of our emotions, we have to refrain from fueling the emotions that come from fear. This is easy to say, but it is very difficult to do. It is difficult because the Judge and the Victim control our mind.

A third solution is called the *initiation of the dead.* The initiation of the dead is found in many traditions and esoteric schools around the world. We find it in Egypt, India, Greece, and America. This is a symbolic death which kills the parasite without harming our physical body. When we "die" symbolically the parasite has to die. This is faster than the first two solutions, but it is even more difficult to do. We need a great deal of courage to face the angel of death. We need to be very strong.

Let's take a closer look at each of these solutions.

THE ART OF TRANSFORMATION: THE DREAM OF THE SECOND ATTENTION

We have learned that the dream you are living now is the result of the outside dream hooking your attention and feeding you all of your beliefs. The process of domestication can be called *the dream of the first attention* because it was how your attention was used for the first time to create the first dream of your life.

One way to change your beliefs is to focus your attention on all those agreements and beliefs, and change the agreements with yourself. In doing this you are using your attention for the second time, thus creating *the dream of the second attention* or the new dream.

The difference is that you are no longer innocent. When you were a child this was not true; you didn't have a choice. But you are no longer a child. Now it's up to you to choose what to believe and what not to believe. You can choose to believe in anything, and that includes believing in yourself.

The first step is to become aware of the fog that is in your mind. You must become aware that you are dreaming all the time. Only with awareness do you have the possibility of transforming your dream. If you have the awareness that the whole drama of your life is the result of what you believe, and what you believe is not real, then you can begin to change it. However, to really change your beliefs you need to focus your attention on what it is that you want to change. You have to know which agreements you want to change before you can change them.

So the next step is to develop awareness of all the self-limiting, fear-based beliefs that make you un-happy. You take an inventory of all that you believe, all your agreements, and through this process you begin the transformation. The Toltecs called this the Art of Transformation, and it's a whole mastery. You achieve the Mastery of Transformation by changing the fear-based agreements that make you suffer, and reprogramming your own mind, in your own way. One of the ways to do this is to explore and adopt alternative beliefs such as the Four Agreements.

The decision to adopt the Four Agreements is a declaration of war to regain your freedom from the parasite. The Four Agreements offer the possibility of ending the emotional pain, which can open the door for you to enjoy your life and begin a new dream. It's up to you to explore the possibilities of your dream, if you are interested. The Four Agree-ments were created to assist you in the Art of

Transformation, to help you break the limiting agreements, gain more personal power, and become stronger. The stronger you get, the more agreements you can break until the moment comes when you make it to the core of all of those agreements.

Going to the core of those agreements is what I call *going into the desert.* When you go into the desert you meet your demons face-to-face. After coming out of the desert, all those demons become angels.

Practicing the four new agreements is a big act of power. Breaking the spell of black magic in your mind requires great personal power. Every time you break an agreement, you gain extra power. You start by breaking agreements that are very small and require less power. As those smaller agreements are broken, your personal power will increase until you reach a point when you can finally face the big demons in your mind.

For example, the little girl who was told not to sing is now twenty years old and she still does not sing. One way she can overcome the belief that her voice is ugly is to say, "Okay, I will try to sing, even if I do sing badly." Then she can pretend that someone is clapping and telling her, "Oh! That was beautiful." This may break the agreement a teeny, tiny bit, but it will still be there. However, now she has a little more power and courage to try again and again until finally she breaks the agreement.

That's one way out of the dream of hell. But for every agreement you break that makes you suffer, you will need to replace it with a new agreement that makes you happy. This will keep the old agreement from coming back. If you occupy the same space with a new agreement, then the old agreement is gone forever and in its place is the new agreement.

There are many strong beliefs in the mind that can make this process look hopeless. This is why you need to go step-by-step and be patient with yourself because this is a slow process. The way you are living now is the result of many years of domestication. You cannot expect to break the domestication in one day. Breaking agreements is very difficult because we put the power of the word (which is the power of our will) into every agreement we have made.

We need the same amount of power to change an agreement. We cannot change an agreement with less power than we used to make the agreement, and almost all our personal power is invested in keeping the agreements we have with ourselves. That's because our agreements are actually like a strong addiction. We are addicted to being the way we are. We are addicted to anger, jealousy, and self-pity. We are addicted to the beliefs that tell us, "I'm not good enough, I'm not intelligent enough. Why even try? Other people will do it because they're better than me."

All of these old agreements which rule our dream of life are the result of repeating them over and over again. Therefore, to adopt the Four Agreements, you need to put repetition in action. Practicing the new agreements in your life is how your best becomes better. Repetition makes the master.

THE DISCIPLINE OF THE WARRIOR: CONTROLLING YOUR OWN BEHAVIOR

Imagine that you awake early one morning overflowing with enthusiasm for the day. You feel good. You are happy and have plenty of energy to face the day. Then at breakfast, you have a big fight with your spouse, and a flood of emotion comes out. You get mad, and in the emotion of anger you spend a lot of personal power. After the fight, you feel drained, and you just want to go and cry. In fact, you feel so tired that you go to your room, collapse, and try to recover. You spend the day wrapped up in your emotions. You have no energy to keep going, and you just want to walk away from everything.

Every day we awake with a certain amount of mental, emotional, and physical energy that we spend throughout the day. If we allow our emotions to deplete our energy, we have no energy to change our lives or to give to others.

The way you see the world will depend upon the emotions you are feeling. When you are angry, everything around you is wrong, nothing is right. You blame everything including the weather; whether it's raining or the sun is shining, nothing pleases you. When you are sad, everything around you is sad and makes you cry. You see the trees and you feel sad; you see the rain and everything looks so sad. Perhaps you feel vulnerable and have a need to protect yourself because you don't know in what moment someone will attack you. You do not trust anything or anyone around you. This is because you see the world with the eyes of fear!

Imagine that the human mind is the same as your skin. You can touch healthy skin and it feels wonderful. Your skin is made for perception and the sensation of touch is wonderful. Now imagine you have an injury and the skin gets cut and infected. If you touch the infected skin, it is going to hurt, so you try to cover and protect the skin. You will not enjoy being touched because it hurts.

Now imagine that all humans have this skin disease. Nobody can touch each other because it is going to hurt. Everyone has wounds on their skin, so the infection is seen as normal, the pain is also considered normal; we believe we are supposed to be that way.

Can you imagine how we would behave with each other if all the humans in the world had this skin disease? Of course we would hardly ever hug each other because it would be too painful. So we would need to create a lot of distance between us.

The human mind is exactly like this description of infected skin. Every human has an emotional body completely covered with infected wounds. Each wound is infected with emotional poison — the poison of all the emotions that makes us suffer, such as hate, anger, envy, and sadness. An action of injustice opens a wound in the mind and we react with emotional poison because of the concepts and beliefs we have about injustice and what is fair. The mind is so wounded and full of poison by the process of domestication, that everyone describes the wounded mind as normal. This is considered normal, but I can tell you it is not normal.

We have a dysfunctional dream of the planet, and humans are mentally sick with a disease called fear. The symptoms of the disease are all the emotions that make humans suffer: anger, hate, sadness, envy, and betrayal. When the fear is too great, the reasoning mind begins to fail, and we call this mental illness. Psychotic behavior occurs when the mind is so frightened and the wounds so painful, that it seems better to break contact with the outside world.

If we can see our state of mind as a disease, we find there is a cure. We don't have to suffer any longer. First we need the truth to open the emotional wounds, take the poison out, and heal the wounds completely. How do we do this? We must forgive those we feel have wronged us, not because they deserve to be forgiven, but because we love ourselves so much we don't want to keep paying for the injustice.

Forgiveness is the only way to heal. We can choose to forgive because we feel compassion for ourselves. We can let go of the resentment and de-clare, "That's enough! I will no longer be the big Judge that goes against myself. I will no longer beat myself up and abuse myself. I will no longer be the Victim."

First, we need to forgive our parents, our broth-ers, our sisters, our friends, and God. Once you forgive God, you can finally forgive yourself. Once you forgive yourself, the self-rejection in your mind is over. Self-acceptance begins, and the self-love will grow so strong that you will finally accept yourself just the way you are. That's the beginning of the free human. Forgiveness is the key.

You will know you have forgiven someone when you see them and you no longer have an emotional reaction. You will hear the name of the person and you will have no emotional reaction. When someone can touch what used to be a wound and it no longer hurts you, then you know you have truly forgiven.

The truth is like a scalpel. The truth is painful, because it opens all of the wounds which are cov-ered by lies so that we can be healed. These lies are what we call *the denial system*. It's a good thing we have the denial system, because it allows us to cover our wounds and still function. But once we no longer have any wounds or any poison, we don't need to lie anymore. We don't need the denial system, because a healthy mind, like healthy skin, can be touched without hurting. It's pleasurable for the mind to be touched when it is clean.

The problem with most people is that they lose control of their emotions. It is the emotions that control the behavior of the human, not the human who controls the emotions. When we lose control we say things that we don't want to say, and do things that we don't want to do. That is why it is so important to be impeccable with our word and to become a spiritual warrior. We must learn to control the emotions so we have enough personal power to change our fear-based agreements, escape from hell, and create our own personal heaven.

How are we to become a warrior? There are certain characteristics of the warrior that are nearly the same around the world. The warrior has aware-ness. That's very important. We are aware that we are at war, and the war in our minds requires discipline. Not the discipline of a soldier, but the discipline of a warrior. Not the discipline from the outside to tell us what to do and what not to do, but the discipline to be ourselves, no matter what.

The warrior has control. Not control over an-other human, but control over one's own emotions, control over one's own self. It is when we lose control that we repress the emotions, not when we are in control. The big difference between a warrior and a victim is that the victim represses, and the warrior refrains. Victims repress because they are afraid to show the emotions, afraid to say what they want to say. To refrain is not the same thing as repression. To refrain is to hold the emotions and to express them in the right moment, not before, not later. That is why warriors are impeccable. They have complete control over their own emotions and therefore over their own behavior.

THE INITIATION OF THE DEAD:
EMBRACING THE ANGEL OF DEATH

The final way to attain personal freedom is to prepare ourselves for the initiation of the dead, to take death itself as our teacher. What the angel of death can teach us is how to be truly alive. We become aware that we can die at any moment; we have just the present to be alive. The truth is that we don't know if we are going to die tomorrow. Who knows? We have the idea that we have many years in the future. But do we?

If we go to the hospital and the doctor tells us that we have one week to live, what are we going to do? As we have said before, we have two choices. One is to suffer because we are going to die, and to tell everyone, "Poor me, I am going to die," and really create a huge drama. The other choice is to use every moment to be happy, to do what we really enjoy doing. If we only have one week to live, let's enjoy life. Let's be alive. We can say, "I'm going to be myself. No longer am I going to run my life trying to please other people.

No longer am I going to be afraid of what they think about me. What do I care what others think if I am going to die in one week? I'm going to be myself."

The angel of death can teach us to live every day as if it is the last day of our lives, as if there may be no tomorrow. We can begin each day by saying, "I am awake, I see the sun. I am going to give my gratitude to the sun and to everything and everyone, because I am still alive. One more day to be myself."

That is the way I see life, that is what the angel of death taught me — to be completely open, to know that there is nothing to be afraid of. And of course I treat the people I love with love because this may be the last day that I can tell you how much I love you. I don't know if I am going to see you again, so I don't want to fight with you.

What if I had a big fight with you and I told you all those emotional poisons that I have against you and you die tomorrow? Oops! Oh my God, the Judge will get me so bad, and I will feel so guilty for everything that I told you. I will even feel guilty for not telling you how much I love you. The love that makes me happy is the love that I can share with you. Why do I need to deny that I love you? It is not important if you love me back. I may die tomorrow or you may die tomorrow. What makes me happy now is to let you know how much I love you.

You can live your life this way. By doing so, you prepare yourself for the initiation of death. What is going to happen in the initiation of death is that the old dream that you have in your mind is going to die forever. Yes, you are going to have memories of the parasite — of the Judge, the Victim, and what you used to believe — but the parasite will be dead.

That is what is going to die in the initiation of death — the parasite. It is not easy to go for the initiation of death because the Judge and the Victim will fight with everything they have. They don't want to die. And we feel we are the ones who are going to die, and we are afraid of this death.

When we live in the dream of the planet, it is as if we are dead. Whoever survives the initiation of the dead receives the most wonderful gift: the resurrection. To receive the resurrection is to arise from the dead, to be alive, to be ourselves again. The resurrection is to be like a child — to be wild and free, but with a difference. The difference is that we have freedom with wisdom instead of innocence. We are able to break our domestication, become free again, and heal our mind. We surrender to the angel of death, knowing that the parasite will die and we will still be alive with a healthy mind and perfect reason. Then we are free to use our own mind and run our own life.

That is what, in the Toltec way, the angel of death teaches us. The angel of death comes to us and says, "You see everything that exists here is mine; it is not yours. Your house, your spouse, your children, your car, your career, your money — everything is mine and I can take it away when I want to, but for now you can use it."

If we surrender to the angel of death we will be happy forever and ever. Why? Because the angel of death takes the past away in order to make it possible for life to continue. For every moment that is past, the angel of death keeps taking the part that is dead and we keep living in the present. The parasite wants us to carry the past with us and that makes it so heavy to be alive. When we try to live in the past, how can we enjoy the present? When we dream of the future, why must we carry the burden of the past? When are we going to live in the present? That is what the angel of death teaches us to do.

7

THE NEW DREAM

Heaven on Earth

I WANT YOU TO FORGET EVERYTHING YOU HAVE learned in your whole life. This is the beginning of a new understanding, a new dream.

The dream you are living is your creation. It is your perception of reality that you can change at any time. You have the power to create hell, and you have the power to create heaven. Why not dream a different dream? Why not use your mind, your imagination, and your emotions to dream heaven?

Just use your imagination and a tremendous thing will happen. Imagine that you have the ability to see the world with different eyes, whenever you choose. Each time you open your eyes, you see the world around you in a different way.

Close your eyes now, and then open them and look outside.

What you will see is love coming out of the trees, love coming out of the sky, love coming out of the light. You will perceive love from everything around you. This is the state of bliss. You perceive love directly from everything, including yourself and other humans. Even when humans are sad or angry, behind these feelings you can see that they are also sending love.

Using your imagination and your new eyes of perception, I want you to see yourself living a new life, a new dream, a life where you don't need to justify your existence and you are free to be who you really are.

Imagine that you have permission to be happy and to really enjoy your life. Your life is free of conflict with yourself and with others.

Imagine living your life without fear of expressing your dreams. You know what you want, what you don't want, and when you want it. You are free to change your life the way you really want to. You are not afraid to ask for what you need, to say yes or no to anything or anyone.

Imagine living your life without the fear of being judged by others. You no longer rule your behavior according to what others may think about you. You are no longer responsible for anyone's opinion. You have no need to control anyone, and no one controls you, either.

Imagine living your life without judging others. You can easily forgive others and let go of any judgments that you have. You don't have the need to be right, and you don't need to make anyone else wrong. You respect yourself and everyone else, and they respect you in return.

Imagine living without the fear of loving and not being loved. You are no longer afraid to be rejected, and you don't have the need to be accepted. You can say "I love you" with no shame or justification. You can walk in the world with your heart completely open, and not be afraid to be hurt.

Imagine living your life without being afraid to take a risk and to explore life. You are not afraid to lose anything. You are not afraid to be alive in the world, and you are not afraid to die.

Imagine that you love yourself just the way you are. You love your body just the way it is, and you love your emotions just the way they are. You know that you are perfect just as you are.

The reason I ask you to imagine these things is because they are all entirely possible! You can live in the state of grace, the state of bliss, the dream of heaven. But in order to experience this dream, you must first understand what it is.

Only love has the ability to put you in that state of bliss. Being in bliss is like being in love. Being in love is like being in bliss. You are floating in the clouds. You are perceiving love wherever you go. It is entirely possible to live this way all the time. It is possible because others have done it and they are no different from you. They live in bliss because they have changed their agreements and are dreaming a different dream.

Once you feel what it means to live in a state of bliss, you will love it. You will know that heaven on earth is truth — that heaven truly exists. Once you know that heaven exists, once you know it is possible to stay there, it's up to you to make the effort to do it. Two thousand years ago, Jesus told us about the kingdom of heaven, the kingdom of love, but hardly anyone was ready to hear this. They said, "What are you talking about? My heart is empty, I don't feel the love that you are talking about; I don't feel the peace that you have." You don't have to do this. Just imagine that his message of love is possible and you will find that it is yours.

The world is very beautiful and very wonderful. Life can be very easy when love is your way of life.

You can be loving all the time. This is your choice. You may not have a reason to love, but you can love because to love makes you so happy. Love in action only produces happiness. Love will give you inner peace. It will change your perception of everything.

You can see everything with the eyes of love. You can be aware that there is love all around you. When you live this way, there is no longer a fog in your mind. The *mitote* has gone on a permanent vacation. This is what humans have been seeking for centuries. For thousands of years we have been searching for happiness. Happiness is the lost paradise. Humans have worked so hard to reach this point, and this is part of the evolution of the mind. This is the future of humanity.

This way of life is possible, and it's in your hands. Moses called it the Promised Land, Buddha called it Nirvana, Jesus called it Heaven, and the Toltecs call it a New Dream. Unfortunately, your identity is mixed with the dream of the planet. All of your beliefs and agreements are there in the fog.

You feel the presence of the parasite and believe it is you. This makes it difficult to let go — to release the parasite and create the space to experience love. You are attached to the Judge, attached to the Victim. Suffering makes you feel safe because you know it so well.

But there is really no reason to suffer. The only reason you suffer is because you choose to suffer. If you look at your life you will find many excuses to suffer, but a good reason to suffer you will not find. The same is true for happiness. The only reason you are happy is because you choose to be happy. Happiness is a choice, and so is suffering.

Maybe we cannot escape from the destiny of the human, but we have a choice: to suffer our destiny or to enjoy our destiny. To suffer, or to love and be happy. To live in hell, or to live in heaven. My choice is to live in heaven. What is yours?

Prayers

PLEASE TAKE A MOMENT TO CLOSE YOUR EYES, OPEN your heart, and feel all the love that comes from your heart.

I want you to join with my words in your mind and in your heart, to feel a very strong connection of love. Together, we are going to do a very special prayer to experience a communion with our Creator.

Focus your attention on your lungs, as if only your lungs exist. Feel the pleasure when your lungs expand to fulfill the biggest need of the human body — to breathe.

Take a deep breath and feel the air as it fills your lungs. Feel how the air is nothing but love. Notice the connection between the air and the lungs, a connection of love. Expand your lungs with air until your body has the need to expel that air. And then exhale, and feel the pleasure again. Because when we fulfill any need of the human body, it gives us pleasure. To breathe gives us much pleasure. Just to breathe is enough for us to always be happy, to enjoy life. Just to be alive is enough. Feel the pleasure to be alive, the pleasure of the feeling of love. . . .

PRAYER FOR FREEDOM

Today, Creator of the Universe, we ask that you come to us and share with us a strong communion of love. We know that your real name is Love, that to have a communion with you means to share the same vibration, the same frequency that you are, because you are the only thing that exists in the universe.

Today, help us to be like you are, to love life, to be life, to be love. Help us to love the way you love, with no conditions, no expectations, no obligations, without any judgment. Help us to love and accept ourselves without any judgment, because when we judge ourselves, we find ourselves guilty and we need to be punished.

Help us to love everything you create unconditionally, especially other human beings, especially those who live around us — all our relatives and people whom we try so hard to love. Because when we reject them, we reject ourselves, and when we reject ourselves, we reject You.

Help us to love others just the way they are with no conditions. Help us to accept them the way they are, without judgment, because if we judge them, we find them guilty, we blame them, and we have the need to punish them.

Today, clean our hearts of any emotional poison that we have, free our minds from any judgment so that we can live in complete peace and complete love.

Today is a very special day. Today we open our hearts to love again so that we can tell each other "I love you," without any fear, and really mean it. Today, we offer ourselves to you. Come to us, use our voices, use our eyes, use our hands, and use our hearts to share ourselves in a communion of love with everyone. Today, Creator, help us to be just like you are. Thank you for everything that we receive this day, especially for the freedom to be who we really are. Amen.

PRAYER FOR LOVE

We are going to share a beautiful dream together — a dream that you will love to have all of the time. In this dream you are in the middle of a beautiful, warm sunny day. You hear the birds, the wind, and a little river. You walk toward the river. At the edge of the river is an old man in meditation, and you see that out of his head comes a beautiful light of different colors. You try not to bother him, but he notices your presence and opens his eyes. He has the kind of eyes that are full of love and a big smile. You ask him how he is able to radiate all that beautiful light. You ask him if he can teach you to do what he is doing. He replies that many, many, years ago he asked the same question of his teacher.

The old man begins to tell you his story: "My teacher opened his chest and took out his heart, and he took a beautiful flame from his heart. Then he opened my chest, opened my heart, and he put that little flame inside it. He put my heart back in my chest, and as soon as my heart was inside me, I felt intense love, because the flame he put in my heart was his own love.

"That flame grew in my heart and became a big, big fire — a fire that doesn't burn, but purifies everything that it touches. And that fire touched each one of the cells of my body, and the cells of my body loved me back. I became one with my body, but my love grew even more. That fire touched every

emotion of my mind, and all the emotions transformed into a strong and intense love. And I loved
myself, completely and unconditionally.

"But the fire kept burning and I had the need to
share my love. I decided to put a little piece of my
love in every tree, and the trees loved me back, and I
became one with the trees, but my love did not stop,
it grew more. I put a piece of love in every flower, in
the grass, in the earth and they loved me back, and
we became one. And my love grew more and more
to love every animal in the world. They responded
to my love and they loved me back, and we became
one. But my love kept growing and growing.

"I put a piece of my love in every crystal, in every
stone in the ground, in the dirt, in the metals, and
they loved me back, and I became one with the earth.
And then I decided to put my love in the water, in
the oceans, in the rivers, in the rain, in the snow. And
they loved me back and we became one. And still my
love grew more and more. I decided to give my love
to the air, to the wind. I felt a strong communion

with the earth, with the wind, with the oceans, with nature, and my love grew and grew.

"I turned my head to the sky, to the sun, to the stars, and put a little piece of my love in every star, in the moon, in the sun, and they loved me back. And I became one with the moon and the sun and the stars, and my love kept growing and growing. And I put a little piece of my love in every human, and I became one with the whole of humanity. Wherever I go, whomever I meet, I see myself in their eyes, because I am a part of everything, because I love."

And then the old man opens his own chest, takes out his heart with that beautiful flame inside, and he puts that flame in your heart. And now that love is growing inside of you. Now you are one with the wind, with the water, with the stars, with all of nature, with all animals, and with all humans. You feel the heat and the light emanating from the flame in your heart. Out of your head shines a beautiful light of different colors. You are radiant with the glow of love and you pray:

Thank you, Creator of the Universe, for the gift of life you have given me. Thank you for giving me everything that I have ever truly needed. Thank you for the opportunity to experience this beautiful body and this wonderful mind. Thank you for living inside me with all your love, with your pure and boundless spirit, with your warm and radiant light.

Thank you for using my words, for using my eyes, for using my heart to share your love wherever I go. I love you just the way you are, and because I am your creation, I love myself just the way I am. Help me to keep the love and the peace in my heart and to make that love a new way of life, that I may live in love the rest of my life. Amen.

The Four Agreements Companion Book*

Additional insights, practice ideas, questions and answers about applying The Four Agreements, and true stories from people who have already transformed their lives.

The Four Agreements Illustrated Edition

A four-color illustrated edition of this classic bestseller.

The Circle of Fire (Formerly published as Prayers)

A beautiful collection of essays, prayers, and guided meditations that will inspire and transform your life.

The Voice of Knowledge*

Ruiz transforms complex human issues into simple common sense. He tells us that all of our emotional suffering is because we believe in lies — mainly about ourselves.

The Mastery of Love*

Ruiz shows us how to heal our emotional wounds, recover the joy and freedom that are our birthright, and restore the spirit of playfulness that is vital to loving relationships.

Toltec Wisdom Card Decks

Each card deck contains 48 beautifully illustrated cards with wisdom from The Four Agreements and The Fifth Agreement.

The Fifth Agreement*

Ruiz and his son, don Jose Ruiz, offer another powerful agreement for transforming our lives. *The Fifth Agreement* encourages us to see the truth, to recover our authenticity, and to change the message we deliver not only to ourselves, but to everyone around us.

The Four Agreements for a Better Life (Online Course)

Take the course and begin a journey of personal transformation unlike any other. Watch inspiring videos, deepen your understanding and practice of The Four Agreements, download a poster, read our blog, and become a member of a worldwide community of people who are dedicated to changing their lives for the better by practicing The Four Agreements. For information about the online course and other ways to support your practice of The Four Agreements, please visit TheFourAgreements.com.

* Also Available in Spanish

For information about other bestselling titles from
Amber-Allen Publishing, please visit:
AmberAllen.com

THE VOICE OF
KNOWLEDGE

A Practical Guide to Inner Peace

A
Toltec

THE VOICE OF
KNOWLEDGE

Wisdom
Book

DON MIGUEL RUIZ

WITH JANET MILLS

AMBER-ALLEN PUBLISHING
SAN RAFAEL, CALIFORNIA

Published by Amber-Allen Publishing, Inc.
P.O. Box 6657
San Rafael, California 94903

Cover Illustration: Nicholas Wilton
Cover Design: Janet Mills
Author Photo: Ellen Denuto

Library of Congress Cataloging-in-Publication Data
Ruiz, Miguel, 1952- The voice of knowledge : a practical guide to inner
peace / Miguel Ruiz with Janet Mills.   p. cm. — (A Toltec wisdom book)
(alk. paper) 1. Conduct of life. 2. Peace of mind. 3. Toltec philosophy.
I. Mills, Janet, 1953- II. Title II. Series: Ruiz, Miguel, 1952 - . Toltec
wisdom book. BJ1595.R745 2004   299.7'92--dc22   2004045051

ISBN 978-1-878424-54-9
Printed in China
Distributed by Hay House, Inc.

18 17 16 15 14 13 12 11 10

I dedicate this book to the angels who have
helped to spread the message of truth
all around the world.

Contents

CONTENTS

Acknowledgments

I WISH TO EXPRESS MY GRATITUDE TO JANET MILLS, the mother of this book. I would also like to thank Gabrielle Rivera, Gail Mills, and Nancy Carleton, who lovingly and generously contributed their time and talents to the realization of this book.

The Toltec

THOUSANDS OF YEARS AGO, THE TOLTEC WERE KNOWN throughout southern Mexico as "women and men of knowledge." Anthropologists have spoken of the Toltec as a nation or a race, but, in fact, the Toltec were scientists and artists who formed a society to explore and conserve the spiritual knowledge and practices of the ancient ones. They came together as masters *(naguals)* and students at Teotihuacan, the ancient city of pyramids outside Mexico City known as the place where "Man Becomes God."

Over the millennia, the *naguals* were forced to conceal the ancestral wisdom and maintain its existence in obscurity. European conquest, coupled with rampant misuse of personal power by a few of the apprentices, made it necessary to shield the knowledge from those who were not prepared to use it wisely or who might intentionally misuse it for personal gain.

Fortunately, the esoteric Toltec knowledge was embodied and passed on through generations by different lineages of *naguals*. Though it remained veiled in secrecy for hundreds of years, ancient prophecies foretold the coming of an age when it would be necessary to return the wisdom to the people. Now, don Miguel Ruiz, a *nagual* from the Eagle Knight lineage, has been guided to share with us the powerful teachings of the Toltec.

Toltec knowledge arises from the same essential unity of truth as all the sacred esoteric traditions found around the world. Though it is not a religion, it honors all the spiritual masters who have taught on the earth. While it does embrace spirit, it is most accurately described as a way of life, distinguished by the ready accessibility of happiness and love.

THE VOICE OF
KNOWLEDGE

What is truth is real.

What is not truth is not real.

It's an illusion, but it looks real.

Love is real.

It's the supreme expression of life.

1

ADAM AND EVE

The story from a different point of view

A BEAUTIFUL AND ANCIENT LEGEND THAT ALMOST everyone has heard before is the story of Adam and Eve. It is one of my favorite stories because it explains with symbolism what I will try to explain with words. The story of Adam and Eve is based on absolute truth, though I never understood it as a child. It is one of the greatest teachings ever, but

I believe that most people misunderstand it. Now I will tell you this story from a different point of view, perhaps from the same point of view as the one who created it.

The story is about you and me. It's about us. It's about all of humanity because, as you know, humanity is only one living being: man, woman — we are only one. In this story, we call ourselves Adam and Eve, and we are the original humans.

The story begins when we were innocent, before we closed our spiritual eyes, which means thousands of years ago. We used to live in Paradise, in the Garden of Eden, which was heaven on earth. Heaven exists when our spiritual eyes are open. It is a place of peace and joy, freedom and eternal love.

For us — Adam and Eve — everything was about love. We loved and respected one another, and we lived in perfect harmony with all of creation. Our relationship with God, our Creator, was a perfect communion of love, which means that we communed with God all of the time, and God communed with us. It was inconceivable to be afraid of God, the one who created us. Our Creator was a God of love and justice, and we put our faith and trust in God. God gave us complete freedom, and we used our free will to love and enjoy all of creation. Life was beautiful in Paradise. The original humans saw everything through the eyes of truth, the way *it is*, and we loved it. That is the way we used to be, and it was effortless.

Well, the legend says that in the middle of Paradise stood two trees. One was the Tree of Life, which gave life to everything in existence, and the other was the Tree of Death, better known as the Tree of Knowledge. The Tree of Knowledge was a beautiful tree with juicy fruit. Very tempting. And God told us, "Don't go near the Tree of Knowledge. If you eat the fruit of that tree, you may die."

Of course, no problem. But by nature we love to explore, and surely we went to pay a visit to the tree. If you remember the story, you can already guess who lived in that tree. The Tree of Knowledge was the home of a big snake full of poison. The snake is just another symbol for what the Toltec call the *Parasite*, and you can imagine why.

The story says that the snake who lived in the Tree of Knowledge was a fallen angel who used to be the most beautiful one. As you know, an angel is a messenger who delivers God's message — a message of truth and love. But for who knows what reason, that fallen angel no longer delivered the truth, which means he delivered the wrong message. The fallen angel's message was fear, instead of love; it was a lie, instead of truth. In fact, the story describes the fallen angel as the Prince of Lies, which means that he was an eternal liar. Every word coming out of his mouth was a lie.

According to the story, the Prince of Lies was living in the Tree of Knowledge, and the fruit of that tree, which was *knowledge*, was contaminated with lies. We went to that tree, and we had the most incredible conversation with the Prince of Lies. We were innocent. We didn't know. We trusted everyone. And there was the Prince of Lies, the first storyteller, a very smart guy. Now the story gets a little more interesting because that snake by itself had a whole story of its own.

That fallen angel talked and talked and talked, and we listened and listened and listened. As you know, when we are children and our grandparents tell us stories, we are eager to hear everything they tell us. We learn, and it's very seductive; we want to know more. But this was the Prince of Lies talking. No doubt about it — he was lying, and we were seduced by the lies. We *believed* the fallen angel's story, and that was our big mistake. That is what it means to eat the fruit of the Tree of Knowledge. We *agreed* and took his word as the truth. We *believed* the lies; we put our *faith* in them.

When we bit into the apple, we ate the lies that came with knowledge. What happens when we eat a lie? We believe it, and boom! Now that lie lives in us. This is easy to understand. The mind is very fertile ground for concepts, ideas, and opinions. If someone tells us a lie and we believe it, that lie takes root in our mind. There it can grow big and strong, just like a tree. One little lie can be very contagious, spreading its seeds from person to person when we share it with others. Well, the lies went into our mind, and reproduced a whole Tree of Knowledge inside our head, which is everything that we know. But what is it that we know? Mostly lies.

The Tree of Knowledge is a powerful symbol. The legend says that whoever eats the fruit of the Tree of Knowledge will have knowledge of good and evil; they will know the difference between what is right and what is wrong, what is beautiful and what is ugly. They will gather all of that knowledge and begin to judge. Well, that is what happened in our head. And the symbolism of the apple is that every concept, every lie, is just like a fruit with a seed. When we place a fruit in fertile ground, the seed of the fruit creates another tree. That tree reproduces more fruit, and by the fruit, we know the tree.

Now each of us has our own Tree of Knowledge, which is our personal belief system. The Tree of

Knowledge is the structure of everything we believe. Every concept, every opinion, forms a little branch of that tree, until we end up with the whole Tree of Knowledge. As soon as that Tree is alive in our mind, we hear the fallen angel talking very loudly. The same fallen angel, the Prince of Lies, lives in our mind. From the Toltec point of view, a Parasite was living in the fruit; we ate the fruit, and the Parasite went inside us. Now the Parasite is living our life. The storyteller, the Parasite, is born inside our head, and it survives inside our head because we feed it with our faith.

The story of Adam and Eve explains how humanity fell from the dream of heaven into the dream of hell; it tells us how we became the way we are right now. The story usually says that we took just one bite of the apple, but this is not true. I think we ate all of the fruit of that tree, and we became sick from being so full of lies and emotional poison. Humans ate every concept, every opinion, and every story the liar told us, even though it was not the truth.

In that moment, our spiritual eyes closed, and we could no longer see the world with the eyes of truth. We began to perceive the world in a completely different way, and everything changed for us. With the Tree of Knowledge in our head, we could only perceive knowledge, we could only perceive lies. We no longer lived in heaven because lies have no place in heaven. This is how humans lost Paradise: We dream lies. We create the whole dream of humanity, individually and collectively, based on lies.

Before humans ate the fruit of the Tree of Knowledge, we lived in truth. We spoke only truth. We lived in love without any fear. After we ate the fruit, we felt guilt and shame. We judged ourselves as no longer good enough, and of course we judged others the same way. With judgment came polarity, separation, and the need to punish and be punished. For the first time we were no longer kind to one another; we no longer respected and loved all of God's creation. Now we suffered, and we began to blame ourselves, to blame other people, and even to blame God. We no longer believed that God was loving and just; we believed that God would punish and hurt us. It was a lie. It was not true, but we believed it, and we separated from God.

From this point, it is easy to understand what is meant by *original sin*. The original sin is not sex. No, that is another lie. The original sin is to believe the lies that come from the snake in the tree, the fallen angel. The meaning of the word *sin* is "to go against." Everything that we say, everything that we do against ourselves is a sin. To sin is not about blame or moral condemnation. To sin is to believe in lies, and to use those lies against ourselves. From that first sin, that original lie, all of our other sins are born.

How many lies do you hear in your head? Who is judging, who is talking, who is the one with all the opinions? If you don't love, it's because that voice doesn't let you love. If you don't enjoy your life, it's because that voice doesn't let you enjoy it.

And not only that — the liar in our head has the need to express all those lies, to tell its story. We share the fruit of our Tree with others, and because others have the same kind of liar, together our lies become more powerful. Now we can hate more. Now we can hurt more. Now we can defend our lies and become fanatics following our lies. Humans even destroy one another in the name of these lies. Who is living our life? Who is making our choices? I think the answer is obvious.

Now we know what is going on in our head. The storyteller is there; it is that voice in our head. That voice is talking and talking and talking, and we are listening and listening and believing every word. That voice never stops judging. It judges whatever we do, whatever we don't do, whatever we feel, whatever we don't feel, whatever everybody else does. It is constantly gossiping in our head, and what comes out of that voice? Lies, mostly lies.

These lies hook our attention, and all we can see are lies. That is the reason we don't see the reality of heaven that exists in this same place, at this same time. Heaven belongs to us because we are the children of heaven. The voice in our head doesn't belong to us. When we are born, we don't have that voice. The voice in our head comes after we learn — first the language, then different points of view, then all the judgments and lies. Even when we first learn to speak, we speak only truth. But little by little, the whole Tree of Knowledge is programmed into our head, and the big liar eventually takes over the dream of our life.

You see, in the moment when we separated from God, we started to search for God. For the first time, we started to search for the love we believed we didn't have. We started to search for justice, for beauty, for truth. The search began thousands of years ago, and humans are still searching for the paradise we lost. We are searching for the way we used to be before we believed in lies: authentic, truthful, loving, joyful. The truth is we are searching for our Self.

You know, it was true what God told us: If we eat the fruit of the Tree of Knowledge, we may die. We did eat it, and we are dead. We are dead because our authentic self is no longer there. The one who is living our life is the big liar, the Prince of Lies, that voice in our head. You can call it *thinking*. I call it *the voice of knowledge*.

⁂

POINTS TO PONDER

• The mind is fertile ground for concepts, ideas, and opinions. If someone tells us a lie and we believe it, that lie takes root in our mind and can grow big and strong, like a tree. One little lie can be very contagious, spreading its seeds from person to person when we share it with others.

• Knowledge goes into our mind and reproduces a structure inside our head, which is everything that we know. With all that knowledge in our head, we only perceive what we *believe*; we only perceive our own knowledge. And what is it that we know? Mostly lies.

• Once the Tree of Knowledge is alive in our mind, we hear the fallen angel talking very loudly. That voice never stops judging. It tells us what is right and what is wrong, what is beautiful and what is ugly. The storyteller is born inside our head, and survives inside our head because we feed it with our faith.

- Heaven exists when our spiritual eyes are open, when we perceive the world through the eyes of truth. Once lies hook our attention, our spiritual eyes are closed. We fall from the dream of heaven and begin to live the dream of hell.

- Heaven belongs to us because we are the children of heaven. The voice in our head doesn't belong to us. When we are born, we don't have that voice. *Thinking* comes after we learn — first the language, then different points of view, then all the judgments and lies. *The voice of knowledge* comes as we accumulate knowledge.

- Before we eat the lies that come with knowledge, we live in truth. We speak only truth. We live in love without any fear. Once we have knowledge, we judge ourselves as no longer good enough; we feel guilt, shame, and the need to be punished. We begin to dream lies, and we separate from God.

- In the moment when we separate from God, we begin to search for God, for the love we believe we don't have. Humans are continually searching for justice, for beauty, for truth — for the way we used to be before we believed in lies. We are searching for our authentic self.

2

A Visit with Grandfather

A simple truth is discovered

I CONSIDER MYSELF LUCKY BECAUSE I GREW UP learning from an ancient tradition known as the Toltec. My mother was a great healer, and to witness miracles was nothing extraordinary because I didn't know anything else. I grew up believing that anything is possible, but what I learned about the Toltec was full of superstition and mythology. I remember seeing superstitions everywhere, and as a teenager, I began to rebel against all of the lies that come from this tradition. I learned to challenge everything until certain experiences opened my eyes to the truth. Then I knew that what I had learned from the ancient Toltec was no longer a theory. I knew, but I could not explain it with words.

In this book, I want to tell you about some of the experiences that changed my point of view completely. With each experience, I realized something that was always obvious, but that I had never seen before. Perhaps the way I will relate these stories to you is not exactly the way they happened, but it's the way I perceive them and try to explain them to myself. Maybe you have had similar moments when you realized, as I did, that most of what we believe is not the truth. Opportunities to perceive the truth always come to us, and my life has been full of these opportunities. Many of them I just let go, but others opened my spiritual eyes and made the transformation in my life possible.

One of these opportunities came from a visit with my grandfather when I was a teenager in college. My grandfather was what they call an old *nagual*, which is like a shaman. He was close to ninety years old, and people used to visit with him just to learn, just to be around him. Grandfather had been teaching me since I was a child, and I had worked hard all my youth to be good enough to earn his respect.

Well, this was a time when I was pretending to be an intellectual, and I wanted to impress my grandfather with my opinions about everything I was learning in school. I was ready to show the one who had been the biggest influence on my life how smart I was. Good luck! I went to my grandfather's house, and he received me the way he always did — with a big smile, with enormous love. I started to tell him my point of view about all of the injustice in the world, about the poverty, about the violence, about the conflict between good and what I then called *evil*.

My grandfather was very patient, and he listened very carefully to everything I said. This encouraged me to speak even more, just to impress him. At a certain point, I saw a little smile on his face. Ooh! I knew something was coming. I was not impressing him at all. I thought, "Oh, he's making fun of me." He noticed my reaction, and looked directly into my eyes. "Well, Miguel, those are very good theories that you've learned," he said. "But they are only theories. Everything you have told me is just a story. It doesn't mean that it's true."

Of course I felt a little badly about this. I took it personally right away, and I tried to defend my point of view. But it was too late because now my grandfather started to talk. He looked at me with a big smile and said, "You know, most people around the world believe that there is a great conflict in the universe, a conflict between good and evil. Well, this is not true. It's true that there is a conflict, but the conflict only exists in the human mind, not in the universe. It's not true for the plants or the animals. It's not true for the stars or the trees, or for the rest of nature. It's only true for humans. And the conflict in the human mind is not really between good and evil. The real conflict in our mind is between the truth and what is not the truth, between the truth and lies. Good and evil are just the result of that conflict. The result of believing in the truth is goodness, love, happiness. When you live your life in truth, you feel good, and your life is wonderful. The result of believing in lies and defending those lies creates what you call *evil*; it creates fanaticism. Believing in lies creates all of the injustice, all of the violence and abuse, all of the suffering, not only in society but also in the individual. The universe is as simple as *it is* or *it is not*, but humans complicate everything."

Hmm. . . . What my grandfather told me was logical, and I understood what he was saying, but I didn't believe him. How could all of the conflict in the world, all of the war, violence, and injustice, be the result of something so simple? Surely it must be more complicated than that.

Grandfather went on to say, "Miguel, all of the drama you suffer in your personal life is the result of believing in lies, mainly about yourself. And the first lie you believe is you *are not:* You *are not* the way you should be, you *are not* good enough, you *are not* perfect. We are born perfect, we grow up perfect, and we will die perfect, because only perfection exists. But the big lie is that you are not perfect, that nobody is perfect. So you start to search for an *image* of perfection that you can never become. You will never reach perfection in that way because that image is false. It's a lie, but you invest your faith in that lie, and then you build a whole structure of lies to support it."

In that moment I didn't realize that my grandfather had given me a great opportunity — something as simple as having the awareness that every drama in my life, all of the suffering in my life, was because I believed in lies. Though I wanted to believe what my grandfather said, I only pretended to believe him. And it was so logical that I said, "Oh yes, Grandfather, you're right. I agree with you." But I was lying. There were too many lies inside my head to accept something as simple as the truth.

Then my grandfather looked at me very kindly and said, "Miguel, I can see that you are trying hard to impress me, to prove that you are good enough for me. And you have the need to do this because you are not good enough for yourself." Ouch. He got me right there. I didn't know why, but I felt as if he had caught me in a lie. I never realized that my grandfather knew about my insecurities, about the self-judgment and self-rejection, about the guilt and shame I felt. How did he know that I was pretending to be what I was not?

Grandfather was smiling again as he told me, "Miguel, everything you've learned in school, everything you know about life, is only knowledge. How can you know if what you've learned is the truth or not? How can you know if what you believe about yourself is the truth?" At that point I reacted and said, "Of course I know the truth about myself. I live with myself every day. I know what I am!" Grandfather really laughed at that and said, "The truth is that you have no idea what you really are, but you know what you *are not*. You have been practicing what you *are not* for so long, that you really believe your *image* is what you are. Your faith is invested in all those lies you believe about yourself. It's a story, but it's not the truth.

"Miguel, what makes you powerful is your faith. Faith is the power of creation that all humans have, and it doesn't have anything to do with religion. Faith is the result of an agreement. When you agree to believe in something without a doubt, you invest your faith. If you have no doubt about what you believe, then for you it is truth, even though it may really be a lie. Your faith is so powerful that if you believe you are not good enough, you are not good enough! If you believe you will fail, you will fail, because that is the power and magic of your faith. As I said before, you suffer because you believe lies. It's that simple. Humanity is the way it is because collectively we believe so many lies. Humans have carried the lies for thousands of years, and we react to the lies with hate, with anger, with violence. But they're only lies."

I was wondering, "Then how can we know the truth?" Before I could ask this question out loud, my grandfather answered it: "The truth needs to be experienced. Humans have the need to describe, to explain, to express what we perceive, but when we experience the truth, there are no words to describe it. Whoever claims, 'This is the truth,' is lying without even knowing it. We can perceive truth with our feelings, but as soon as we try to describe it with words, we distort it, and it's no longer the truth. It's our story! It's a projection based on reality that is only true for us, but still we try to put our experience into words, and this is something wonderful, really. It's the greatest art of every human."

Grandfather could see that what he had just said wasn't clear to me. "Miguel, if you are an artist, a painter, you try to express what you perceive through your art. What you paint may not be exactly what you perceive, but it is close enough to remind you of what you perceive. Well, imagine that you are very lucky and you are Pablo Picasso's friend. And because

Picasso loves you, he decides to make a portrait of you. You pose for Picasso, and after many days, he finally shows you your portrait. You will say, 'This is not me,' and Picasso will say, 'Of course it is you. This is how I see you.' For Picasso, this is true; he is expressing what he is perceiving. But you will say, 'I don't look like that.'

"Well, every human is the same as Picasso. Every human is a storyteller, which means that every human is an artist. What Picasso does with colors, we do with words. Humans witness life happening inside us and all around us, and we use words to make a portrait of what we witness. Humans make up stories about everything we perceive, and just like Picasso we distort the truth; but for us, it *is* the truth. Of course, the way we express our distortion could be something other people enjoy. Picasso's art is highly valued by many people.

"All humans create their story with their own unique point of view. Why try to impose your story on other people when for them your story is not true? When you understand that, you no longer have the need to defend what you believe. It's not important to be right or to make others wrong. Instead, you see everybody as an artist, a storyteller. You know that whatever they believe is just their point of view. It has nothing to do with you."

Well, I had wanted to impress my grandfather, but he had impressed me once again. I had so much respect for my elders. Later in my life I understood the smile on my grandfather's face. He had not been making fun of me. The smile was because I reminded him of a time when, just like me, he had tried to impress his elders.

After this conversation with my grandfather, I felt the need to make sense of things. I wanted to understand my personal life, and to find out when I began to invest my faith in lies. It was not easy. That conversation took me years to digest. To see myself in the present moment, to see what I believed, was not that obvious and not so easy to give up. But I wanted answers because this is my nature. I needed to know, and the only point of reference was my memories.

❦

POINTS TO PONDER

• There is a conflict in the human mind between the truth and what is not the truth, between the truth and lies. The result of believing in the truth is goodness, love, happiness. The result of believing and defending lies is injustice and suffering — not only in society, but also in the individual.

• All of the drama humans suffer is the result of believing in lies, mainly about ourselves. The first lie we believe is *I am not:* I am not the way I *should* be, I am not perfect. The truth is that every human is born perfect because only perfection exists.

• We humans have no idea what we really are, but we know what we *are not*. We create an image of perfection, a story about what we *should* be, and we begin to search for a false image. The image is a lie, but we invest our faith in that lie. Then we build a whole structure of lies to support it.

• Faith is a powerful force in humans. If we invest our faith in a lie, that lie becomes truth for us. If we believe we are not good enough, then *thy will be done*, we are not good enough. If we believe we will fail, we will fail, because that is the power and magic of our faith.

• Humans can perceive truth with our feelings, but when we try to describe the truth, we can only tell a story that we distort with our word. The story may be true for us, but that doesn't mean it is true for anyone else.

• All humans are storytellers with their own unique point of view. When we understand this, we no longer feel the need to impose our story on others or to defend what we believe. Instead, we see all of us as artists with the right to create our own art.

3

THE LIE OF OUR IMPERFECTION

Childhood memories are recalled

I REMEMBER WHEN I WAS A CHILD. I WAS SO FREE. It was wonderful to be a child. I remember that I learned to walk before I learned to talk. I was like a little sponge trying to learn everything. I also remember the way I used to be before I learned to speak.

As a little child I was completely authentic. I never pretended to be what I am not. My tendency was to play, to explore, to be happy. My emotions ruled everything. I only wanted to do what I liked to do, and I tried to avoid what I didn't like. All of my attention was focused on what I was feeling, and I could perceive the emotions coming out of other people. We can call it *instinct* if we want to, but it was a kind of perception. Some people I would run to because I trusted them. I wouldn't get close to others because I felt uncomfortable. I had many emotions that I couldn't explain because I didn't have words, of course.

I remember waking up, seeing my mother's face, and feeling overwhelmed with a desire to grab her. I didn't know that this emotion was called *love*. It was completely natural to love. I felt the same way about my toys, and about the cat and the dog, too. I remember seeing my father come back from work and running to him and jumping on him with so much joy, with a big and beautiful smile. Completely authentic. I could be naked and I didn't care what people thought. I used to be myself, whatever

I was, because I didn't have *knowledge*. I didn't have a program in my head. I didn't know what I was, and I didn't care to know. Just as a dog doesn't know that it's a dog. But it acts like a dog. Barks like a dog. Well, I used to be like that. I lived my life through my integrity. This was my true nature before I learned to speak.

I continued to explore my childhood memories, and I discovered that something happens to all of us. What happens? Well, knowledge happens. I can remember starting to learn words. I learn the names of every object I perceive. I learn a language, which is great. Now I can use words to ask for what I want. Months later, or maybe years later, my mind is mature enough for abstract concepts. With these concepts, something incredible happens. I start to create stories by qualifying everything: what is right or wrong, what I should or shouldn't be, what is good or bad, beautiful or ugly. I learn from my parents not just what they say, but what they do. I learn what they say not just to me, but what they say about other people. I learn how to interact. I copy everything that I see. I see my father, very powerful, with his strong opinions, and I want to be like him. I can hardly wait to grow up to have an opinion of my own.

When I finally understand the language, almost everybody begins to tell me what I am. The way I learn about myself is by hearing the opinions of the storytellers around me. My mother creates an image of me based on what she believes I am. She tells me what I am, and I believe her. Then my father tells me what I am, and it's something completely different, but I agree with him, too. Of course, each of my brothers and sisters has an opinion of me, and I agree with them. Surely they know more than I do, even though I'm the one who lives in this physical body. None of this makes sense, but I'm having fun.

Then I go to school, and the teacher tells me what I am, which is still okay until she tells me the way I should be, but *I am not*. I agree, and the problem begins in that moment. I hear the teacher say,

"Children, you need to work hard to become some-body, to be a success in life. The world is divided into winners and losers, and you are here to prepare yourself to become a winner. If you work hard, perhaps you will be a lawyer, a doctor, an engineer." My teacher tells me stories about all of the past presidents and what they did when they were chil-dren. Of course all of the heroes are winners. I am a child; I am innocent. I learn the concept of *winner*. I agree that I should become a winner, and that's it — that agreement is stored in my memory.

At home, I hear my parents say, "Miguel, you have to behave this way to be a good boy," which means that if I don't behave that way, *I am not* a good boy. They don't say this, but I understand this. You have to do this, this, and that to be a good boy. Then you will get a reward. And if you are not that way, you will be punished. Oops! I am too small; they are so big. I try to rebel, and I fail. They win. I start pretending to be what *I am not* to avoid the punishment, but also to get the reward. I have to be what they tell me to be because the reward only goes to good boys. I remember trying so hard to become what they want me to be, just to have the reward of their attention, just to hear them say, "Miguel, you are such a good boy."

What I don't notice behind all of the messages I hear are the silent messages that are never said, but that I can understand: *I am not the way I should be; it is not okay to be me.* If the message is "Miguel, you have to work hard to become somebody," that means that right now I am nobody. In a child's mind the silent message I understand is *I am not good enough.* And not just that; I never will be good enough because *I am not perfect.* I agree, and in that moment, like most of us, I start searching for perfection.

That's how the image of perfection is introduced in my mind. This is when I stop being myself, and start pretending to be what *I am not.* That first lie happens in my first year of school, almost right away. Sitting in that classroom and seeing my first teacher impresses me deeply. The teacher is a grown-up.

Whatever she says must be the truth, just as whatever my father or mother says must be the truth. She is a great teacher who really cares about children, and even though the message I receive is mostly positive, the consequence is a little different. Behind that message is something very subtle. I call it *the lie of my imperfection*. It is the main lie that I agree to believe about myself, and from that lie, more lies are invented to support it.

This is the moment of my fall, when I start to come out of heaven, when my faith in the lie begins to work its magic. Just like a miracle, it starts to take effect all around me: I have to work hard to be good enough for my mother, to be good enough for my father, to be good enough for my older brothers and sisters, to be good enough for my teachers. This is overwhelming, but it's not over yet. I turn on the television and they also tell me the way I should look, the way I should dress, the way I should be, but *I am not*. Television gives me more images of heroes and villains. I see people trying hard to be winners. I see them striving for perfection, wanting to be somebody important, wanting to be what they are not.

The real drama begins when I am a teenager because now it's not only that I'm not good enough for other people; I am no longer good enough for myself. The result is self-rejection. I try to prove my worth to myself by working hard to get A's in school. I try hard to be the best at sports, the best at playing chess, the best at everything. At first I do this to try to impress my father and my older brothers; later, I do this to impress myself. At this point, I am no longer authentic. I have lost my integrity, my authenticity, because I no longer make decisions based on what is good for me. It is more important to satisfy other people's points of view.

When I change schools from elementary to the next level, I am told, "You are not a child anymore; you cannot act like a child. Now you have to behave this way." Over and over, I try to please other people by pretending to be what they want me to be.

I start searching for opinions from everybody. How do I look? What do you think of me? Did I do a good job? I am looking for support, for someone to tell me, "Miguel, you are so good." And if I'm with somebody who tells me how good I am, that person can manipulate my life so easily because I need that recognition. I need somebody to tell me that I'm intelligent, that I'm wonderful, that I'm a winner.

I can't stand to be alone with myself. When I'm alone, I see myself as a loser, and my self-judgment is strong. Because *I am not* the way I should be according to my story, I judge myself and find myself guilty. Then I begin to use everything around me as an instrument for self-punishment. I have the tendency to compare myself with other people. "Oh, they are better than I am. Well, they are worse." That makes me feel a little better, but then I see myself in the mirror — ugh! I don't like what I see. I reject myself; of course I don't love myself. But I pretend that I love myself. With enough practice, I even begin to believe what I pretend.

Later, when I really try to prove myself in society, I become a medical doctor. Does becoming a medical doctor finally make me a winner? No, oh no. There are cardiologists, neurologists, surgeons. Then I become a surgeon, but I'm still not good enough according to my story. I have an image of myself that I believe when I'm alone, and I project different images around other people, depending on what I want them to believe about me. In trying to project my images, I have to defend these images. I have to become very intelligent just to cover all of the lies!

I keep pretending to be all of those images, and from years and years of practice, I become a great actor. If I have a broken heart, I tell myself, "It doesn't hurt. I don't care." I am lying. I am pretending. I could almost win an Academy Award for my performance. What a character, what a drama! And I could say that the drama of my life begins when I agree that I am not good enough — when I hear my teachers, my family, the television tell me, "Miguel, you have to be *this* way," but *I am not*.

I am searching for appreciation, for acceptance, for love — not knowing that it's just a story. I am searching for perfection, and I find it very interesting how "not being perfect" becomes the biggest excuse people use to justify their actions. Every time they make a mistake and need to defend their image, I hear them say, "Well, I'm only human; I'm not perfect. Only God is perfect." This also becomes the biggest excuse for every mistake I make. "Oh well, nobody's perfect." What a great justification.

I go to church, and they show me pictures of saints: "This is perfection." But in the faces of the saints I see suffering and pain. Ooh! To be perfect, do I need to be like them? Yes, I am here to suffer, and if I suffer with patience, maybe when I die I can receive my reward in heaven. Maybe then I'll be perfect!

I used to believe that because I heard it so often. But it's just a story. I had so many superstitions in my head about myself, about everything. Lies that come from thousands of years ago still affect the way we create our own story. What I was told as a

THE VOICE OF KNOWLEDGE

child is "Only God is perfect. All of God's creation is perfect except humans." At the same time, I was told that God put humans at the very top of creation. But how can humans be at the top of creation, when everything is perfect except humans? It didn't make sense to me. After I grew up, I thought about the contradiction. This is not possible. If God is perfect, well, God is the one who creates everything. If I really believe in the perfection of God's creation, then I think that all of us are perfect or God is not perfect either.

I love and respect all of God's creation. How can I say, "God, you have created billions of people, and they are not perfect"? For me to say that I am not perfect or that you are not perfect is the greatest insult to God, from my point of view. If we don't see the perfection, it's because our attention is focused on the lie, on that image of perfection that we can never be. And how many of us give up trying to be the image of perfection, but in giving up we don't go as warriors? We just accept that we are failures, that we will never make it, and we blame everything out-side of us. "I didn't make it because nobody helped me — because of this or that or whatever." There are hundreds of excuses, but now the self-judgment is even worse than before. When we are still trying to be perfect, the judgment is there, but it's not as bad as when we give up. Then we try to cover our frustration, and say, "I'm okay; this is the kind of life I want," but we know that we have failed, and we can't hide what we believe from ourselves.

Of course, any time we try to be what we are not, we fail. It's so difficult to be what we are not, to *pretend* to be what we are not. I used to pretend that I was very happy and very strong and very important. Wow! Living that way is truly a deep hell. It's a setup, it's a no-win situation. You can never be what you are not, and that is the main point. You can only be *you*, and that's it. And you are *you* right now, and it's effortless.

There is no need to justify what we are. There is no need to work hard to become what we are not.

We just need to return to our integrity, to the way we were before we learned to speak. Perfect. As little children, we are authentic. When we are hungry, we only want to eat. When we are tired, we just want to rest. Only the present time is real for us; we don't care about the past, and we aren't worried about the future. We enjoy life; we want to explore and have fun. Nobody teaches us to be that way; we are born that way.

We are born in truth, but we grow up believing in lies. This is the whole drama of humanity, the whole problem with storytellers. One of the biggest lies in the story of humanity is the lie of our imperfection. That lie had a big effect in my own life. And though I tell others not to make assumptions, I have to assume that in one way or another this happens to all of us. Of course there are differences in the story, but I think the pattern is more or less the same for everyone. Hardly anyone can escape from the setup.

I was a perfect little child. I was innocent, and I ate the lie that *I am not* what I should be. I believed that I would have to work hard to become what I should be. This is how I learned to create my story, and because I had faith in the story, the story became truth for me. And the story, even if it is full of lies, is perfect. It is wonderful and beautiful. The story is not right or wrong or good or bad — it's just a story, that's all. But with awareness, we can change the story. Step by step, we can return to the truth.

❧

POINTS TO PONDER

• As little children, we are completely authentic. We never pretend to be what we are not. Our tendency is to play and explore, to live in the moment, to enjoy life. Nobody teaches us to be that way; we are born that way. This is our true nature before we learn to speak.

• When the human mind is mature enough for abstract concepts, we learn to qualify everything: right or wrong, good or bad, beautiful or ugly. We create a story about what we *should* be, we put our faith in the story, and the story becomes the truth for us.

• Behind all of the messages that we hear as children are the silent messages that are never said, but that we can understand: *It is not okay to be me. I am not good enough.* The moment we agree, we stop being ourselves and start pretending to be what we are not, just to please other people, just to fit an image they create for us according to their story.

• You can never be what you are not. You can only be *you*, and that's it. And you are *you* right now, and it's effortless.

• Humans are born in truth, but we grow up believing in lies. One of the biggest lies in the story of humanity is the lie of our imperfection. It's just a story, but we believe it, and we use the story to judge ourselves, to punish ourselves, and to justify our mistakes.

• Everything in God's creation is perfect. If we don't see our own perfection, it's because our attention is focused on our story. The lies in our story keep us from seeing the truth. But with awareness, we can change the story and return to the truth.

4

A Night in the Desert

An encounter with the infinite

ANOTHER OPPORTUNITY TO PERCEIVE THE TRUTH came along when I was doing my social service as a medical doctor. I was in the little town of Altar Sonora in the Sonoran desert. It was summer, and the heat was so intense that I couldn't sleep. I decided to leave the clinic and take a walk in the desert. There was a new moon that night, and I could see millions of stars in the sky. I was alone in the middle of the desert, perceiving so much beauty. I saw eternity, the endless, the infinite in those stars, and I knew without a doubt that the stars are alive. The infinite, our Mother Earth, all of creation, is alive. It is one living being.

Surely I had seen those stars many times before, but never in that way, from that point of view. My emotional reaction was overwhelming. I felt intense joy mixed with the most exquisite peace in my heart. Then something incredible happened. I had the sensation that I was not alone in the desert. While I was perceiving the immensity of the infinite, the infinite was perceiving me. All of those millions of stars were part of one living being who knows everything and perceives everything. The universe knew that I existed!

Then something even more extraordinary happened. My perception shifted, and for a moment I was the immensity of the stars perceiving the infinite in my physical body. I could see myself in the middle of the desert — so small. I saw that my physical body was made of billions of tiny stars, which I knew were atoms, and they were as vast as all of the stars in the sky.

That night, I knew that the infinite inside my physical body is just a continuation of the infinite all around me. I am part of that infinite, and so is every object I perceive. There is no difference between any of us, or between us and any object. We are only one because everything is made of light. Light expresses itself in billions of different forms to create the material universe. More than that, I knew that there is only one force that moves and transforms everything. The force that moves the stars is the same force that moves the atoms in my body. I call it *life*, and light is the messenger or carrier of *life* because light is sending information all the time to everything in existence.

And it was incredible to understand that light is alive. Light is a living being that contains all of the wisdom of the universe and occupies every space. There is no empty space between the stars, just as there is no empty space between the atoms in my body. The space between the stars is filled with light; it only appears empty when there is no object to reflect the light. Any object we send into space will reflect light because all matter reflects light, just like a mirror.

Then I looked in my pocket for a little mirror that I always carried with me in my practice. In the mirror, I could see an exact copy of all of creation, a virtual reality made by light. In that moment I knew that my eyes were just like a couple of mirrors. Light projects a virtual reality inside my brain, just the way it projects a virtual reality inside a mirror. It was obvious that everything I perceive is a virtual reality made by images of light. The only difference between my eyes and a mirror is that my eyes have a brain behind them. And with that brain I have the capacity to analyze, interpret, and describe the virtual reality I perceive at any moment.

I co-create with God, with *life*. God creates what is real, and I create the virtual reality inside my mind.

Through light, life sends all of that information into my eyes, and I make a story about what I perceive. The story is how I qualify, justify, and explain what I perceive. If I see a tree, I don't just *see* the tree; I qualify the tree, I describe the tree, I have an opinion about the tree. I like the tree or I don't like the tree. I may feel that the tree is beautiful or not, but my point of view, my opinion about the tree, is a story of my own creation. Once I interpret, qualify, or judge what I perceive, it is no longer real; it is a virtual world. This is what the Toltec call *dreaming*.

Now everything started to make sense in my mind. I finally understood what my mother and my grandfather had tried to teach me for so long about the ancient philosophy of the Toltec. The Toltec believe that humans are living in a dream. The dream is a world of illusion made by images of light, and the mind dreams when the brain is both asleep and awake.

Then I remembered that the word *Toltec* means "artist of the spirit." In the Toltec tradition, every human is an artist, and the supreme art is the expression of the beauty of our spirit. If we understand this point of view, we can see how wonderful it is to call ourselves artists instead of humans. When we think of ourselves as human, we limit the way we express ourselves in life. We hear, "I'm just a human; I'm not perfect." But if we call ourselves artists, where is that limitation? As artists, we no longer have any limitation; we are creators, just like the one who created us.

The Toltec believe that the force of life working through us is what really creates the art, and that everyone is an instrument of this force. Every manifestation of the supreme artist becomes an artist itself that manifests art through its own manifestations. The art is alive, and it has self-awareness because it comes from life. The creation is ongoing, it is endless, it is happening in every moment, everywhere.

How do we live our life? This is our art, the art of living. With our power of creation, we express the force of life in everything we say, everything we feel, everything we do. But there are two kinds of artists: the ones who create their story without awareness, and the ones who recover awareness and create their story with truth and with love.

You are dreaming your life in this moment. You perceive not only your own dream, but the dream of the supreme artist reflected in everything you perceive. You react and try to make sense of what you perceive. You try to explain it in your own way, depending on the knowledge stored in the memory of your mind. This is something wonderful from my point of view. You live in the story that you create, and I live in the story that I create. Your story is your reality — a virtual reality that is only true for you, the one who creates it.

Long ago, somebody said, "Every head is a world," and it's true. You live in your own world, and that world is so private. Nobody knows what you have in your world. Only you know, and sometimes even you don't know. Your world is your creation, and it's a masterpiece of art.

That night in the Sonoran desert changed the way I perceive myself and humanity, the way I perceive the entire world. In a moment of inspiration, I saw the infinite, the force of life in action. That force is always present and obvious for anyone to see, but there was no way I could see it with my attention focused on lies. What my grandfather had tried to tell me was true: "Only perfection exists." It took a long time for me to put it into words, of course, but I finally understood what he meant when I experienced this truth for myself. I realized that I am perfect because I am inseparable from the infinite, the force of life that creates the stars and the entire universe of light. I am God's creation. I don't need to be what *I am not*.

This was my reencounter with love, which is how I felt before I denied myself love. I recovered my authenticity, which is how I lived before I learned any lies. In that moment of inspiration everything made sense to me without thinking at all. I was pure awareness. I was perceiving with my feelings, and if

I had tried to use words to explain what I felt, the experience would have been over.

I believe that all humans have moments of inspiration when we perceive truth. These moments usually occur when the mind is quiet — when we perceive the force of life through our feelings. Of course, the voices inside our head that we call *thinking* will invalidate our experience almost right away. These voices will try to justify and deny what we feel. Why? Because when we witness the truth, all of the lies that we believe cannot survive. Humans are afraid of the truth, and when we say that we are afraid, the one who is speaking is the liar. Yes, because the lies that speak through that voice cannot survive the truth, and they don't want to die.

That is why it takes such courage to face our own lies, to face what we believe. The structure of our knowledge makes us feel safe. We have the need to *know*, even if what we know is not the truth. And if what we believe about ourselves is no longer true, we don't feel safe because we don't know how to be any other way. When we discover that we are not what we believe we are, the foundation of our entire reality begins to collapse. The whole story loses its meaning, and this is very frightening.

I was not afraid in the desert that night. But when I recovered, I felt fear because nothing in my story was important any longer and I still had to function in the world. Later, I discovered that I could rewrite the story of my life. I could recover the structure of what I believed and rebuild it without all the lies. Then life went on as it did before, but the lies no longer ruled my life.

POINTS TO PONDER

• Light is a living being that contains all of the wisdom of the universe and occupies every space. Light, the supreme messenger of God, constantly sends information to everything in existence, and expresses itself in billions of different forms.

• Life, the force of transformation that creates and transforms the stars, is the same force that creates and transforms the atoms in our physical body. This force is always present and obvious for us to see, but we cannot see it when our attention is focused on lies.

• Every human is a part of the infinite, and so is every object we perceive. There is no difference between any of us, or between us and any object. We are only one because everything is made of light.

• Life creates what is real, and humans create a virtual reality — a story about what is real. We perceive images of *light*, and we interpret, qualify, and judge what we perceive. This ongoing reflection in the mirror of our mind is what the Toltec call *dreaming*.

• God, the supreme artist, uses our life for the creation of art. We are the instruments through which the force of life expresses itself.

• The art of dreaming is the art of living. Everything we say and do is an expression of the force of life. The creation is ongoing. It is endless. It is happening in every moment.

5

THE STORYTELLER

Exploring the characters in the story

THAT NIGHT IN THE DESERT IS WHAT I CALL MY *return to common sense.* I had been living in a story of my own creation my entire life without even noticing it! Once I had this awareness, I started to question everything in my story. Is it true that I am what I believe I am? Is what I believe about everybody else true? I reviewed the story of my life, and

I didn't like all of the drama that I had created. I wanted to reinvent myself.

The first step was to take away from my story what I felt was not true, and to find out what was true. I discovered that what I call the *frame* of the dream is true because our Creator creates the frame, and it's the same for everybody. Our agreements about what to call the objects in the frame are also true because this is how we describe our virtual reality. The letter *A* is an *A* because we say so and we agree. The word *dog* describes a type of animal that we agree to call a *dog*.

Knowledge used in this way is just a *tool for communication*. But almost everything that is abstract is a lie: what is right or wrong, what is good or bad, what is beautiful or ugly. I discovered that more than 90 percent of the concepts I had stored in my mind were based on lies, especially the concepts I believed about myself: I can do this; I cannot do that. I am this way; I will never be that way. The problem is not really knowledge; the problem is what *contaminates* knowledge — and that is the lie. I could see that there was a lot of nonsense in the way we learn to write our stories. How did this happen?

Before I was born in this physical body, a whole society of storytellers was already here. The story was ongoing, and from their story I learned how to create my own. The storytellers who are here before us teach us how to be human. First they tell us what we are — a boy or a girl — then they tell us who we are, and who we should or shouldn't be. They teach us how to be a woman or how to be a man. They tell us to be a *proper* woman, a *decent* woman, a *strong* man, a *brave* man. They give us a name, an identity, and they tell us the role that we are playing in their story. They prepare us to live in the human jungle, to compete with one another, to control one another, to impose our will, to fight against our own kind.

Of course I believed what the storytellers told me. Why would I not believe them? They filled me with knowledge, and I used that knowledge to copy their style and create my art in a similar way. I heard my older brothers sharing their strong opinions with my father. I tried to talk, and they shut me up right away — forget it, I had no voice. As I said before, I could hardly wait to have an opinion of my own. It didn't matter what the opinion was; I just wanted to impose my opinion and to defend my opinion with all of that self-righteousness.

As children, we witness the way other people relate to one another, and this becomes normal behavior for us. We see our older sisters and brothers, our aunts and uncles, our parents and neighbors in romantic relationships. They suffer, but they believe they love. We see them fight, and we can't wait to grow up and do the same thing. The mentality when we are children is "Wow, that looks like fun!" All of the drama we suffer in our relationships is because we witness so many lies when we are innocent, and we use these lies to form our own story.

I continued to study the story of my life, and what I discovered is that everything in my story is about me. Of course, it has to be that way because I am the center of my perception, and the story is from my point of view. The main character who lives in my story is based on someone who really exists — that is true. But what I believe about me is not true — it's a story. I create the character of "Miguel," and it's just an image based on what I agree to believe about myself. I project my image to other people in society, and other people perceive that projection, modify it, and react to me according to their stories.

Then I discovered that because it's my story, I also create an image for every secondary character who lives in my story. The secondary characters are based on people who really exist, but everything I believe about them is a story of my own creation. I create the character of my mother, the character of my father, the character of each of my brothers and sisters, my friends, my beloved, even my dog and my cat. I meet a person; I qualify the person. I make judgments about the person based on all of the knowledge in my mind. This is how I keep their image in my memory.

In my story, you are a secondary character who is my creation, and I interact with you. You project what you want me to believe about you, and I modify it depending on what I believe. Now I am sure that you are what I believe you are. I might even say, "I know you," when the truth is that I don't know you at all. I only know the story I create about you. And it took some time for me to understand that I only know the story I create about myself.

For years I thought that I knew myself until I discovered that it was not the truth. I only knew what I believed about myself. Then I discovered that I am not what I believe I am! And it was very interesting, and also very frightening, when I discovered that I really don't know anybody, and they don't know me either.

The truth is that we only know what we *know*, and the only thing we really know is our story. But how many times have you heard people say, "I know my children very well; they would never do something like that!" Do you think that you really know your children? Do you think that you really know your partner? Well, you are probably certain that your partner doesn't know you! You may be certain that nobody really knows you, but do you really know yourself? Do you really know anybody?

I used to believe that I knew my mother, but the only thing I know about her is the role I assign her to play in my story. I have an image for the character who plays the role of my mother. Everything I know about her is what I *believe* about her. I have no idea what she has in her head. Only my mother knows what she is, and surely she doesn't know either.

The same is true for you. Your mother can swear that she knows you very well. But is it true? I don't think so. You know that she has no idea what you have in your mind. She only knows what she believes about you, which means she knows almost nothing. You are a secondary character in her story, and you play the role of the son or the daughter. Your mother creates an image of you, and she wants you to fit the image she creates. If you are not what she wants you to be according to her story, guess what happens? She feels hurt by you, and she tries to make you fit her image. That is why she feels the need to control you, to tell you what to do and what not to do, to give you all of her opinions about the way you should live your life.

When you know that it's just her story, why bother defending your point of view? It doesn't matter what you say; she will not believe you anyway. How can she believe your story when it isn't her point of view? The best you can do is to change the conversation, enjoy her presence, and love her the way she is. When you have this awareness, you will forgive your mother for whatever she did to you, according to your story, of course. Just through the act of forgiveness, your relationship with your mother will change completely.

Once I discovered that people are creating and living in their own story, how could I judge them any longer? How could I take anything personally when I know that I am only a secondary character in their story? I know that when they talk to me they are really talking to the secondary character in their story. And whatever people say about me is just a projection of their *image* of me. It has nothing to do with me. I don't waste my time taking anything personally. I focus my attention on creating my own story.

Each of us has the right to create our own life story, to express ourselves through our art. But how many times do we try to make the secondary characters in our story fit the images and roles we create for them? We want our children to be the way we want them to be. Well, bad news! That will never happen. And when our partner doesn't fit the image we create for him or her, we feel angry or hurt. Then we try to control our partner; we have to tell our partner what to do, what not to do, what to believe, what not to believe. We even tell our partner how to walk, how to dress, how to speak. We do the same thing with our children, and it becomes a war of control.

Life in this physical body is very short, even if we live to be one hundred years old. When I discovered this, I decided not to waste my time creating conflict, mainly with the people I love. I want to enjoy them, and I do that by loving them for who they are, not for what they believe. The story they create is not important. I don't care if my mother's story doesn't agree with my story; I love her and I enjoy her presence. I know not to impose my story on her; I don't impose my story on anybody. I respect her story, I listen to her story, and I don't make it wrong.

If other people try to write your story, it means they don't respect you. They don't respect you because they consider that you are not a good artist, that you cannot write your own story, even though you were born to write your own story. Respect comes directly from love; it is one of the greatest expressions of love.

I also respect myself, and I don't allow anybody to write my story. My story is my responsibility; it's my creation. I am the artist, and I respect my own art. I can compare my art with other people's art, but I make my own choices, and I take responsibility for my creation. When I first had the awareness that I didn't like my story, I thought, "Okay, I am the author. I will change my story." And I tried and I failed. And I tried again and I failed again many times because I was trying to change all of the secondary characters in my story. I thought that if I changed the secondary characters, I was changing my story, and it was not true at all!

The problem is not with the secondary characters in our story. What we see in them is just a projection of what we believe, and that's a secondary problem. Our main problem is with the main character of the story. If we don't like our story, it's because we don't like what we believe about the main character. There is only one way to change our story, and that is by changing what we believe about ourselves.

This is a big step in awareness. If we clean up the lies that we believe about ourselves, almost like magic the lies that we believe about everybody else will change. Then the secondary characters in our story will change, but this doesn't mean that we exchange one person for another person. The secondary characters stay the same; what changes is what we *believe* about them. This changes what we project onto them, and with that change, the interaction we have with them changes. And with that change, the way they perceive us changes. And with that change, the secondary character who we represent in their story changes. Just like a wave that ripples across the water, we change ourselves, and everything else changes.

You are the only one who can change your story, and you do this by changing your relationship with yourself. Every time you change the main character in your story, just like magic the whole story starts to change in order to adapt to the new main character. This is easy to prove because the main character is changing anyway, but it's changing by itself, without your awareness.

The way you perceive the world when you are eight or nine years old is not the same way you perceive the world at fifteen or sixteen. When you are in your early twenties, your perception changes again. You see the world differently when you are first married, or when you have your first child. You change what you *believe* about yourself. Your point of view changes, the way you express yourself changes, and your reactions change. Everything changes, and the change can be so dramatic that it seems like two different dreams and two different people.

You also change the secondary characters in your story. The way you see your father and your mother when you are ten changes when you are twenty, and thirty, and forty, and it keeps changing. Every single day, you rewrite the story. As soon as you wake up in the morning, you have to find out what day it is. You have to find out where you are and where the story was before you went to sleep just to keep going with the story, with your life. You have to go to work, you have to do whatever activity you have planned for that day, and you keep writing your own story, but without awareness.

Everything in your story is constantly changing, including the story you tell yourself about who you are. Twenty years ago, the storyteller told you who you are, and you believed it. Today the storyteller is telling you another story about yourself, and it's completely different. Of course the storyteller will say, "Oh, that's because I have more experience. Now I know more; now I am wiser." It's just another story. Your whole life has been a story.

If you talk about something that happened to you when you were a child, your father or mother or brother or sister will have a different story. This is because we only share the frame of the dream. If two of you start talking about something that happened twenty years ago, it may sound as if you are talking about two different events. Your father claims, "This is what happened; this is the truth." And you say, "No, no, no; you're wrong. This is what really happened." Who is right and who is wrong? Well, both of you are right, according to your stories.

If one hundred people perceive the same event,

you hear one hundred different stories, and everybody claims that his or her story is the true story. Of course, it's only true for that person, and your story is only true for you. But the voice of knowledge starts searching for everything in your mind to make yourself right. You even look for allies from the outside to join you in your crusade to be right and to make the other person wrong. Why try to justify what you believe? You don't need to make others wrong because you already know that in their story they are right. In your story, you are right. Then being right or wrong is over; you no longer have to defend what you believe.

When we reach this level of awareness, it is easier not to take what other people say personally. We know that every human around us is a storyteller, and that everyone distorts the truth. What we share with one another is just our perception; it is just our point of view. And it's completely normal because the only thing we have is our point of view. This is how we describe whatever we witness.

Our point of view depends upon our programming, which is everything in our personal Tree of Knowledge. Our point of view also depends upon how we are feeling emotionally and physically, and it changes from one moment to the next. It changes when we are angry or upset, and it changes again when we are happy. Our perception changes when we are tired or hungry. We humans are constantly modifying what we say, how we react, what we project. We even modify what everybody else says!

You know, the way we create our stories is very interesting. We have a tendency to distort everything we perceive to make it agree with what we *already* believe; we "fix it" to make it agree with our lies. It is amazing how we do this. We distort the image of each of our children, we distort the image of our partner, and we distort the image of our parents. We even distort the image of our dog or our cat! People come to me and say, "Oh, I have learned so much from my dog. My dog is almost human. He's almost talking now." And they really mean it!

How many people take their dog to a pet psychologist because the dog has so many issues? Do you see how we distort our story? The story is based in reality because, yes, we have an emotional connection with our dog, but it's not true that our dog almost talks or that our dog is almost human.

When we talk about our children, we say, "My children are the best. They do this and this and that." Another person hearing this may say, "No, look at mine." As artists with our own style, we have the right to distort our story, and this is the best we can do anyway. That distortion is our point of view, and for us it has meaning. We project our story, and by seeing the distortion, we can sometimes return to our own truth. Then who says that the distortion of our story is not art? It is art, and it is beautiful.

Humans are the storytellers of God. There is something that exists inside all of us that can make an interpretation of everything we perceive. We are like God's journalists trying to explain whatever happens around us. It is our nature to make up stories, and this is why we create languages. This is why all of the world religions create beautiful mythology. We try to express what we perceive and share what we perceive, and this action is happening all of the time.

When we meet somebody new, we want to know that person's story almost right away. We ask all of the key questions: "What do you do? Where do you live? How many children do you have?" This interrogation goes both ways. We can hardly wait to tell that person our point of view, to express what we feel, to share our own story. When we experience something we like, we want to tell everybody about it. That's why we talk so much to one another. Even when we are by ourselves, we have the need to share our story, and we share it with ourselves. We see a beautiful sunset and we say, "Oh, what a beautiful sunset!" Nobody is listening except us, but we talk to ourselves anyway.

We also have the need to know other people's stories because we like to compare notes, or we can say that as artists we like to compare our art. We see a movie, we like it, and we ask the friend who went with us, "What did you think about the movie?" Well, maybe our friend has another point of view and tells us things about the movie that we didn't see. Very soon we change our mind and say, "Well, that movie was not as good as I thought it was." We are constantly exchanging information and modifying our story in this way. This is how the dream of humanity evolves. Our personal dream mixes with the dream of other dreamers, and this modifies the bigger dream of society.

You are dreaming the story of your life, and I can assure you that it's an art. Your art is the art of creating stories and sharing stories. If I met you today, I would see the real you behind your story. I would see you as the force of life creating art through you. Your story could be the best screenplay for any movie because all of us are professional storytellers. But I know that whatever you tell me is just a story. I don't have to believe your story, but I can listen to your story and enjoy it. I can go to the movies to see *The Godfather*, and I don't believe it, but I can enjoy it, right?

What I'm sharing with you is my personal process about how I recovered my personal freedom. I am grateful for the opportunity to share my story, but it's just a story, and it's only true for me. Something I find very interesting is that every time I share this story it is different. I try to distort it as little as possible, but even my own story changes. Despite the distortion, if you can understand it, you can compare it to your own art.

Many times we don't see our own creation; we don't see our own lies. But sometimes in the reflection of somebody else, we can see our own magnificence. By experiencing the love of another person, we can see how great we are. From one artist to another artist, we might see that it's possible to improve our own art.

Once we have the awareness to see our own story, we discover there is another way of creating the main character. Without awareness, there is nothing we can do, because the story is so powerful that the story writes itself. We create the story, we give our personal power to the story, and then the story is living our lives. But with awareness, we recover the control of our story. That is the good news. If we don't like our story, we are the authors; we can change it.

POINTS TO PONDER

• You are the author of an ongoing story you tell yourself. In your story, everything is about you, and it has to be that way because you are the center of your perception. The story is told from your point of view.

• You create an image for the secondary characters in your story, and you assign them a role to play. The only thing you know about the secondary characters is the story you create about them. The truth is that you don't know anyone, and nobody knows you either.

• Respect is one of the greatest expressions of love. If other people try to write your story, it means they don't respect you. They consider that you are not a good artist who can write your own story, even though you were born to write your own story.

• The only way to change your story is to change what you believe about yourself. If you clean up the lies you believe about yourself, the lies you believe about everybody else will change. Every time you change the main character of your story, the whole story changes to adapt to the new main character.

• Don't waste your time taking anything personally. When other people talk to you, they are really talking to the secondary character in their story. Whatever people say about you is just a projection of their *image* of you. It has nothing to do with you.

• Humans are the storytellers of God. It is our nature to make up stories, to interpret everything we perceive. Without awareness, we give our personal power to the story, and the story writes itself. With awareness, we recover the control of our story. We see that we are the authors, and if we don't like our story, we change it.

6

INNER PEACE

Taming the voice with two rules

MORE AND MORE, I KEPT EXPLORING THE WHOLE
dynamic of the story that humans create. What I
discovered is that the story has a voice — a voice so
loud, yet only we can hear it. As I said before, you
can call it *thinking* if you want; I call it *the voice of
knowledge*. That voice is always there. It never stops.
It's not even real, but we hear it. Of course you can

say, "Well, it's me. I'm the one who is talking." But if you are the voice that is talking, then who is listening?

The voice of knowledge can also be called *the liar who lives in your head.* A beautiful Tree of Knowledge lives in your head, and it's the home for guess who? The Prince of Lies. Oh yes, and this is the problem because the voice of the liar speaks in your language, but your integrity, your spirit, the truth, has no language. You just know truth; you feel it. The voice of your spirit tries to come out, but the voice of the liar is stronger and louder and it hooks your attention almost all of the time.

You hear the voice — and not just one voice, but an entire *mitote,* which is like a thousand voices talking all at once. And what are these voices telling you? "Look at you. Who do you think you are? You will never make it. You aren't smart enough. Why should I try? Nobody understands me. What is he doing? What is she doing? What if he doesn't love me? I'm so lonely. Nobody wants to be with me. Nobody really likes me. I wonder if those people are talking about me. What will they think about me? Look at all the injustice in the world. How can I be happy when millions of people are dying of starvation?"

The voice of knowledge is telling you what you are and what you are not. It's always trying to make sense out of everything. I call it *the voice of knowledge* because it's telling you everything you know. It's telling you your point of view in a conversation that never ends. For many people it's even worse because the voice is not just talking nonsense; the voice is judging and criticizing. It's constantly gossiping in your head about you and the people around you.

That voice is usually lying because it's the voice of what you have learned, and you have learned so many lies, mainly about yourself. You cannot see the liar, but you can hear the voice. The voice of knowledge can come from your own head, or it can come from people around you. It can be your own opinion, or it can be the opinion of somebody else, but your emotional reaction to that voice is telling you, "I'm being abused."

Every time we judge ourselves, find ourselves guilty, and punish ourselves, it's because the voice in our head is telling us lies. Every time we have a conflict with our father, our mother, our children, or our beloved, it's because we believe in these lies, and they believe in them, too. But it's not just that. When we believe in lies, we cannot see the truth, so we make thousands of assumptions and we take them as truth.

One of the biggest assumptions we make is that the lies we believe are the truth! For example, we believe that we know what we are. When we get angry we say, "Oh, that's the way I am." When we get jealous: "Oh, that's the way I am." When we hate: "Oh, that's the way I am." But is this true? I'm not sure about that. I used to make the assumption that I was the one who was talking, that I was the one who said all of those things that I didn't want to say. It was a big surprise when I discovered that it was not me; it was the way I learned to be. And I practiced and practiced until I mastered that performance.

The voice that says, "That's the way I am," is the voice of knowledge. It's the voice of the liar living in the Tree of Knowledge in your head. The Toltec consider it a mental disease that is highly contagious because it's transmitted from human to human through knowledge. The symptoms of the disease are fear, anger, hatred, sadness, jealousy, conflict, and separation between humans. Again, these lies are controlling the dream of our life. I think this is obvious.

My grandfather told me in the simplest way, "Miguel, the conflict is between the truth and what is not the truth," and this was nothing new. Two thousand years ago one of the greatest masters, at least in my story, said, "And you will know the truth, and the truth will set you free." Free from what? From all those lies. Especially from the liar who lives in your head and talks to you all the time. And we call it *thinking!* I used to tell my apprentices, "Just because you hear a voice in your head it doesn't mean that it's speaking the truth. Well, don't believe that voice, and that voice won't have any power over you."

There is a movie that illustrates my point beautifully. It's called *A Beautiful Mind*. At first I thought, "Oh, another spy movie," but I became more interested when I realized that the main character is schizophrenic. He is a brilliant man, a genius, but he sees people who don't exist. These people are controlling his life because he listens to their opinions and follows whatever they tell him to do. They are lying to him, and by listening to what they tell him, he is ruining his life. He has no idea that these people are hallucinations until his wife puts him in a mental hospital, where he is diagnosed as schizophrenic and given medication. The visions disappear, but the drug has secondary effects, and he decides to stop taking it. Without the drug, the visions come back, and he finds out that it's true that nobody else can see the people he sees. Now he has to make a choice: go back to the hospital, lose his wife, and accept that he is mentally ill, or face the visions and overcome them.

When he finally has the awareness that the people he sees are not real, he makes a very smart decision. He says, "I will not pay attention to them. I will not believe what they tell me." The power the visions have over him is lost when he no longer believes in them. With this awareness, he finds peace, and after many years of not putting his attention on them, the visions hardly talk to him anymore. Even though he still sees them, they don't waste their time because he doesn't listen to them anyway.

This movie is wonderful because it shows that if you don't believe the voice in your head, it loses the power it has over you, and you become authentic again. The voice in your head isn't even real, but it's ruling your life, and it's a tyrant. Once that voice hooks your attention, it makes you do whatever it wants you to do.

How many times has the voice made you say *yes* when you really wanted to say *no*? Or the opposite —the voice made you say *no* when you really wanted to say *yes*? How many times has the voice made you doubt what you feel in your heart? How many times have you missed opportunities to do what you really want to do in your life because of fear — fear that was a reaction to believing the voice in your head? How many times have you broken up with someone you really loved just because the voice of knowledge told you to do it? How many times have you tried to control the people you love because you follow that voice? How many times have you gotten angry or jealous or lost control and hurt the people you really love just because you believed that voice?

You can see what you have done by following instructions from the voice of knowledge — by following the lies. That voice tells you so many things to do that go against yourself, just like the visions of the character in the movie. The only difference between you and that man is that maybe you don't see the visions, but you hear the voice. It's overwhelming, it never stops, and we pretend that we are mentally sane!

It is obvious that the voice of knowledge is the story talking by itself. As soon as an idea hooks your attention, your story goes in that direction. Then it takes you anywhere and everywhere without any direction. Every idea is repeating itself, and there are so many ideas in your head competing for your attention that the voice is changing from one moment to the next — boom, boom, boom!

I compare the voice of knowledge to a wild horse that is taking you wherever it wants to go. You have no control over that horse. But if you cannot *stop* the horse, at least you can try to *tame* the horse. I tell my apprentices, "Once you learn to tame the horse, you will ride the horse, and thinking becomes a tool that takes you where *you* want to go. If you don't believe that voice, it becomes quieter and quieter, and speaks to you less and less until it stops talking to you."

If you have to talk to yourself, then why not be friendly? Why not tell yourself how beautiful and wonderful you are? Then at least you have someone to talk to when you're alone. But if the voice in your head is nasty and abusive, then it's no fun at all. If that voice is telling you lies, if it's letting you know why you should be ashamed of yourself or why your beloved doesn't love you, then it's better to be quiet.

If you don't like a person, you can walk away from that person. If you don't like yourself, you can't escape yourself; you are with yourself wherever you go. This is why some people try to numb themselves with alcohol or drugs. Or maybe they overeat or gamble to make themselves forget who they are with. Of course this doesn't work because the story-teller judges everything we do, and this only leads to more shame and self-rejection.

Long ago I stopped listening to the voice of knowledge. I remember that I used to go outside and tell myself, "Oh, look at the beautiful clouds, the flowers, mmm, they smell so good" — as if I didn't know that! I no longer make up stories for myself. I know what I know. Why tell myself what I already know? Does that make sense? It's just a habit. I don't waste my time and energy by talking to myself. I no longer have that ongoing voice in my head, and I can assure you that it's wonderful.

You don't need internal dialogue; you can know without thinking. The value of cultivating a silent mind has been known for thousands of years. In India, people use meditation and the chanting of mantras to stop the internal dialogue. To have peace in your head is incredible. Imagine being in an environment where there is a constant sound — bzzzz, bzzzz, bzzzz. The moment comes when you don't even notice the noise. You know something is bothering you, but you no longer notice what it is. The moment the noise stops, you notice the silence and feel the relief, "Ahhh . . ." When the voice in your head finally stops talking, it feels something like that. I call it *inner peace.*

When I shared this with my apprentices, they understood what I was telling them. They said, "We know the voice of knowledge lives in our head, and we know that it's a liar, but how do we stop it from

THE VOICE OF KNOWLEDGE

talking to us? Can you give us a little more help?" By that time, I had already won over the voice, and I was completely at peace. I said, "Okay, I will give you two simple rules. If you follow these rules, there is a chance that you will tame the voice or even win the challenge against the liar."

The solution for taming the liar is to *stop believing* what it tells you. What happens when someone tells you a lie, and you know it's a lie? It doesn't affect you because you don't *believe* the lie. If you don't believe it, the lie cannot survive the test of your skepticism, and boom! The lie disappears. Simple. But in that simplicity there is also a big challenge. Why? Because believing your own lies makes you feel safe, and believing the lies of other people is very tempting. When you are ready for the challenge, the following two rules will accelerate the process of purifying your belief system, which is everything in your personal Tree of Knowledge.

Rule number one: *Don't believe yourself.* But keep your mind open. Keep your heart open. Listen to yourself, listen to your story, but don't *believe* it because now you know that the story you are writing is fiction. It's not real. When you hear the voice in your head, don't take it personally. You know that knowledge is usually lying to you. Listen, and ask if it's speaking the truth or not. If you don't believe your own lies, your lies will not survive, and you can make better choices based on truth.

Don't believe yourself, but learn to listen because sometimes the voice of knowledge can have a brilliant idea, and if you agree with the idea, then take it. It could be a moment of inspiration that leads to a great opportunity in life. Respect your story, and learn to *really* listen. When you listen to your story, the communication with yourself will improve 100 percent. You will see your story with clarity, and if you don't like the story, you can change it.

Don't believe yourself mainly when you are using the voice against yourself. The voice can make you afraid to be alive, to express who you really are. It can stop you from doing what you really want to do with your life. That voice has been in control of your head for so many years, and, no, that voice will not give up just because you want it to leave you alone. But at least you can challenge that voice by not believing what it's telling you. That's why I say, "Don't believe yourself."

Rule number two: *Don't believe anybody else.* And that includes me for the same reason. You know that if you lie to yourself, surely other people lie to themselves. And if they lie to themselves, surely they will lie to you as well. When people talk to you, who is speaking through them? Who is dictating what they say? You have no idea if what they are saying is coming from their heart or from the Prince of Lies who lives in their head. You don't know, so don't believe them. But learn to listen without judging. You don't need to judge people because they lie. How many times have you heard someone say, "Oh, he's a pathological liar," when in reality everybody is possessed by the Prince of Lies? There are lies everywhere. People are always lying, and when they don't have awareness, they don't even know it. Sometimes they really believe that what they are saying is true. And they can really *believe* it, but it doesn't mean that it's true.

Don't believe anybody, but this doesn't mean closing your mind or your heart. Listen to other people tell their story. You know that it's just a story, and that it's only true for them. When you listen, you can understand their story; you can see where people are coming from, and the communication can be wonderful. Other people need to express their story, to project what they believe, but you don't have to agree with what they say. *Don't believe*, but learn to listen. Even if it's just a story, sometimes the words that come from other storytellers come from their integrity. When this happens, your own integrity recognizes it right away, and you agree with what they are saying. Their voice goes directly to your spirit, and you feel you already know that what they are telling you is the truth.

Don't believe anybody else, but listen because sometimes a moment of inspiration or opportunity can come through the voice of someone else. The way other people create their story might reflect the way you create your story, and when they are exposed, you can see how they invest their faith in lies. You might see the lies right away, when you couldn't see them in yourself. By listening to their story, you might recognize the truth about something you do all the time, and that truth can change your own story. Listen to their story, but *don't believe it*. That is the key.

If other people tell you, "Look at the way you are dressed!" that remark doesn't ruin your day. You listen to their story, but you *don't believe it*. You can decide if it's true or not according to your story, but you don't have an emotional reaction anymore. If you decide that it's true, you can change what you are wearing, and there's no more problem. This is something simple that is happening all the time. People constantly express their point of view, and we may even ask for their point of view, but *don't believe them!*

When people talk about you, now you know they are talking about a secondary character in their story who represents you. They are talking about an *image* they create for you. You know that it has nothing to do with you. But if you agree, if you *believe* what they say, then their story becomes a part of your story. If you take it personally, it modifies your story. If you don't take it personally, the opinions of others do not affect you the way they used to, and you have more patience with people. This helps you to avoid a great deal of conflict.

If you follow these two rules — *don't believe yourself*, and *don't believe anybody else* — all of the lies that come from the voice of knowledge won't survive your skepticism. Being skeptical is not about being judgmental; it is not about taking the position that you are more intelligent than others. You just don't believe, and what is true will become obvious. This is very interesting because the truth survives your skepticism even if you don't believe it. That is the beauty of the truth. The truth doesn't need anybody to believe it. The truth is still the truth whether or not you believe it. Can we say the same about lies? No, lies only exist because we believe them. If we don't believe in lies, they simply disappear.

Every day the sun is in the sky whether we believe it or not. The Earth is round, even if the entire world believes that it's flat. Hundreds of years ago, everyone believed this lie. They would swear that the Earth was flat, and they were certain that the Earth was the center of the universe, with the sun revolving around it. People really believed this; they had no doubt about it. But just because they believed it, did that make it true? No, but believing those lies made them feel safe.

Humans believe so many lies. Some of these lies are so subtle and convincing that we base our entire virtual reality on them without even noticing that they are lies. The lies we believe about ourselves can be difficult to see because we are so used to them that they seem normal.

For example, if you believe the common lie

"I'm not worth it," that lie lives in your mind because you believe it. You don't believe people who tell you how great you are, and you don't believe them because you believe the opposite. Your faith is already invested in a belief that is not the truth; it's a lie, but your faith guides your actions. By not feeling worthy, how do you express yourself with other people? You are shy. How can you ask for something when you do not believe you are worth it? What you believe about yourself is what you project to other people, and that is what others then believe about you. Of course, that is how they treat you, which only reinforces the belief that you aren't worth it. And what is the truth? The truth is that you are worth it; everybody is worth it.

If you believe the lie that you cannot speak in public then *thy will be done:* When you try to speak in public, you are afraid. The only way to break your faith in this agreement is by taking the action and doing it. Then you prove that it's a lie, and you are no longer afraid.

If you believe that you cannot have a loving relationship, *thy will be done.* If you feel that you don't deserve love, even if love is in front of you, you just don't take it because you are blind to it. You only see what you want to see, and you only hear what you want to hear. Everything you perceive is just more support for your lies.

If you understand these examples, you can just imagine how many lies you believe about yourself, and how many lies you believe about your parents, your children, your siblings, or your partner. Every time you judge them, you give voice to the false beliefs in your own Tree of Knowledge. You give your power to these lies, and what is the result? Anger or jealousy or even hate. Then you accumulate all of that emotional poison, and the moment comes when you lose control and say something that you don't want to say.

Can you see the power of what I'm sharing with you? You can change your life by refusing to believe your own lies. You can start with the main lies that limit the expression of your happiness and your love. If you take your faith away from these lies, they lose their power over you. Then you can recover your faith and invest it in different beliefs. If you stop believing in lies, everything in your life changes, just like magic.

There is a part of *The Iliad* by Homer that I really love: "We, the gods, will live as long as the humans believe in us. The day the humans no longer believe in us, all the gods will disappear." This is beautiful. Centuries ago, the Greek gods were worshiped by hundreds of thousands of people; today, they are just legends. When we don't believe in lies, the lies disappear, and the truth becomes obvious.

Many lies enslave us, but only one thing can free us, and it's the truth. Only the truth can set us free from the fear, the drama, and the conflict in our lives. This is the absolute truth, and I cannot put it more simply than that.

꙰

POINTS TO PONDER

• What you call *thinking* is the voice of knowledge making up stories, telling you what you know, and trying to make sense out of everything you don't know. The problem is that the voice makes you do many things that go against yourself.

• The voice in your head is like a wild horse taking you wherever *it* wants to go. Once you tame the horse, you can ride the horse, and knowledge becomes a tool for communication that takes you where *you* want to go.

• You don't need internal dialogue; you can know without thinking. You can perceive with your feelings. Why waste energy telling yourself what you already know or worrying about what you don't know? When the voice in your head finally stops talking, you experience *inner peace*.

• The solution for taming the liar in your head is to *stop believing* what it tells you. If you follow two rules — *don't believe yourself*, and *don't believe anybody else* — all of the lies you believe won't survive your skepticism and will simply disappear.

• The truth survives our skepticism, but we cannot say the same about lies. Lies can only survive if we believe them. The truth is still the truth, whether or not we believe it. That is the beauty of the truth.

• The voice of knowledge rules your life, and it is a tyrant. If you refuse to obey that voice, it becomes quieter and quieter, and speaks to you less and less until it no longer controls you. When the voice loses power over you, lies no longer rule your life, and you become authentic again.

7

EMOTIONS ARE REAL

The voice of knowledge is not real

BEFORE YOU LEARN TO SPEAK, YOUR BRAIN IS LIKE a perfect computer, but without a program. When you are born, you don't know a language. It takes several years for your brain to mature enough to receive a program. Then the program is introduced to you, mainly through your parents, as well as other people around you. They hook your attention and teach you the meaning of words. You learn to speak, and the program goes inside you little by little by agreement. You agree, and now you have the program.

Well, if you are the computer, then knowledge is the program. Everything you know, all of the knowledge in your head, was already in the program before you were born. I can assure you that none of us ever has an original idea. Every letter, every word, every concept in your belief system is part of the program, and that program is contaminated with a virus called *lies*.

There's no need to judge the program as good or bad or right or wrong. Even if we don't like the program, nobody is guilty for sharing it with us. It's just the way it is, and it's wonderful because we use the program to create our stories. But who is running our life? The program! The program has a voice, and it's lying to us all the time.

How can we know what the truth is when almost everything we have learned is a lie? How can we recognize what is real in us? Well, it took some time for me to find out, but I found out. Our emotions are real. Every emotion that we feel is real, it is truth, *it is*. I discovered that every emotion comes directly from our spirit, from our integrity; it is completely authentic.

You cannot fake what you feel. You can try to repress your emotions, you can try to justify what you feel or lie about what you feel, but what you feel is authentic. It is real, and you are feeling it. There is nothing wrong with whatever you feel. There are no good emotions or bad emotions; there is nothing wrong with anger or jealousy or envy. Even if you are feeling hate, it comes from your integrity. Even if it's sadness or depression that you are suffering, if you feel it, there is always a reason for feeling it.

I discovered something very interesting about the human mind, something logical and important to understand. Everything you perceive causes an emotional reaction — *everything*. If you perceive beauty, your emotional reaction is wonderful; you feel great. When you are hurt, your emotional reaction is not so great. But you perceive not just the outside world;

you perceive the virtual world you create in your head. You perceive not only your feelings, but your knowledge — your own thoughts, judgments, and beliefs. You perceive the voice in your head, and you have an emotional reaction to that voice.

Now the question is this: What is the voice in your head telling you? How many times has it told you, "God, I'm so stupid, how could I do that? I will never learn!" The voice of knowledge judges you, you perceive the judgment, and you have an emotional reaction. You feel the shame; you feel the guilt. The emotion is true, but what causes the emotion, which is the judgment that you are stupid, is not true; it's a story. Again, this is just action–reaction. What is the action? The action is the perception of your point of view, which means the perception of your own judgment. What is the reaction? Your feelings are the reaction, and you react to the lies with emotional poison.

Let's see if we can understand this a little better. Imagine that you have a dog. As you know, the dog is just a dog, and it's a perfect dog, isn't it? But what happens if you abuse the dog? What if every time you see the dog, you kick the dog? Very soon the dog will be afraid. You can see the emotions coming from the dog. It is angry; it might try to bite you or run away. Is there something wrong with the dog's emotions? Does the dog's anger make the dog evil? No, the dog's reaction is just the result of being abused. The emotion is helping the dog to defend itself. It comes from the dog's integrity.

Now imagine a dog living in the most beautiful environment with people who always love and respect the dog. That dog is the sweetest animal in the whole world, the most wonderful dog. Because that dog is not abused, he follows his nature; he loves everybody who loves him. Well, your physical body is just like that dog. It reacts emotionally in the same way. Why do you react with anger? Well, because somebody kicked you, right? But who kicked you? The voice in your head, the main character of your story — what you *believe* you are.

You also perceive your image of perfection, what you believe you *are not*, and this also creates an emotional reaction. How do you feel when you cannot live up to that image? The emotion is not pleasant, but your emotional reaction is real; it's what you feel. But is it true that you need to fit that image? No, it's a lie. What you are perceiving is just a lie that you agreed to believe in. You agreed, and that lie has become a part of your story.

Humans are victimized by knowledge, by what we *know*. If we make a mistake in front of someone, we try to justify the mistake to protect the image we project. Later, when we are alone, we remember what happened, and we punish ourselves all over again. Why? Because the voice of knowledge keeps telling us what we did from the same point of view that we had when we did it. The voice becomes a powerful judge, and it's telling us, "Look what you did!" And it's telling this to whom? It was the voice that made us do it in the first place!

The voice of knowledge is abusing the emotional body. What is not real is abusing what is real. The action is to believe a lie; the reaction is to feel emotional pain. The emotional body perceives the voice, reacts to the voice, and just like a tiger, it attacks. We lose control, and we do things and say things that we really don't want to do or say. Now the voice of knowledge is afraid of our emotional reaction; it judges our reaction, and makes us feel ashamed of our own feelings.

Then we perceive the emotion of shame, and use knowledge to try to justify the emotion, which means the voice of knowledge is talking about what we feel. The voice starts lying about our feelings, and even tries to deny what we feel. Then we perceive that voice, we perceive the judgment, and we have another emotional reaction. Now we feel guilty because we reacted emotionally. Then knowledge tries to explain the emotion of guilt. The emotional pain is growing, and now we are depressed. Can you see the cycle?

The voice of knowledge makes a story about our emotions, we perceive the story, and we try to repress our emotions. Perceiving that repression creates another emotional reaction, and soon we just want to repress everything we feel. "I shouldn't feel this way. What kind of man are you? Are you a wimp or what? Real men don't cry." We pretend it doesn't hurt. Yes it hurts, but it hurts because we make a story, perceive the story, and drag more emotions into the story.

Why do we hate? Because someone is abusing us. That's why we hate. Why do we suffer? Because something is hurting us. That's why we suffer. It's a normal reaction to being hurt. But what is hurting us? Well, now the answer is easy. What hurts us is the voice of the liar in our head that keeps telling us the way we *should* be, but we *are not*. The hate, the anger, and the jealousy are normal emotional reactions that come from what is real, which means they come from our integrity, not from who we are pretending to be.

That's why there is nothing wrong with hate. If we feel hate, the voice of knowledge speaking in our head is causing us to hate. The hate is completely normal; it's just a reaction to what we believe. If we change the belief, then the hate will transform into love. All of our emotions change when we no longer believe the voice because the emotions are the effect, not the cause. Emotional pain is a symptom of being abused; the pain is letting us know that we have to do something to stop the abuse.

Why do people abuse us? Because we allow them to abuse us, because in our judgment we believe we deserve to be abused. But if we go a little deeper, we see that we abuse ourselves far more than anybody else abuses us. We can blame other people who hurt us and say, "I grew up being abused," and we can make many excuses. But in the present moment, who is abusing you? If you are truthful, you find that mostly it's your own voice of knowledge.

Every time we lie to ourselves, we abuse ourselves. Every time we curse ourselves, we abuse ourselves. Every time we judge ourselves, every time we reject ourselves, of course we have an emotional reaction, and it isn't pleasant! Again, if we don't like the emotional reaction, it's not about repressing what we feel; it's about cleaning up the lies that cause the emotional reaction.

The message coming from our integrity is clear. The voice of integrity is screaming to us, "Please, save me!" That reminds me of the movie *The Exorcist*, about a little girl who is possessed by demons. Well, there is a little girl inside us saying, "Help me! I'm being possessed by the main character of my story!" Oh, my goodness — and it's true! Humans are possessed by knowledge. We are possessed by a distorted image of ourselves, and that is why we are no longer free. How many times have you heard someone say, "If the real me comes out, I don't know what's going to happen"? We are afraid that something inside of us will come out and destroy everything. And you know what? It is true. If the real you comes out, it will destroy all of the lies, and that *is* frightening.

I used to be possessed by the main character of my story. I was abused by that character for so many years, yet I pretended to love myself. What a joke! And not just that, I pretended to love somebody else. How could I love somebody else when I didn't love myself? I can only give to others what I have for myself.

People have asked me, "Miguel, why can't I feel love? How can I learn to create love?" I thought about this. Hmm . . . Create love? Then a little idea came into my mind. We don't need to learn how to love. By nature, we love. Before we learn to speak, love is the main emotion we feel. It is natural to express our love, but then we learn to repress our love. And I tell them, "You don't need to create love. Your heart is made to produce so much love that you can send your love to the entire world. If you can't feel love, it's because you are resisting love; it's because you've learned how to stop expressing your love."

When we are little children and people tell us that we shouldn't be the way we are, we begin to repress the expression of our authentic self. We repress our integrity, our own emotional body. We practice hiding our emotions and pretending that we don't feel them. When we feel ashamed of our emotions, we begin to justify and explain and judge our emotions. We believe in so many lies that we no longer express the beautiful emotion of love.

The voice of knowledge tells us, "It's not safe to love. I'm afraid to love because love makes me vulnerable. If I love, my heart will be broken." So many lies. It's not the truth, but knowledge tells you, "Of course it's true. I have a lot of experience with this. Every time I love, my heart is broken." Well, this isn't the truth because nobody can break your heart if you love yourself. If your heart was broken in the past, you broke it with the lies you believed about love. Love makes you strong; selfishness makes you weak. Love doesn't hurt. What hurts is the fear, selfishness, and control that come from the lies you believe in. If you no longer believe in lies, automatically love starts coming out of you.

After my experience in the desert, it was clear to me that every emotion I feel comes directly from my integrity. When I noticed this, I no longer repressed my emotions. Now my emotions are the most important part of my story because I know that my feelings are authentic. When I feel an emotion, I know it's a reaction to what I perceive. My emotions are telling me how I am doing in my life, and by following my emotions, I can change my circumstances.

Whatever the feeling — from joy to anger, from love to hate — it is just a reaction. But being a reaction, it is important to see the action. If I am not happy, it's because there is something in my story that is suppressing my happiness. Then I have to take a step back and see what is causing it. If I have the awareness, I can face the problem, fix the problem, and be happy again. As soon as any problem arises in my life, I resolve it in one way or another without even trying to make a story about it.

The universe is simple: it's about cause and effect, action and reaction. If you don't like the way you are living your life, this is a reaction to the program that is ruling your life. The liar, the program, is not even part of you, but at the same time, it *is* part of you because it's the way you identify yourself. The program creates the story, then it tries to make sense of the story by explaining and justifying everything to the main character of the story. What a setup. What a creation. Humans create an entire culture, a whole philosophy of humanity. We create history, science, art, Olympic games, Miss Universe, you name it. It's our creation, and it's beautiful and wonderful, but it's just a *story!*

The main character of your story is you, but the role that you are playing is not you. You have practiced that role for so long that you have mastered the performance. You have become the best actor in the entire world, but I can assure you that you are not what you believe you are. Thank God, because you are much better than what you believe you are.

I remember when my Grandfather told me, "Miguel, you will know that you are free when you no longer have to be you." At that moment, I didn't understand him, but later I knew exactly what he meant. I don't have to be the way everybody wants me to be. I don't have to be what I believe *I should be* according to my own lies.

Your story is your creation. You are the artist with the force of life flowing through you. If you don't like your art, you have the power to change it. That's the good news. You don't have to be you anymore, and that's the maximum freedom. You don't have to be what you *believe* you are. You don't have to be that anger or that jealousy or that hate. You can recover the sense of what you really are, return to paradise, and live again in heaven on earth.

✂

POINTS TO PONDER

• Every emotion that you feel is real. It is truth. It comes directly from the integrity of your spirit. You cannot fake what you feel. You can try to justify or repress your emotions, you can try to lie about what you feel, but what you feel is authentic.

• The voice of knowledge can make you feel ashamed of your feelings, but there is nothing wrong with whatever you feel. There are no good emotions or bad emotions. Even if what you feel is anger or hate, it comes from your integrity. If you feel it, there is always a reason for feeling it.

• Everything you perceive causes an emotional reaction. You perceive not only your feelings, but your knowledge

— your own thoughts, judgments, and beliefs. You perceive the voice in your head, and you have an emotional reaction to that voice.

• Every time you lie to yourself, or judge yourself, or reject yourself, you have an emotional reaction, and it isn't pleasant. If you don't like the emotional reaction, it's not about repressing what you feel; it's about cleaning up the lies that cause it. All of your emotions change when you no longer believe in lies because the emotions are the effect, not the cause.

• Our emotions are real; the voice of knowledge that makes us suffer is not. Our suffering is true, but the reason why we suffer may not be true at all.

• Humans are possessed by knowledge, by a distorted image of ourselves. That is why we are no longer free.

• Emotional pain is a symptom of being abused; the pain is letting you know that you have to do something to stop the abuse. The emotions are the most important part of your story because they are telling you how you are doing in your life. By following your emotions, you can change your circumstances.

8

COMMON SENSE AND BLIND FAITH

Recovering our faith and free will

WHEN I STARTED TEACHING THIS PHILOSOPHY, one of my challenges was to share the wisdom of my tradition without the superstition. I wanted to take away all of the superstition, all of the things about evil and witchcraft from the Toltec tradition. Who cares about all the lies? I wanted to take away the nonsense, and only keep the common sense.

If we take away the superstition and mythology from the traditions around the world, the result is pure common sense. When it comes to common sense, there is no difference between the Toltec tradition, the Egyptian tradition, the Christian tradition, the Buddhist tradition, the Islamic tradition, or any other tradition, because all of these philosophies come from the same place. They come directly from human integrity.

The difference is in the story. Each philosophy has tried to explain with symbols something that is so difficult to say with words. The masters witnessed the truth and created a story, depending on what they believed. The story became mythology, and the people who were not masters created all of the superstition and lies. That is why I don't believe in following gurus or idolizing heroes. We are our own gurus, our own heroes. What I am sharing with you is the way I live my life, but I'm not telling you how to live your life. It's not my business; it's your business. But seeing the way that I dream can give you an idea of what you can do with your dream.

As you read this book, perhaps you will feel as if you are reading something you already know: your own common sense. In one moment, you can return to your common sense, to your own integrity. You can have clarity again, and see what others cannot see. You can live with awareness and recover a wonderful power that humans gave up long ago: faith.

Faith is a force that comes from our integrity. It is the expression of what we really are. Faith is the power of our creation because we use faith to create our life story and to transform our life story. Different traditions have called this power by different names. The Toltec call it *intent*, but I prefer to call it *faith*.

Let's see if we can understand why our faith is so important. When we talk about faith or intent, we are also talking about the power of the word. The word is pure magic. It is a power that comes directly from God, and faith is the force that directs this power. We can say that everything in our virtual reality is created with the word because we use the word for the creation of our story. Humans have the most wonderful imagination. Beginning with the word, we form a language. With a language, we try to make sense out of everything we experience.

First we agree about the sound and meaning of each word. Then just by remembering the sound of the words, we can communicate with other dreamers about our virtual reality. We give names to everything we perceive; we choose words as symbols, and these symbols have the power to reproduce a dream in our head. For example, just hearing the word *horse* can reproduce an entire image in our mind. That's how a symbol works. But it can even be more powerful than that. Just by saying two words, *"The Godfather,"* a whole movie can appear in our mind. The word, as a symbol, has the magic and power of creation because it can reproduce an image, a concept, or an entire situation in our imagination.

It is amazing what the word can do. The word creates images of objects in our mind. The word creates complex concepts. The word evokes feelings.

The word creates every belief that we store in our mind. The structure of our language shapes how we perceive our entire virtual reality.

Faith is so important because it is the force that gives life to every word, to every concept that we store in our mind. We can say that life manifests through faith, and that faith is a messenger of life. Life goes through our faith, and then our faith gives life to everything we agree to believe in. Remember, we invest our faith by making an agreement. When we agree with a concept, we accept the concept without any doubt, and the concept becomes a part of us. If we don't agree with a concept, our faith is not there, and we don't keep it in our memory. Every concept is alive just because our faith is there, just because we *believe* in the concept. Faith is the force that holds all of these symbols together and gives sense and direction to the entire dream.

If you can imagine that every belief, every concept, every opinion is like a brick, then our faith is the mortar that holds the bricks together. The way we start getting these bricks and putting them together is by using our attention. Humans can perceive millions of things simultaneously, but with our attention we have the power to discriminate and focus only on what we want to perceive. The attention is also the part of our mind that we use to transfer information from person to person. By hooking someone's attention, we create a channel of communication, and through that channel we can send and receive information. This is how we teach, and this is how we learn.

As I have said, our parents hook our attention and teach us the meaning of words; we agree, and we learn a language. Through language, the word, we start to build the edifice of knowledge. Together, all of our beliefs form a structure that tells us what we believe we are. The Toltec call this shape that our mind takes *the human form*. The human form is not the form of our physical body. The human form is the structure of our personal Tree of Knowledge. It is everything we believe about being a human; it is the structure of our whole story. This structure is almost as solid as our physical body because our faith makes it rigid.

You call yourself a human, and that is what makes you a human. Your faith is invested in your story — mostly in the main character of your story — and that is the main problem! The most powerful part of you, your faith, is invested in the liar who lives in your head. Through your faith, you give life to all of those lies. The result is the way you live your life in the present moment because you have faith in the main character of your story. This means that you believe in what you believe you are without any doubt. The rest is just action–reaction. Every habit is a setup for you to perform the role of your main character.

The storyteller has power over you because you have faith in the story that it tells you. Once you support the story with your faith, it doesn't matter whether the story is the truth or not the truth. You believe it; you are done. *Thy will be done.* That is why Jesus said that if you have just a little faith you can move mountains. Humans are powerful because we have a strong faith; we have the capacity to believe strongly, but where is our faith invested? Why do we feel that we have hardly any faith? I can tell you that it's not true that we have so little faith. Our faith is strong and powerful, but our faith is not free. Our faith is invested in all of the knowledge in our head. It is trapped in the structure of our Tree of Knowledge.

The structure is what really controls the dream of our life because our faith lives in that structure. Our faith is not in the voice of our story, and it's not in our reasoning mind. Just because we say, "I will succeed," doesn't mean that our faith follows those words. No, there may be another belief that is stronger and deeper, and that belief is telling us, "You will not succeed." And that is what happens. It doesn't matter what we do; we fail.

That is why you cannot change yourself just by wishing to change. No, you need to really challenge what you believe you are, especially the beliefs that limit the expression of your life. You need to challenge every belief that you use to judge yourself, to reject yourself, to make yourself little.

I remember one of my apprentices asking me, "Miguel, why is it so difficult to change my beliefs?" And I told him, "Well, you understand the concept that what you believe you are is not the truth; it's a story. You understand that very well, but you don't *believe* it. And that is what makes the difference. If you really believe it, if your faith is there, then you change."

So yes, it is possible to change what we believe, to recreate the dream of our life, but first we need to free our faith. And there is only one way to free our faith, and that way is through the truth. The truth is our sword, and it's the only weapon we have against the lies. Nothing but the truth can free the faith that is trapped in the structure of our lies. But with our faith invested in the lies, we no longer see the truth. The lies blind our faith, the power of our creation.

Blind faith is a powerful concept. When our faith is blind, we no longer follow the truth. That is what happened when we ate the fruit of the Tree of Knowledge. We believed the lies, our faith was blinded, and we followed an illusion that was not true. God told us, "You may die." And our faith in lies is death because we lose our power of creation, which is our connection with life or God. We fall into the illusion that we are separate from life, and this leads to self-destruction and death.

If your faith is blind, it is leading you nowhere. That is why Jesus said if the blind lead the blind, both fall. Now you know why other people's stories do not really help you; it is just like the blind leading the blind. If you have blind faith and you teach blind faith, both fall. If you believe that life is against you, and you teach that life is against you, both are blind because you don't see the truth. Now both believe the lie!

Real faith, or free faith, is what you are feeling in this moment. This moment is real; you have faith in life, faith in yourself, faith for no reason. This is the power of your creation in the moment. From that point of power, you can create whatever you want to create in any direction.

Blind faith is faith without awareness, but when your faith has awareness, that's a different story. When your faith has awareness, you never use the power of your faith against yourself, which means you are impeccable with your word. When you are impeccable with your word, your entire life improves in every direction. Why? Because the impeccability of your word goes directly to the main character of your story, where most of your faith is invested. To be impeccable with your word means that you never use the word against yourself in the creation of your story. I will talk more about this in the next chapter.

The way to change what you believe about yourself is to take your faith out of the lies. This is the key to changing your story, this is your dream quest, and nobody can do it but you. It's just you and your story. You have to face your own story, and what you will face, of course, is the main character of your story.

Begin by looking at the main character as if it is somebody else, not you. Your whole life story is like a book about you. Detach from the story and become aware of your own creation. Review the story of your life without any judgment so you won't have any emotional reaction. See your own story since you were a child — all of the growth you have experienced, all of your relationships. Simply take an inventory and perceive the images if you can do that. Imagine that all you have are your lungs to breathe, your eyes to see the beauty, your ears to hear the sounds of nature. It is all about love. Face your life story with your love, and you will experience the most incredible dream quest.

The dream quest is what Buddha did under the bodhi tree, what Jesus did in the desert, and what Moses did on the mountain. All world religions say the same thing because they come from humans who have opened their spiritual eyes and whose faith is no longer blind. But how can they explain the truth to anybody else? Can you imagine Jesus trying to explain the truth two thousand years ago? He talked about truth, forgiveness, and love. He told everybody, "You have to forgive one another. Love is the only way." He gave us the solution for healing the mind, but who was ready back then? Well, the question is: Are we ready now? Do we still want to believe our own lies, and be so blind that we are willing to die for our lies, for our fanaticism, for our dogmas?

Blind faith, as I said before, is leading us to be fanatics, to impose what we believe onto other people without respecting what they believe. We don't need to impose what we believe. We can respect what each of us believes and know that each of us is dreaming our own dream that has nothing to do with anyone else. Just by having this awareness, we are taking a big step toward healing the mind.

The challenge is to recover the power of your faith and no longer be blinded by lies. But if you want to face the tyrant that you have created, you need to have faith. And the problem is that the faith you have invested in your creation is a thousand times stronger than the faith you now have left. So where are you going to find the faith to face your own creation if your creation is eating every ounce of your faith?

Well, if you cannot find faith within you, from what you believe you are, there is a lot of faith outside of you, everywhere. The point is to learn how to gather all of the faith that you need to free yourself from the structure of your lies. That is why humans perform rituals: to gather more faith. When you go to any church and you pray or chant or sing or play the drums or dance, you are gathering power and faith from these rituals. This is really powerful. When you focus your attention on your ritual, this opens a channel to your faith. Your faith follows the ritual, and with your attention hooked into that channel, it is possible to recover your faith.

Ritual can help us to gather faith from nature,

and to build faith with one another as a human community. When people gather together, when they love, they experience tremendous faith. This is what you are doing every time you go to church, any time you pray. When you pray and perform rituals, you gather faith that is not really your own faith, but it is faith that you can use to recover your own. And if you believe 100 percent in what you want to accomplish with a prayer or ritual, you multiply your intent.

When you pray, you commune with the divine spirit. Prayer creates a bridge that goes from the real you into the divine spirit, pushing aside the main character of your story. This is the key, because the main character of your story is the only thing between you and the divine spirit. Prayer and ritual help to stop the judgments and all the voices talking in your head that tell you why something isn't possible. Both prayer and ritual offer an intense action to stop the voice of knowledge from abusing the emotional body.

All the religions with all of their different rituals are wonderful because they provide a way for you to gather the power to break at least some of the self-limiting agreements you have made. Every time you break an agreement, the faith invested in that agreement comes back to you, and you recover a little more of your faith. That is what this book is about. My intent is for you to recover at least part of the faith that you have invested in the main character of your story. But if you gather all of that faith and you don't use it to change the main character of your story, soon all of the faith you have gathered is consumed by the main character.

That is why you need to reclaim your life from the superstition of what you believe you are. There is only one way to do this, and that is to stop believing the storyteller, the voice of knowledge in your head. When you restore your faith in the truth, and you take it out of the lies, the result is that you become authentic. Your emotional body becomes the way it was when you were a child, and you return to your own common sense. I cannot say that I invented this or that I've discovered something new. As an artist, I only rearrange what already exists. Everything I'm sharing with you has been in this world for thousands of years, not only in Mexico, but in Egypt, India, Greece, Rome. Common sense exists in all of us, but we cannot see it with our attention focused on the lies we believe.

Lies make everything complicated, when the truth is very simple. I think now is the time to return to the truth, to common sense, to the simplicity of life itself. Now we know that the lies are so powerful that they blind us. Well, the truth is so powerful that when we finally return to the truth, our entire reality changes. Truth brings us back to paradise, where we experience a strong communion of love with God, with life, with all of creation.

When you release your faith from all the lies, the result is that you free your will. And when your will is free, you can finally make a choice. The voice in your head gives you the illusion that you can make a choice, that you have free will. Well, do you really believe that it's your conscious choice to hurt yourself, to make yourself suffer, to reject and abuse yourself? How can you say that you have free will when you choose to hurt the people you love, when you judge your partner or your children, and make them miserable with your judgment?

Just imagine if you really have free will, which is the power to make your own choices. Do you really choose to sabotage your own happiness or your own love? Do you choose to judge yourself, to blame yourself, to live your life in shame and in guilt? Do you choose to believe that you are bad, that you are not beautiful, that you don't deserve to be happy or healthy or prosperous because you are not worth it? Do you choose to constantly fight with the people you love the most? If you have free will, you choose the opposite. I think it is obvious that our will is *not* free.

When you put your faith in truth instead of in lies, your choices change. When your will is free, your choices come from your integrity, not from the program, that liar in your head. Now you believe whatever you want to believe, and when you have the power to believe whatever you want, something very interesting happens. What you want is to love. You don't want anything else but love because you know that what is not love is not the truth!

When your will is free, you choose happiness and love, peace and harmony. You choose to play; you choose to enjoy life. You no longer choose drama. If in the present moment you are choosing drama, it's because you have no choice; it's a habit. It's because you were programmed to be that way, and you don't even know that you have the power to make a different choice. Something else in your head is making the choice, and it's the voice of the liar. Just like that man in the movie *A Beautiful Mind*, whose visions made the choices for him, your voice is making the choices for you.

Why would we consciously decide to have a fight with our parents or our children or our beloved? It's not that we want to fight. You know, when we are children and we gather with other children, it's because we want to play; we want to have fun and enjoy life. When we grow up and decide to get into a relationship — mainly a romantic relationship — is it because we want to create emotional pain and drama? No, common sense tells us that we want to play together; we want to have fun exploring life together. But the Prince of Lies who controls the voice of knowledge represses our common sense.

Common sense is wisdom, and wisdom is different from knowledge. You are wise when you no longer act against yourself. You are wise when you live in harmony with yourself, with your own kind, with all of creation.

Right now you have a choice. What are you going to do with this information? What happens if you don't believe in lies? Take a moment to put your attention on your feelings, to feel all of the possibilities for your life if your faith is no longer blind. If you recover your faith from lies, your suffering is over, your judgments are over. You no longer live with guilt, with shame, with anger, with jealousy. You no longer have the need to be good enough for anybody, including yourself. You accept what you are, whatever you are, even if you don't know what you are. And you don't care to know anymore. It's not important to know, and that is wisdom.

Just imagine that because you don't believe in lies, your whole life changes. You live your life without trying to control everybody around you, and your integrity doesn't allow anybody to control you. You no longer judge other people or need to complain about whatever they do because you know you can't control what people do. Just imagine that you choose to forgive whoever hurt you in your life because you no longer want to carry all of that emotional poison in your heart. And just by forgiving everybody, even yourself, you heal your mind, you heal your heart, and you no longer have emotional pain.

Just imagine that you recover the power to make your own choices because you no longer believe the storyteller. You enjoy your life with plenitude, with inner peace, with love. Imagine how you treat your partner, how you treat your children, what you teach the new generation, if you no longer believe in lies. Just imagine the change in the whole of humanity out of something so simple: not believing in lies.

❧

POINTS TO PONDER

• The word is pure magic. It is a power that comes directly from God, and faith is the force that directs that power. Everything in our virtual reality is created with the word; we use the word for the creation of our story, to make sense out of everything we experience.

• Faith is the force that gives life to every word, to every belief that we store in our mind. If we agree with a concept, our faith is there, and we keep it in our memory. Faith is the mortar that holds our beliefs together and gives sense and direction to the entire dream.

• The attention is that part of our mind that we use to transfer information from person to person. By hooking the attention, we create a channel of communication, and through that channel we can send and receive information.

- The structure of our knowledge controls the dream of our life because our faith lives in that structure. Our faith is not in the voice of our story, and it's not in our reasoning mind. Our faith is trapped in the structure of our knowledge, and only the truth can set it free.

- Real faith, or free faith, is what you are feeling in this moment. This moment is real; you have faith in life, faith in yourself, faith for no reason. This is the power of your creation in the moment. From this point of power, you can create whatever you want to create in any direction.

- Blind faith leads us nowhere because it doesn't follow the truth. With lies blinding our faith, we fall into the illusion that we are separate from God, and we lose our power of creation.

- When we release our faith from the lies, we recover free will and make our own choices. We recover the power to believe whatever we want to believe. And when we have the power to believe whatever we want, all we want is to love.

9

TRANSFORMING THE STORYTELLER

The Four Agreements as favorite tools

YOU HAVE SEEN HOW YOU CREATE A VIRTUAL REALITY, the dream of your life, and you know that your life is a story. Now with that awareness, the question is: Are you happy with your story? Something important to understand is that you can be whatever you want to be because you are the artist and your life is your creation. It's your story. It's your comedy or your drama, and if the story is changing anyway, then why not direct the change with awareness?

Now that you are an artist with awareness, you can see if you like your art, and you can practice making it better. Practice makes the master. But it's action that makes the difference. When I discovered this, my action was to take responsibility for my art and purify my program. As an artist I started exploring the possibilities — every action and every reaction. And by the way, this is our real nature: to explore. Explore what? Life! What else can we explore?

To change the story of your life is what the Toltec call *the mastery of transformation*. It's about transforming you, the storyteller, the dreamer. Life is changing so fast, and you can see that you are always transforming, but you master transformation when you no longer resist change. Instead, you take advantage of change, and you enjoy change. To master transformation is to live in the present moment, all the time. Life is an eternal *now* because the force of life is creating everything right now, and it is transforming everything right now.

How are you going to change your story? Well, now you know that you are creating your story according to what you believe about yourself. The way to transform what you believe about yourself is to unlearn what you have already learned. When you unlearn, your faith returns to you, your personal power increases, and you can invest your faith in new beliefs.

If you want to know the truth, if you are ready to take your faith out of the lies, then remember: *Don't believe yourself,* and *don't believe anybody else.* This will give you clarity about many things. But you may need a little support to stop believing the lies, and to start breaking all of the agreements that go against yourself. The Four Agreements offer this support. They are just for you, the main character of your story. These four simple agreements can take you all the way to your integrity: *Be impeccable with*

*your word. Don't take anything personally. Don't make
assumptions. Always do your best.*

Many tools can help you change your story, but
the Four Agreements are my favorite tools for transformation. Why? Because they have the power to help
you unlearn the many ways you have learned to use
the word against yourself. Just by following these
agreements, you challenge all of the opinions that are
nothing but superstition and lies. *Be impeccable with
your word* because you use the word to create your
story. *Don't take anything personally* because you live
in your own story and other people live in their own
story. *Don't make assumptions* because most assumptions are not the truth; they are fiction, and when the
storyteller makes up stories — especially about other
storytellers — this creates big drama. *Always do your
best* because this keeps the voice of knowledge from
judging you, and by taking action, you keep the voice
from talking to you.

The storyteller, the liar in your head, makes you
use your word against yourself. It makes you take

everything personally, it makes a lot of assumptions, and it makes you fail to do your best. The first agreement, *be impeccable with your word*, is the supreme agreement because it helps you to recognize all of the lies that rule your life. To be impeccable is to use the power of your word in the direction of truth and love. The other three agreements are more support for the first agreement — they are the practice that makes the master — but the goal is the first agreement. By practicing all Four Agreements, the moment comes when you experience the truth and your emotional reaction is incredible.

I have written a book about the Four Agreements, and I tried to keep it as simple as possible. The book can make you feel as if you already know the Four Agreements. And this is true because the agreements come from the real you, and the real you is exactly the real me, too. Your spirit is telling you the same thing, and it's pure common sense. The book is a messenger of love. It is like an open doorway that will take you all the way to the real you, but you are the one who needs to walk the way. You need to have the courage to apply the tools to find yourself, and to recreate your own story in your own way. You can transform your entire story just by practicing the Four Agreements. Let's take a closer look at each agreement.

The first agreement, *be impeccable with your word*, means you never use the power of the word against yourself in the creation of your story. *Impeccable* means "without sin." Anything you do that goes against yourself is a sin. When you believe in lies, you are using the power of the word against yourself. When you believe that nobody likes you, that nobody understands you, that you will never make it, you are using the word against yourself.

Many philosophies around the world have known that lies are a distortion of the word, and some traditions call this distortion *evil*. I prefer to say that we are *using the word against ourselves* because we do not call it *evil* when we judge ourselves and find ourselves guilty. We do not call it *evil* when we reject ourselves and treat ourselves much worse than the way we treat our pets. When you are impeccable, you never speak against yourself, you have no beliefs that go against yourself, and you never help anybody else to go against you. To be impeccable means that you don't use your own knowledge against yourself, and you don't allow the voice in your head to abuse you. Maybe the first agreement, *be impeccable with your word*, makes a little more sense now.

Remember, the word is your power because you use the word for the creation of your virtual world. You use the word to create the main character of your story. Every self-opinion, every belief, is made by words: "I am smart, I am stupid, I am beautiful, I am ugly." This is powerful. But your word is even more powerful because it also represents you when you interact with other dreamers. Every time you speak, your thought becomes sound, your thought becomes the word, and now it can go into other people's minds. If their minds are fertile for that kind of seed, they eat it, and now that thought lives inside of them, too.

The word is a force that you cannot see, but you can see the manifestation of the force, the expression of the word, which is your own life. The way to measure how you use the word is by your emotional reaction. How do you know when you are using the word impeccably? Well, you are happy. You feel good about yourself. You feel love. How do you know when you are using the word against yourself? Well, when you are suffering with envy, with anger, with sadness. Suffering of all kinds is the result of misusing the word; it is the result of believing in knowledge contaminated with lies. If you clean up the word, you recover the impeccability of the word, and you never betray yourself. If you agree to be impeccable with your word, this is enough for you to return to the paradise that humans lost. It is enough to bring you back to the truth and to transform your whole story. Be impeccable with your word. Very simple.

The second agreement, *don't take anything personally*, helps you to break the many lies you agreed to believe in. When you take things personally, you react and feel hurt, and this creates emotional poison. Then you want revenge, you want to get even, and you use the word against other people. Now you know that whatever somebody projects onto you is just like Picasso saying, "This is you." You know that it's just the person's storyteller, simply telling you a story. Not taking anything personally gives you immunity to emotional poison in all your relationships. You no longer lose control and react because you are emotionally hurt. This gives you clarity, which puts you a step ahead of other people who cannot see their own stories.

The second agreement guides you in breaking hundreds of little lies until it hits the core of all of the lies in your life. When this happens, the whole edifice of knowledge collapses, and you have a second chance to create another story, in your own way. The Toltec call this *losing the human form.*

When you lose the human form, you have the opportunity to choose what to believe according to your integrity. When you were a child, you used your attention to create the first dream of your life. You never had the opportunity to make a choice about what to believe; everything you agreed to believe was imposed upon you. Now you have an opportunity you didn't have when you were a child. You can use your attention for the second time to base your story on the truth instead of on lies. The Toltec call this *the dream of the second attention.* I call it *your second story* because it's still a dream, it's still a story! But now it's your choice.

When you lose the human form, your will is free again. You recover the power of your faith, and what you can do with that faith has no limits. You can recreate your life in a big way if this is what you want. But the goal is not to save the world. No, the only mission that you have in life is to make yourself happy. That's it. It's that simple. And the only way that you can make yourself happy is to create a story that will make you happy. Anything can happen to any of us. You cannot control what is happening around you, but you can control the way you tell the story. You can relate the story as a big melodrama and be sad and depressed about everything that happens to you, or you can relate the story without all of the drama.

The third agreement, *don't make assumptions*, is a big ticket to personal freedom. What is going on when we make assumptions? The storyteller is making up a story, we believe the story, and we fail to ask questions that might shed some light on the truth. Most of our dream is based on assumptions, and these assumptions create a whole world of illusion that is not true at all, but we believe it. Making assumptions and then taking them personally is the beginning of hell in this world. Humans create so many problems because we make assumptions and believe they are the truth! Almost all of our conflicts are based on this.

To be aware is to see what is truth, to see everything the way it is, not the way we want it to be to justify what we already believe. The *mastery of awareness* is the first mastery of the Toltec, and we can also call it the *mastery of truth*. First, you need to be aware that the voice in your head is always telling you a story. You are dreaming all the time. It is true that you perceive, but the way the storyteller justifies, explains, and makes assumptions about what you perceive is not the truth; it's just a story.

Next, you need to have the awareness that the voice of the storyteller in your head is not necessarily your voice. Every concept in your head has a voice that wants to express itself. It is dreaming. It is just a story trying to catch your attention and justify its own existence. The other part of you, the part who is listening, the one who is dreaming the dream, is the one who is being abused.

Finally, you need to practice awareness until you master awareness. When you master awareness as a habit, you always see life the way it is, not the way you want to see it. You no longer try to put things into words, to explain anything to yourself, and this keeps you from making assumptions. You only use the word to communicate with others, knowing that what you are communicating is just a point of view based on what you believe. And what you believe is just a program; it is nothing but ideas that are mostly lies. That is why you need to listen and ask questions. With clear communication, people will give you all of the information you need, and you won't have to make assumptions.

The fourth agreement is *always do your best*. When you do your best, you don't give the voice of knowledge an opportunity to judge you. If the voice doesn't judge you, there's no need to feel guilty or to punish yourself. Doing your best, you are going to be productive, which means you are going to take action. Doing your best is about taking action and doing what you love to do because it's the action that makes you happy. You are doing it because you want to, not because you have to.

The best moments of your life are when you are authentic, when you are being yourself. When you are in your creation and you are doing what you love to do, you become what you really are again. You are not thinking in that moment; you are expressing. When you are doing your best in your creation, the mind stops. You are alive again. Your emotions are coming out and you don't even notice how great you feel. The action, just the action, makes you feel great. When you have inaction, your mind has to have action, and that is an open invitation for the voice of knowledge to talk to you. But when you are absorbed in what you are doing, the mind hardly speaks.

When you are creating, the voice of knowledge is not there, even if you are using words in your art. If you are writing a poem, you are not thinking about the words you will use to write the poem; you are simply expressing your emotions. The words are the instrument; they are the code that you use for expression. If you are a musician who is playing music, there is no difference between you and the music. At the same time you are creating the music, you are the one who is enjoying every note, every sound. You become one with what you are doing, and it's a supreme pleasure. Anyone who is a musician will know what I am talking about. You are expressing what you really are, and this is the greatest thing that can happen to anybody. Just expressing yourself leads you into ecstasy because you are creating. This is life as an art.

Doing your best is about trusting in yourself and trusting in creation, the force of life. You set a goal and go for it 100 percent without any attachment to attaining it. You don't know if you are going to reach your goal, and you don't care if you do. You go for it, and when you reach the goal it's wonderful. And if you don't reach the goal, that's wonderful, too. Either way, you are complete because love in motion is a wonderful thing. Taking action is an expression of yourself, it's the expression of the spirit, and it's your creation.

I encourage you to take responsibility for every decision you make in life. No decision is right or wrong; what matters is the action that follows your choice. Everything in life is just a choice. You control the dream by making choices. Every choice has a consequence, and a dream master is aware of the consequences. We can also say that for every action, we experience a reaction. If your knowledge is the action, and your emotions are the reaction, then you can see why becoming aware of the voice of knowledge is so important.

The voice of knowledge is always sabotaging your happiness. In the happiest moments of your life, you are playing; you are acting like a child. But the voice comes into your head and says, "This is too good to be true. Let's put our feet back on the ground and get back to reality." And the reality that the voice of knowledge is talking about is suffering.

Life can be so wonderful. If you love yourself, if you practice doing your best, very soon it becomes a habit. When doing your best becomes a habit, everything is a set up for you to always be happy, just as you were when you were a very young child. But first you need to stop the internal dialogue. This is one of the biggest miracles that any human can experience. If you can stop the voice from talking to you, then you are almost free from being abused by all of the lies.

People have asked me if I encourage the use of a mantra to eliminate the internal dialogue. Well, I encourage you to use any trick that you can find to stop the chatter. There is no kitchen recipe. You can explore any number of ways until you find your own way. For some people, a mantra might be the miracle. For other people, meditation, contemplation, or music could be the miracle. For others, walking outdoors or just surrounding themselves with natural beauty could be the miracle. It could be dancing, yoga, running, swimming, or any exercise. It's up to you.

When I was a teenager, my grandfather told me, "Music is the solution to stopping the voice in your head. Replace the voice with music, because you cannot explain music. How can you explain the Fifth Symphony of Beethoven? You can use your opinions, but you can't explain it. You need to play it."

I understood what my grandfather said, but I didn't like his music. My grandfather liked classical music, so I refused that method completely. I told him, "I don't think so. It's boring." Of course, I was listening to music anyway, but the music I liked was the Beatles. Well, the lyrics were in English, and I only spoke Spanish at the time. I knew every word to the songs, but the words had no meaning for me. If there was any drama in those songs, I didn't perceive it as drama; I perceived it as beauty.

Listening to the Beatles really worked for me because the voices were just like another instrument, and the music occupied the space of the voice of knowledge. There were times when the voice was there, but there were times when there was no voice. I liked the music so much that if I was not putting my attention on anything else, there was only music in my head. I started doing this without awareness because although I had heard what my grandfather said, I had made the assumption that he was talking about classical music! Well, the music can be drums, trumpets, or any kind of instrument as long as there are no words in a language that you know to hook your attention. The problem is when the music has words that have meaning to you, and you can think about the words.

There are many ways to quiet the mind if you just use them, but from my point of view, practicing the Four Agreements is the best way. These agreements have the power to break thousands of little agreements that go against yourself, but they are not as simple as they look. Many people say, "I understand the Four Agreements, and they are changing my life, but at a certain point I cannot keep going." Well, you cannot keep going because in that moment you are facing a strong belief. And the faith you invested in that belief is stronger than the faith you have available to change that belief. That is why it's important to practice recovering your faith with little beliefs. Then you can go for the stronger beliefs.

Every time you practice the Four Agreements, their meaning goes a little deeper. When you read the book *The Four Agreements* for the second time, or the third time, at a certain point it seems as if you are reading a different book. And it seems like a different book because you have already broken many little agreements. Now you can go a little deeper, and you go deeper and deeper until the moment comes when you open your spiritual eyes. When you finally transform, your life becomes a masterpiece of dreaming, an expression of your emotional body, just the way it was before knowledge.

❧

POINTS TO PONDER

• The way to transform what you believe about yourself is to unlearn what you have already learned. When you unlearn, your faith returns to you, your personal power increases, and you can invest your faith in new beliefs.

• The Four Agreements have the power to help you unlearn the many ways you have learned to use the word against yourself. By following these agreements, you challenge all of the opinions that are nothing but superstition and lies: *Be impeccable with your word. Don't take anything personally. Don't make assumptions. Always do your best.*

• When the edifice of knowledge collapses, you have a second chance to create a story according to your integrity. You can use your attention for the second time to make a story based on the truth instead of on lies. In *the dream of the second attention*, you recover the power of your faith, your will is free again, and what you can do with that has no limits.

• When you are absorbed in what you are doing, the mind hardly speaks. You are expressing what you really are, and just the action makes it great. When there is inaction, your mind has to have action, and that is an open invitation for the voice of knowledge to talk to you.

• The best moments of your life are when you are authentic, when you are being yourself. When you are in your creation and you are doing what you love to do, you become what you really are again. You are not thinking in that moment; you are expressing. Your emotions are coming out and you feel great.

• Every time you practice the Four Agreements, their meaning goes deeper and deeper until the moment comes when you open your spiritual eyes. Then your life becomes an expression of your emotional body, just the way it was before knowledge.

10

Writing Our Story with Love

Life as an ongoing romance

WHAT IS THE BEST WAY TO WRITE YOUR LIFE story? There is only one way, and that way is with love. Love is the material I use to write my story because love comes directly from my integrity, from what I really am. I love the main character of my story, and the main character loves and enjoys every secondary character. I am not afraid to tell you, "I love you."

Your mind may say, "How can you love me when you don't even know me?" I don't need to know you. I don't need to justify my love. I love you because this is my pleasure. Love coming out of me makes me happy, and it's not important if you reject me because I don't reject myself. In my story, I live in an ongoing romance, and everything is beautiful for me.

To live in love is to be alive again. It is to return to your integrity, to what you were before knowledge. When you recover your integrity, you always follow love. You live your life as an eternal romance because when you love yourself, it is easy to love everybody else. You feel so good just being by yourself, and when you gather with other people, it's because you want to share your happiness. You love so much that you don't need anybody's love to make you happy. But this doesn't mean that you don't accept love. Of course you accept love. You accept good food, good wine, good music, why not good love?

If you can see yourself as an artist, and you can

see that your life is your own creation, then why not create the most beautiful story for yourself? It's your story, and it's just a choice. You can write a story based on love and romance, but that love has to begin with yourself. I suggest that you start a brand-new relationship between you and yourself. You can have the most wonderful, romantic love relationship, and the way to have it is by changing your agreements.

One agreement you can make is to treat yourself with respect. Introduce the agreement of self-respect, and tell the voice in your head, "It's time for us to respect each other." Many of the judgments will end there, and most of the self-rejection will end there, too. Then you can allow the voice to talk, but the dialogue will be much better. You will have all of these great ideas, these great dialogues in your head, and when you express them to other people, they will love what you are saying. You will find yourself smiling and having fun, even when you are just by yourself.

You can see why the relationship with yourself is so important. When you have conflict with yourself, when you don't like yourself, or even worse, when you hate yourself, the internal dialogue is contaminated with poison, and that is the way you talk to yourself. When you love yourself, even if the voice of knowledge is in your head, it is nice to you. When you love yourself, when you are kind to yourself, that is a good relationship with yourself. Then every relationship you have will improve, but it always begins with yourself.

How can we expect to be kind when we speak with other people if we are not kind to ourselves? We have the need to express what we feel, and we express our emotions through our voice. If we don't feel good, if we are full of emotional poison, we need to release it. That is why we have the need to curse, to release all of the emotions that are trapped in our head. If we have anger or jealousy that needs to come out, our words will carry those emotions. If the voice of knowledge is abusing us, then that voice will treat others the same way. If we are having fun with ourselves, that is what we project to the outside.

The first step toward improving your relationship with yourself is to accept yourself just the way you are. You don't need to learn *how* to love yourself. You need to unlearn all of the reasons why you reject yourself, and by nature you love yourself. You love not the *image* you project or the *way* you are, but you love yourself because of *what* you are. Then you start to enjoy yourself until you love yourself so much that you give yourself everything you need. You don't leave yourself until last anymore. The more you enjoy the presence of yourself, the more you enjoy your life, and the more you enjoy the presence of everyone around you.

When you love, you honor and respect *life*. When you live your life with love, honor, and respect, the story you create is an ongoing romance. To love life is to enjoy every manifestation of life, and it is effortless. It is as easy as inhaling and exhaling. To breathe is the greatest need of the human body, and air is the greatest gift. You can be so grateful for the air that just to breathe is enough to love. How can you show your gratitude for the gift of air? By enjoying every breath. When you focus on that enjoyment, you can make it a habit to enjoy the air, and you can enjoy it at least seventeen or eighteen times per minute. Just to breathe is enough to always be happy, to always be in love.

But this is just one direction that love can take. Every activity of our life can become a ritual of love. We have the need for food, and we can do the same thing with food that we do with air. Food is also love, and when we enjoy our food, when we really taste it and feel the texture, it is one of the most sensual experiences we can have. There is so much love in the action of eating, and if we use a new mantra every time we eat, we increase the pleasure. The mantra is just one sound: "Mmmm." If we practice loving our food every time we eat, soon it becomes a habit. It becomes a ritual that we use to give our thanks, to express our love, and to receive love without resistance.

Communication can be another way to express

our love. Every time we share our story or listen to another person's story, we can practice sharing our love. One of the assignments I used to give my apprentices was to find at least a thousand different ways of saying "I love you" in one week. When you practice all of these different ways of saying "I love you," your heart opens completely to hear the whole of creation telling you, "I love you." And you don't need to justify or explain that love. You just receive love and give love without even trying to understand or make a story about it.

When you have the courage to open your heart completely to love, a miracle happens. You start perceiving the reflection of your love in everything. Then eating, walking, talking, singing, dancing, showering, working, playing — everything you do becomes a ritual of love. When everything becomes a ritual of love, you are no longer thinking; you are feeling and enjoying life. You find pleasure in every activity you do because you love to do it. Just to be alive is wonderful, and you feel intensely happy.

People have asked me, "Miguel, are you happy all the time? Don't you ever get cranky?" Well, to be cranky is completely normal. Sometimes I'm cranky when I don't get enough sleep. If I only sleep two hours in the night, I don't feel good when I awaken; I feel *rrrraar!* But that *rrraar* is not directed toward anybody. Why should I be unkind to anybody just because I'm feeling bad and my body is telling me I want to sleep more? If in that moment I cannot satisfy my body, I finish doing whatever I have to do, and then I take my body to a bed and put my body to sleep.

I have the right to feel cranky, but that doesn't mean I'm going to hurt my beloved or my children or my friends or the people who work for me. If we are selfish and we feel cranky, then we believe that nobody has the right to be happy around us. Then we say, "Why are you laughing when I feel so bad?" This is nothing but selfishness, and we are selfish with others because we are selfish with ourselves. Whatever we feel for ourselves, we project onto others. The way we treat ourselves is the way we treat others.

Writing your story with love is so easy to do. Why make it complicated and difficult when love is your true nature? By not being what you are, you resist love, and you are afraid to love because you believe one of the biggest lies, and that lie is "love hurts." As I said before, love doesn't hurt. Love gives us pleasure. But you can even use love to hurt yourself. Someone may really love you, but you don't appreciate that love because you are hearing your own lies. You can say, "What does that person want from me? He wants to take advantage of me." Who knows what the storyteller will tell you?

If you don't perceive love, if you cannot recognize love, it's because you only recognize the poison inside you. I am responsible for what I say, but I am not responsible for what you understand. I can give you my love, but you can make the interpretation that you are receiving judgments, or who knows? Only your storyteller knows. When we no longer believe our own stories, we find it so easy to enjoy one another.

Humans are made for love. Before knowledge, it was easy to open our heart and to love, and we just walked away from whatever was not love. But with the voice of knowledge in our head, we walk away from love, and we go for what is not love. We always have a choice, and if we love ourselves, we choose love. We do not allow ourselves to be hurt by accepting other people's opinions or abuse. If other people abuse us, they are abusing us because we stay there, because we allow that to happen. And if we stay, it's because we believe that we deserve the abuse, and we are using them for self-punishment. If we don't have awareness, we blame, when the solution is not to blame. The solution is to step aside and not be there.

How can you believe someone who says, "I love you," and then treats you with disrespect and emotional violence? How can someone say, "I love you," when that person wants to control your life, to tell you what you have to do, what you have to believe? How can someone claim to love you, and then give you emotional garbage, jealousy, and envy?

How can we tell someone, "I love you," and then send all our opinions against the person we love and try to make that person suffer? I have to tell you what is wrong with you because "I love you." I have to judge you, find you guilty, and punish you because "I love you." I have to make you wrong all the time, and make you feel like you are good for nothing because "I love you." And because you love me, you have to put up with my anger, with my jealousy, with all my stupidity.

Do you think this is love? This is not love. This is nothing but selfishness, and we call it love. And we say "love hurts," but we are hurting ourselves with our own lies. All of the struggle in romantic relationships is just nonsense. It is not love, and that is why people are starving for love.

When you are needy, this is what you share in a relationship. But when you are open to love, you receive love, and if it's not love, you don't have to be there. You are open to receiving love, but you are not open to receiving abuse. You are not open to being blamed; you are not open to receiving anybody's poison because your mind is no longer fertile ground for that. When you love and respect yourself, there is no way that you ever allow anybody to disrespect you or dishonor you.

Many people come to me and say, "Gosh, I want someone who loves me. I want the right man or the right woman to come into my life." Who is the right man or the right woman? It's not about them; it's about you. If that person comes into your life, and you treat that person the way you treat yourself, which means with selfishness, then you are going to use that person to hurt yourself.

How can we want a romantic relationship when we don't even like ourselves? How can we pretend to love somebody else when we don't love ourselves? When you feel unworthy, when you don't respect yourself, you don't respect your partner either. If you don't honor yourself, how can you honor your partner? How can you give anything that you don't have for yourself?

The most beautiful and romantic relationship has to begin with you. You are responsible for one half of the relationship: your half. When you respect yourself, you respect your beloved. When you honor yourself, you honor your beloved. And you give love and accept love. But when you are full of poison, this is what you give. When you abuse yourself, you want to abuse your beloved. It's just nonsense.

When you hear people's stories, including your own, you hear nothing but lies. But behind the story, everything is love, which means everything and everybody is divine. You are divine, you are perfect, but as an artist, you create your own story and you have the illusion that the story is real. You live your life by justifying that story. And by justifying the story, you are wasting your life.

As I've said before, life is very short. You don't know if your children, or your friends, or your beloved will still be here tomorrow. Just imagine that your opinion is so important that you have a big fight with your partner or your child. You lose control because of all of the lies you believe, and you really hurt your loved one. The next day you discover that your loved one is dead. How will you feel about telling your loved one all of those things you didn't really mean?

Our life is so short that every time I see my children, I enjoy them as much as I can. Whenever I can, I enjoy my beloved, my family, my friends, my apprentices. But mainly I enjoy myself, because I am with myself all the time. Why should I spend my precious time with myself judging myself, rejecting myself, creating guilt and shame? Why should I push myself to be angry or jealous? If I don't feel good emotionally, I find out what is causing it and I fix it. Then I can recover my happiness and keep going with my story.

When you write your story with love, you love the main character unconditionally. That is the biggest difference between the old story based on lies and the new story based on love. When you love yourself unconditionally, you justify and explain everything you perceive through the eyes of love. When that new main character hooks your attention, your attention is focused on love. Now it is easy to love all the secondary characters of the story unconditionally because that is the nature of the new main character. This is wisdom; it is simple common sense, and it's the goal of all the different traditions and religions around the world.

Love is so simple, so easy and wonderful, but love begins with you. Every relationship improves when you love yourself and live with awareness of your love. Few people know how to love with awareness, but everybody knows how to love without awareness. When you love without awareness, you don't even notice that it's love you're feeling. You see a little child smiling at you, and you feel something for that child. This is love, but of course the voice of knowledge tells you, "This is not love."

You love so many times, and you don't even notice that you love.

Love and respect are what we should also teach our children, but the only way to teach them love and respect is to love and respect ourselves. There is no other way. Again, we can only give what we have, not what we don't have. I can only share what I know. I cannot tell you anything that I don't know. My parents taught me what they learned from their parents. How could they teach me something different? They could not do better than that. I cannot blame my parents for the programming I received. I cannot blame my teachers for the training I received in school. They did their best; it was the only thing they knew, and they passed it on to the next generation.

The only chance to break the chain of lies is to change the adults, to change ourselves. Children are very aware. They learn from what we do; they learn what they see, not just what we say. We tell them, "Never lie to anybody." Later, somebody is knocking on the door, and we say, "Tell them I'm not here."

Whatever we do at home, the way we behave, the way we treat one another, is what our children learn. If we are never at home, that becomes normal behavior for them. When they grow up, they are not at home either, and their children are alone. The way we speak is the way they speak. If we curse at home, they curse, too. If they receive violence, they deliver violence. If we fight and share our anger and our poison, our children learn that this is the normal way of being, and this is how they learn to write their own stories. But if there is respect and honor at home, if there is love at home, this is what they learn.

By changing ourselves, by loving ourselves, the message we deliver to our children carries the seeds of love and truth. These seeds go into our children, and these seeds can change their lives. Imagine how our children will grow up when we share with them the seeds of love instead of the seeds of fear, judgment, shame, or blame. Imagine how they will grow up when we finally respect them as humans just like us, and we don't try to break their integrity because we are bigger and stronger. Imagine when we teach our children to be secure in themselves, and to have their own voice. Imagine how everything will change if we bring respect to any relationship.

People have asked me why I don't work with children, and the reason is because they have parents. It doesn't matter what I tell children; it is undone by their parents. I prefer to teach parents and teachers because our children learn from them. Our future as a human race depends on children. Children will take our place one day, and we are training them to be like us. Just imagine if your parents had told you a different story when you were a child. Your life story would be completely different. But you can still change your story, and if you have children, the only way to change their story is to change your own.

To love is so easy; it's not work at all. But we have so much work to do, and that work is to unlearn all of the lies that we believe. Unlearning lies is not easy because we feel safe with our lies; we are very attached to them. But the more we practice seeing the truth, the easier it becomes to detach from our lies. Transforming our life gets easier with practice, and our life gets better and better.

The more love we have, the more love we can share and receive. To give to one another and receive from one another is the purpose of a relationship. We don't need a lot of words. When we share time with someone, what is important is to communicate with feelings, not with words. But if we want to share words, we don't need anything complicated. It's just three words: "I love you." That's it. What makes you happy is not the love that other people feel for you, but the love you feel for other people.

Once we experience love, we can't find the words to explain what we really feel, but to love is the greatest experience that any of us can have. To experience love is to experience God; it is to experience heaven right here and now. When the voice of knowledge is no longer hooking our attention, our perception becomes much wider. We start perceiving our own emotional reactions, and we start perceiving other people's emotional reactions. Then we start perceiving the emotions that come from the trees, from the flowers, from the clouds, from everything. We see love coming from everywhere, even from other people. At a certain point, we are simply in ecstasy, and there are no words to explain it because there are no agreements yet about how to explain it.

What we call *love* is something that is so generic that it's not even what love really is. Love is much more than words can describe. As I said before, we cannot really talk about the truth; we need to experience the truth. The same is true of love. The only way to really know love is to experience love, to have the courage to jump into the ocean of love, and perceive it in its totality. That is the only way, but we are programmed with so much fear that we don't see the love coming from all around us. We look for love in other people when they don't love themselves. Of course we won't find love there; we only find selfishness and a war of control.

You don't have to search for love. Love is here because God is here; the force of *life* is everywhere. We humans create the story of separation, and we search for what we believe we don't have. We search for perfection, for love, for truth, for justice, and we search and search when everything is inside of us. Everything is here; we just need to open our spiritual eyes to see it.

There is nothing you need to do to improve what you really are. The only thing left for all of us to do is to create a beautiful story and enjoy a better life. How do you create a beautiful story? By being authentic. When the main character is authentic, it is easy to write your story with integrity, with common sense, with love.

Life is the greatest gift that we receive, and the art of living is the greatest art. How do you master the art of living? Practice makes the master. It's not about learning; it's about taking action and practicing your art. As an artist, if you practice love, and you keep practicing and practicing, the moment comes when everything you do is an expression of your love. How will you know when you have mastered love? When the story you tell yourself is an ongoing romance.

✖

POINTS TO PONDER

• The best way to write your story is with love. Love is the material that comes directly from your integrity, from what you really are.

• When you introduce the agreement of self-respect, many self-judgments end there, and most of the self-rejection ends there, too. Then you can allow the voice to talk, but the dialogue is much better. You find yourself smiling and having fun, even when you are just by yourself.

• When you enjoy the presence of yourself, you love yourself not because of the way you are, but because of *what* you are. The more you love yourself, the more you enjoy your life, and the more you enjoy the presence of everyone around you.

• Every activity of your life can become a ritual of love — eating, walking, talking, working, playing. When everything becomes a ritual of love, you are no longer thinking; you are feeling. Just to be alive makes you intensely happy.

• When you love yourself unconditionally, you justify and explain everything you perceive through the eyes of love. Your attention is focused on love, and this makes it easy to feel unconditional love for all of the secondary characters in your story.

• The only way to know love is to experience love, to have the courage to jump into the ocean of love, and perceive it in its totality. Once you experience love, you can't find the words to explain what you feel, but you see love coming from everyone, from everything, from everywhere.

11

OPENING OUR SPIRITUAL EYES

A reality of love all around us

ANOTHER OPPORTUNITY FOR ME TO ENCOUNTER the truth occurred during a car accident that was so dramatic that I almost died. There are no words to explain what I experienced, but the truth made it obvious that what I believed was a lie. Like most people, I used to believe that I am my mind and I am my physical body. I live in my physical body; it is home, and I can touch it. Then, in my near-death experience, I could see my physical body asleep at the wheel of my car. If I was perceiving my physical body from outside my body, then it was obvious that I am not my mind, and I am not my physical body. Then the question became: *What am I?*

In the moment when I came face to face with death, I started to perceive another reality. My attention expanded so much that there was no future or past; there was only the eternal now. Light was everywhere, and everything was full of light. I could feel my perception go through all of these different realities until I recovered the attention and could focus on one universe at a time. I was in the light, and it was a moment of total awareness, of pure perception. At a certain point, I knew that the light has all the information about everything and that everything is alive. I can say that I was with God, that I was in bliss, that I was in a state of ecstasy, but these are just words that I know.

After the accident, my perception of the world

changed again because I knew, not just as a theory, that I am not this physical body. And I began a search that was different from my search before the accident. Before the accident, I was still searching for perfection, for an image to satisfy the main character of my story. After the accident, I knew that what I was searching for was something I had lost: myself.

It took more than a year for me to recover from the impact of seeing my own creation from outside my body. My first reaction after the accident was to try to deny what had happened. I tried to feel safe in my world of lies and tell myself, "This is not true; it is just an illusion." I thought that surely it was just a hallucination caused by the accident. I created all kinds of stories to justify that experience, and I know that many people do the same thing. They try to forget about it, to keep going with their ordinary story. But something deep inside was telling me, "No, this is real." Fortunately for me, I felt the doubt and thought, "What if that experience was real and everything else in my life was the illusion?"

After that experience, I wasn't the same because I couldn't believe my own story anymore. I needed many answers, and I started to read every kind of book to try to find them. Some people described a similar experience, but hardly anybody could explain what happened. I finished medical school, returned to my home, and went directly to my grandfather to tell him about my experience. He just laughed and said, "I knew that life would have to make you see the truth the hard way. And that is what happened to you because you have always been very stubborn."

I told my grandfather that I wanted to experience that reality again to see if it was true — without an accident, of course. My grandfather told me, "Well, the only way you can do it is to let go of everything, just the way you did in the moment when you died. When you die, you lose everything, and if you live your life as if you've already lost everything, you will have the experience again." He gave me many clues, and I tried many times to do what he told me, but I failed. My grandfather died, and I hadn't made it yet.

The next in line was my mother, and her explanation was a little different. She told me, "The only way for you to experience that reality is to master *dreaming*. To do this, you have to completely detach from what you believe you are; you have to let go of the story of your life. It's just like the moment right before your brain goes to sleep — when you are so tired that you cannot keep your eyes open any longer. In that moment, you detach from everything; you don't care about anything in your story because you just want to sleep. When you can do this without falling asleep, you will have the experience again."

I asked my mother to help me, and because she felt compassion for me, she chose twenty-one people to train in dreaming. Every Sunday for three years, we went into dreaming for eight to twelve hours. Not one of the twenty-one people ever missed a Sunday. There were eight or nine medical doctors, lawyers, and a variety of people with a lot of personal importance in the group. But according to my mother, only three of us really made it. Fortunately, I was one of them, and after the first year of dreaming, I finally had the experience again with full awareness. That was it; after that point, the other two years of dreaming were the greatest experience of my life.

Each time I went into the state of ecstasy, I was able to stay there a little longer. Then, a few days later, I would lose it again and be back to the way I had been almost all of my life. Errrh! I was determined to experience that state all the time. There was no way I could live my life any differently. It took me three or four months to have the experience for the third time, but it happened again, and now I was staying longer. It became easier and easier, and every time I stayed longer and longer until that state became my normal reality.

At first it was difficult to function in ordinary reality, especially in a hospital as a medical doctor.

I felt like nothing made sense to me, but in some ways, I was functioning better. It was as though I could see two realities at the same time. I could see what really is, but I could also see the stories. And it was a big shock at a certain point just to see myself lying, and to see everybody around me lying. Though I didn't have any judgment about it, I could see that people were making nonsense of their life. I could see them creating drama and emotional pain. They would get so upset over something that wasn't important. They would make up stories and lie about everything. It was amazing and even kind of funny to watch them do it. But I had to refrain from laughing because I knew they would take it personally. They could not see their own stories because they were blind.

People have the right to live their life in any way they want to live it. But if you have had the experience I've been describing, you understand. Certainly many people have had the same experience, but then fear makes them try to deny what happened. Many times when I've given workshops, I see people go so high into love, and they understand a great deal. But if they see something in their story that they don't like, they just deny the whole experience and run away. And if the truth hits their personal importance, they devalue everything, and run away with a lot of judgments. I see this happen all the time, but it's okay because that is all the truth they can handle.

It took many years for me to win the conflict between the truth and what is not the truth because our lies are so seductive. The temptation to believe in lies is very strong, but the car accident pushed me to another point of reference. And, yes, now I know that there is another reality right here and right now, and it is more than the reality of light and sound that we normally perceive. There are many realities that exist, but we only perceive the reality where we focus our attention.

I can say according to my story that the reality I experienced is a reality of love. The energy of love is just like the light that comes from the sun. The sunlight splits into thousands of different colors, and the light looks different depending on what is reflecting the light. That is why we can see different colors, different shapes, and different forms. Well, for me, the same thing happens in this reality of love. You perceive the reflection of the emotions coming from every object, and as with light, the emotion of love looks different depending on what is reflecting the love. The emotional body creates an entire reality right in front of your eyes, in the same place that the reality of light exists. Of course, it's almost impossible to put it into words, but I think it's worth trying.

I want you to use your imagination to try to understand what I am saying. I want you to imagine that humans have been blind for thousands of years. We have no idea that light exists because we just don't open our eyes. But we develop the rest of our senses, and we create an entire virtual reality through sound. Like bats, we recognize objects through the reflection of sound. We give names to every object

and emotion; we create a language, we create knowledge, and we communicate through sound. That is
our reality — a reality of sound.

Then imagine that for the first time in your life,
you open your eyes and you perceive light. Suddenly
a reality full of objects, shapes, and colors appears in
front of you. You cannot comprehend this reality
because you have never seen light before. For the first
time, you see flowers and clouds and grass and butterflies. You see the rain, the snow, the oceans, the
stars, the moon, the sun. Perhaps you don't even perceive these things as separate objects because you have
no idea what you are perceiving. You cannot name
anything you see; there are no words to describe your
experience. You have to use the universe of sound to
explain the universe of light. You try to compare
colors with sounds, shapes with melodies. You say,
"The color red is like this kind of tone in the musi-
cal scale. The ocean is like this symphony."

Imagine your emotional reaction to seeing so
much color and beauty for the first time. You are

overwhelmed with emotion, and tears flow out of your eyes. Just by perceiving all of this beauty, your heart begins to open wide and love starts pouring out of you. If you try to describe your emotions, you say, "I'm in bliss. I'm in ecstasy. I'm in a state of grace." Then you close your eyes, and again you perceive only the reality of sound. Now even if you want to, you cannot open your eyes again.

How can you explain that experience to yourself when there are no words to explain it? How can you explain a color or a shape or the form of a butterfly? How can you share this experience with other people if they have never seen light? How can you believe that the reality of sound is the only reality that exists?

Now we can understand why Moses came down from the mountain and talked about the Promised Land. What else could he say? Or we can understand what Jesus felt after spending forty days in the desert, when he talked about the Kingdom of Heaven. Or when Buddha awoke from under the bodhi tree and talked about Nirvana. When you open your spiritual eyes, the first thing you say is "I am with God and the angels. I am in heaven, in paradise, where everything is so beautiful. In the city of God, only beauty and goodness exist; there is no place for fear or suffering. It's just beautiful." People see that you have changed. They see your emotional reaction and know that something profound has happened to you.

From my point of view, the reality I experienced is all of that together; it is ecstasy all the time. In my personal mythology, I experienced the reality of truth, the reality of love. It's a reality that belongs to all of us, but we just don't see it. And if we don't see it, it's because we are blinded by all of the lies from thousands of years ago. If you can open what I call *the spiritual eyes*, you will perceive *what is* without the lies, and I can assure you that your emotional reaction will be overwhelming. For you it is no longer a theory that your story is just a dream. Heaven is the truth, but the story you are perceiving right now is not the truth; it's an illusion.

What is real is so beautiful and there are no words to explain it, but it's there. There is a whole reality created by the reflection of emotions, and in that reality you can see that what is real is your love. I know that I used to perceive that reality before I learned to speak. I know that before the voice of knowledge, all of us perceived that reality all of the time. What you are is something incredibly magnificent. And not just humans, but every animal, every flower, every rock, because everything is the same. When you open your spiritual eyes, you see the simplicity of life. I am life, and you are life. There is no empty space in the universe because everything is full of life. But life is a force that you cannot see. You only see the effects of life, the process of life in action.

You see a flower opening or a tree with the leaves changing colors and falling to the ground. You see a child growing. You see a human becoming old. You have the sense of time, but it's nothing but the reaction of life passing through matter. You don't see yourself, but you see the manifestation of life in your physical body. If you can move your hand, you can see the manifestation of being alive. If you hear your voice, you hear the manifestation of being alive. You see your own physical body when you used to have little hands and very fresh skin, then big hands. You see all these changes in your own physical body, but you still feel that you are the same person.

The closest I can come to describing what you are is that you are a force of life that is transforming everything. This force is moving every atom of your physical body. This force is creating every thought. The spirit of life expresses itself through your physical body, and your physical body can say, "I am alive," because that force of transformation lives in every cell of your physical body. That force has the awareness to perceive an entire reality, that force feels everything. Your physical body is perceiving you right now. Your body can feel you, and when your body feels you, it goes into ecstasy. Your mind can also feel you, and when your mind feels you,

you can experience such intense love and compassion that you don't think any longer.

I see my physical body as a mirror where life, through light, can see itself. I see my physical body as the evolution of life. Life is evolving, it is pushing matter, it is creating. The creation of humanity is not over yet. The creation of humanity is happening right now in your physical body. That force is helping you evolve. That force makes you perceive, analyze, dream, and create a story about everything you perceive.

Life is the force that God uses to create everything at every moment. There is no difference between humans, dogs, cats, trees. Everything is moved by the same force of life. From my point of view, I am that force. Thanks to life, I create my art, I create my whole experience, and it's amazing. Because of me, I have emotions. Because of me, I create knowledge and I can talk. Because of me, I create the story. The force that makes me think and tell my story is the same force that makes you read and understand. There is no difference, and it's happening right now.

I see myself growing older, and I know that some day I will leave this physical body. When I leave this physical body, the body will return to the earth, but life cannot be destroyed. Life is eternal. It was so clear to me when I encountered the truth that life is only one force acting in billions of directions in the creation of the universe. That force never dies. We are life, and life is immortal. We are indestructible, and I think this is very good news.

Once you open your spiritual eyes, you see the dream of your life, you see how much time you waste by playing with petty concerns, by playing with all of that nonsense and meaningless drama. You see how you keep yourself from enjoying a reality of love, a reality of joy.

With your attention focused on what you believe, you cannot perceive this other reality. If your attention is hooked by the voice of knowledge, you only see your knowledge. You only see what you want to see, not what is really there. You only hear what you want to hear, not what is really expressing its love to you. You only relate with what you believe, with what you know, with what you think you are, which means you relate with your story. And you think you are the story, but are you really? You are neither the physical body nor the story. The story is your creation, and, believe it or not, your physical body is also your creation because what you really are is that force of life.

All of us are only one living being, and we come from the same place. There is no difference between any of us; we are the same. You can look at your hand and see that there are five fingers. If you focus your eyes on one finger at a time, you might believe they are different, but it's only one hand. It's the same thing with humanity. There is only one living being, and that being is a force that is moving each of us like a finger on a hand. But all of the fingers belong to one hand. Humans share the same spirit; we share the same soul. There is no difference between me and you — not in my eyes. I know that I am you, and I have no doubt at all because I can see that way.

Behind your story is the real you, and it's full of love. The goodness is right there because what you are is goodness. You don't have to try to be good; you just need to stop pretending to be what you are not. You are one with God, and it is effortless. God is here, and you can feel the presence of God. Of course, if you don't feel God's presence, you need to detach from the story because the only thing between you and God is your story.

Once you find yourself, what you *really* are, you cannot explain what you are because there are no words to explain it. If you use knowledge, you never know what you are, but you know that you are because you exist. You are alive, and you don't need to justify your existence. You can be the biggest mystery in your own story.

POINTS TO PONDER

• There is another reality right here and now, and it is more than the reality of light and sound that we normally perceive. In this reality, we can perceive the reflection of emotions coming from every object. In this reality, what is real is our love.

• The reality of truth, the reality of love, is a reality that belongs to us. Before the voice of knowledge, all of us perceived this reality all of the time. If we don't see it now, it's because we are being blinded by all of the lies from thousands of years ago.

• The energy of love is just like the light that comes from the sun. Like sunlight, the emotion of love looks different depending on what is reflecting the love.

• If you open your spiritual eyes, you perceive *what is* without the lies. For you it is no longer a theory that your story is just a dream. Heaven is the truth, but the story you are perceiving right now is not the truth; it's an illusion.

• Life is a force that you cannot see. You only see the effects of life, the process of life in action. You don't see yourself, but you see the manifestation of life in your physical body. You have the sense of time, but it's nothing but the reaction of life passing through you.

• What you are is something incredibly magnificent. You are life, and not just you, but every animal, every flower, every rock is life, because everything is full of life. All of us are only one living being, and we come from the same place.

12

THE TREE OF LIFE

The story comes full circle

I BELIEVE THAT EVERY HUMAN IS AN ANGEL WITH a message to deliver. I am an angel. Right now I am delivering a message to you. You are also an angel — perhaps you don't know it, but you're still an angel. Humans are always sharing opinions and delivering messages. Is this not true? We can hardly wait for our children to grow up so we can teach them what we know. We want to put all of those seeds in their little heads: what is right, what is wrong; what is good, what is bad. And what is the message that we deliver to our own kids? Do what I say, but not what I do? Tell me the truth when I lie all the time?

There are two kinds of angels: angels who share truth and angels who share lies. The question is: What kind of angels are we? What kind of message do we deliver? When humans lived in Paradise before knowledge, we were angels who shared truth. When we ate the fruit of the Tree of Knowledge and the fallen angel reproduced itself in our mind, we humans also became fallen angels. We are fallen angels because we deliver lies, even if we don't know that we are lying.

The voice of the fallen angel is so loud that we cannot hear the other voice that is silent, what I call *the voice of the spirit*, our *integrity, the voice of love*. This silent voice is always there. Before we learned to speak, when we were one and two years old, we listened to this voice.

THE TREE OF LIFE

When I was a child, I used to watch Walt Disney's Donald Duck cartoons. On one side of Donald Duck's head was an angel, and on the other side of his head was a devil, and both were talking to him. Well, this is real. The storyteller is that little devil. You have a voice that is telling you why you are not good enough, why you don't deserve love, why you cannot trust, why you will never be great or beautiful or perfect. That voice is lying, and the only power that it has is the power that you give it.

The voice of knowledge is loud; it's not silent. The voice of your spirit is silent because it doesn't need to talk to you. Your body doesn't need to know how to be perfect from your point of view because it *is* perfect. When you are born, you don't know what you are, not with words. But your body knows what it is, and it doesn't need to explain it with words, just as your liver doesn't need to go to medical school to function with the rest of your body. It just knows what to do.

There are other things that you just know. If you are a woman, you don't need to learn how to be a woman; you don't need to learn how to develop a fetus or how to deliver a baby. Just by nature, you are what you are; you don't need to learn to be what you are. This is silent knowledge. You just know. You can feel silent knowledge when you close your eyes. You can feel silent knowledge every time you breathe.

You are an angel, and your life is your message. But what kind of angel do you want to be? You cannot serve two masters. You cannot share lies and share truth at the same time. Doesn't that make sense?

Knowledge used to be the greatest tyrant in my life. I used to be a slave of knowledge, but knowledge no longer has power over me. And it doesn't have power over me because I no longer believe knowledge. I no longer accept that voice in my head telling me why nobody likes me, why I'm not worth it, why I'm not perfect. Now knowledge is just a tool of communication in my pocket. What I know is wonderful because, thanks to knowledge, I can talk to you and you can understand me. That is what I am doing right now — communicating through knowledge. Everything I'm telling you is the expression of my art. In the same way that Picasso uses color to make a portrait, I use knowledge to make a portrait of what I see and feel.

Three or four thousand years ago, humans discovered that knowledge is contaminated by lies. If we clean all of the lies from our knowledge, we will go back to the paradise that we lost. We will return to truth, return to love, and reunite with God. Now we can see that the story of Adam and Eve is not just a fable, but a symbol that was created by a master who discovered the same thing that the Toltec discovered. The creator of this story obviously knew the truth, and the symbolism is so beautiful.

Yes, the fallen angel who lived in the original Tree of Knowledge was reproduced in every human and it's controlling people's lives even now. We are possessed, but there's no reason to be afraid. The big demon is merely a lie, and its lies haven't destroyed us yet. They have done their best, but they have failed because we are more powerful than that fallen angel. We are only one living being, and we have been living in this world for thousands of years.

Adam and Eve didn't die. They are here because we are here. You are Adam, and you are Eve. And we are trying so hard to go back to the place we came from — Paradise, that place of love and truth. You know that it's there because you have it in your memory. You were there when you were born, and during the first and second years of your life, you were physically there.

Prophecies from many different philosophies of the world tell us that we are going back to that place of love. Some call it the Kingdom of Heaven; others call it Nirvana or the Promised Land. The Toltec call it the Dream of the Second Attention. Every philosophy has a different name, but the meaning is the same: It is a place of joy and love. It is a place of unity, the unity of all our hearts. It is the reunion with life because we are the manifestation of the one living being that exists.

The Toltec believe that one day common sense will rule the dream of humanity. When that happens, we will discover that everything, and everybody, is perfect. It will take time to fulfill the dreams of these prophets who knew what would happen. When they talked about a society of love and happiness, it's because they lived their lives in that way, and they knew that we are all the same. If one person can reach a place like that, everybody can do it. There are also prophets who talk about destruction and fear, but I believe that we, the humans, are evolving in the right direction. The only problem is that there are billions of us, and in order for the entire society to change, there has to be a great effort. But it's not impossible.

Everything can change, and everything will change. It just takes time. In the last century, we have witnessed rapid changes in science and technology. Psychology has stayed a little behind, but it will catch up. The world in our present-day society is completely different from the society we lived in forty or fifty years ago. There are fewer lies today than there were eight hundred years ago. Just by seeing our evolution, I have faith that we will recover paradise.

Just imagine waking up and finding yourself in Europe during the Middle Ages. You see people suffering because their lives are ruled by superstition; they live in constant fear because of the lies they believe. Do you think you could live your life the way you are living it now? I don't think so. Imagine that you are a woman wanting to tell everybody about the beliefs that rule your life right now. You can see that you don't fit in their dream. For you, their dream is a real nightmare. You want to tell the women that they don't need to suffer anymore, that they don't need to be abused. You want to tell them that they are humans, too, that they have a soul, that they have the right to be happy, that they have the right to express themselves in life.

How do you think everybody will judge you if you take these ideas to them? Surely they will say that you are evil, that you are possessed, that the devil is speaking through your mouth. How long do you think you would survive? Yes, not long, because they would burn you alive. If you think that our present society is hell, that society really was hell. For us, it is obvious that the social, moral, and religious rules of that time were based on lies, but for them it was not that obvious.

Perhaps the lies you believe about yourself are not so obvious to you, but you can see the result of what you believe. And what is the result? Well, how you live your life. When you believe the truth, the result is happiness, love, goodness. You feel good about yourself and you feel good about everything. If you are not happy, it's because you believe in lies. That is the origin of all human conflict. All of our suffering comes from believing in lies.

How can we stop all the human injustice, all the war, all the destruction of our Mother Earth? Well, by not believing in lies. It sounds very simple, but you can just imagine how complicated it is to rearrange the belief system of an entire country or all of humanity. Humans don't want their lies to be challenged because they are not in control of their mind. Who is controlling the human mind? Lies have total control of humanity. This is what you learn in any mystery school when you reach a certain level of preparation. It is something so simple, yet it is one of the highest revelations in any mystery school.

The real enemy is lies, and this used to be top secret in most traditions because people believed that whoever knew this would have power over other people, and they might misuse the power. That was the excuse, but I think that those who understood the truth were probably afraid to share it. Why? Because the people who believed in lies would be frightened of the truth and burn them alive. In fact, that is what happened in many parts of the world.

Then how will we recover the paradise we lost? The solution is simple: The truth will set us free. That is the whole key to going back to heaven.

When you recover the truth, *your* truth, a miracle happens. You open your spiritual eyes and return to heaven. Heaven is the most beautiful story made with love, and guess who creates heaven? We create our own heaven. Heaven is a story; it is a dream that we, as life, can create. But for life to create heaven, the main character of the story needs to surrender to life, and allow life to manifest without the lies.

Heaven is here, and it's available for everybody. Paradise is here, but we need to have the eyes to perceive it. This is exactly what Jesus and Buddha and Moses and Krishna promised so long ago, and all of the great masters in the world who created heaven in their own mind. They are all telling you that it's up to you. If they can do it, you can do it, and if you can do it, everybody can do it.

The truth will set us free, but lies keep us in this reality. I don't know how long ago humans first understood this, but it's so simple that nobody wants to understand it. They want something more complicated than this because the storyteller works that way. If we don't believe in lies, we are already in the healing process. The Christian Mystery School knew this, the Egyptians knew this, and the Toltec knew this, but it was difficult to put it into words. Then they created legends such as the story of Adam and Eve.

And that reminds me of the other half of the story of Adam and Eve. In Paradise, there is another tree, and it is the Tree of Life, or the Tree of Truth. The legend says that whoever eats the fruit of the Tree of Life, which is truth, will live forever in Paradise because life is the eternal truth. The fruit of the Tree of Life is the message that comes directly from life or from God. Life is the only truth; it is the force that is creating all of the time. When you see that force in yourself, and when you put your faith in that force, you are truly alive.

Now we can understand what Jesus meant when he said, "I am life, and only through me can you reach heaven." He was not talking about the person Jesus; he was talking about being the Tree of Life.

What he was trying to say is: "I am the Tree of Life. Whoever eats my fruit will live with me in the kingdom of heaven. The kingdom of heaven is a kingdom where everybody is a king."

Isn't this the same thing we are saying here? You are the king in your own reality; you are responsible for your own dream of life. Jesus also said, "The kingdom of heaven is just like a wedding where you are the bride, and truth or God is the groom, and you live in an eternal honeymoon." Isn't that beautiful?

The truth cannot be explained with words, so Jesus tried to use a concept that everybody could understand. He compared the reality that we spoke of before to a honeymoon. When you are married to the truth, you live in an eternal honeymoon. In the honeymoon, everything in your life is about love. When you are in love, you see everything with the eyes of love. When you are making love all the time, everything is wonderful and beautiful, and you can grasp heaven.

Now we can understand what Jesus meant when he spoke about forgiveness, about love, about heaven. He said, "Let the children come with me because the ones who are like them can enter the kingdom of heaven." When you are a child before you have knowledge, which means before you eat all of the lies, you live in heaven. When you fall, it is because you are innocent. And when you recover that paradise, you become like a child again, but with a big difference. Now you are no longer innocent; you are wise. This gives you immunity; you cannot fall again.

We can also say that you become wise when you finally eat the fruit of the Tree of Life. To eat the fruit of this tree is symbolic of illumination. Illumination is when you become light, but there are no words to describe this experience. That is why we have to use mythology and our imagination to grasp what it means. To really know what it is, we need to experience it, to be there. The truth is the real you; it's your own integrity. Nobody can guide you to that place. Only you can take yourself there.

You can change your own story, but it begins with you, the main character of your story. You can transform yourself from a messenger of lies, fear, and destruction to a messenger of truth, love, and creation. When you return to the truth, the way you express yourself in society is much better. Your communication improves. Your creation is stronger and more powerful. In all directions, life as you know it changes for the better.

You don't need to change the world; you need to change yourself. And you have to do it in your own way because only you have the possibility of knowing yourself. It's obvious that you cannot change the world, at least not yet, because the world is not prepared for the truth. You can only change yourself, but that is a big step. By returning to the truth, you take a big step for everybody else.

The gates of heaven are open, and heaven is waiting for you. But if you don't enter heaven, it's because you believe that you are not worthy of heaven. You believe that you are not worthy of living in a place of truth, joy, and love. This is a lie, but if you believe it, that lie controls your story, and you cannot pass through the gates of heaven.

The truth is not in the story. The truth is in the power that creates the story. That power is life; it is God. I discovered this long ago, and my hope is that you can understand what I am saying. To really understand, it's not enough for your reasoning mind to say, "Oh yes, it's true, it's logical." No, you need to understand with your heart. I really wish that you would take this into your heart because it can change your whole life. Don't believe me with your head, but feel what I am saying with your heart. Focus your attention on what you feel, and what you will perceive is your own integrity speaking to you. What is truth is truth, and a very powerful part of you can recognize truth. Believe your heart.

Your life will become a masterpiece of art when the storyteller finally tells you only truth. When the voice of knowledge becomes the voice of integrity, you return to the truth, you return to heaven, you return to love, and the cycle is over. When this happens, you no longer believe your own storyteller or anybody else's storyteller. This is my story, and you don't have to believe my story either. It's up to you to believe it or not, but this is the way that I see the world.

The moment when I perceived the infinite, I saw that there is only one living being in the universe. That one living being is God, and because everything and everybody is a manifestation of that one living being, everything and everybody will return to that source.

There is nothing to fear anymore; we don't have to be afraid to die. There is only one force that exists, and when we die, everybody is going back to the same place. Even if we don't want to, even if we resist, we will return to that place because there is no other place to go. This is the greatest news for everybody. There's no need to be afraid that we will be condemned when we die. In the moment of our death, I am going back to God, you are going back to God, everybody is going back to God, and that's it.

And it's not about being good enough for God. God doesn't care if we are good enough. God just loves us.

Our life is a story; our life is a dream. The kingdom of heaven is in our mind, and it's just a choice to return to our authentic self, to live our life in love and in truth. There is no reason for our life to be controlled by fear and lies. If we recover the control of our story, that gives us the freedom to create our life as beautifully as we can, as an artist of the spirit. Once we know that everybody is returning to God, which is truth, then believing in lies is just nonsense. The lies in our story are not important. What is important is to enjoy our time in this reality, to live in happiness while we are alive.

The question is: What are you going to do with your story? My choice is to write my story with truth and with love. What is yours?

❧

POINTS TO PONDER

• The voice of the fallen angel is so loud that we cannot hear the voice of our spirit, our integrity, our love. This silent voice is always there. Before we learned to speak, when we were one and two years old, we listened to this voice.

• When you are born, you don't know what you are, but your body knows what it is, and it knows what to do. This is silent knowledge. You can feel silent knowledge every time you breathe.

• You are an angel, and your life is your message. You can be a messenger of lies, fear, and destruction, or a messenger of truth, love, and creation. But you cannot deliver lies and truth at the same time.

• Heaven is a story that we can create when we surrender to life and allow life to manifest without lies. Heaven is here, and it's available for everybody, but we need to have the eyes to perceive it.

- The fruit of the Tree of Life is life; it is truth. Life is the only truth; it is the force that is creating all the time. When you see this force in yourself, and you put your faith in this force, you are truly alive.

- The truth is not in the story. The truth is in the power that creates the story. The truth is the real you; it's your own integrity, and nobody can guide you to that place. Only you can take yourself there.

- When the voice of knowledge becomes the voice of integrity, you return to the truth, you return to love, you return to heaven, and live in happiness again.

Prayers

PLEASE TAKE A MOMENT TO CLOSE YOUR EYES, OPEN
your heart, and feel the love that is all around you.
I invite you to join me in a special prayer to experience a communion with our Creator.

Focus your attention on your lungs, as if only
your lungs exist. Take a deep breath and feel the air
as it fills your lungs. Notice the connection of love
between the air and your lungs. Feel the pleasure
when your lungs expand to fulfill the biggest need
of the human body — to breathe. Take another deep
breath, then exhale and feel the pleasure again.

Just to breathe is enough for us to always enjoy
life. Feel the pleasure of being alive, the pleasure of
the feeling of love. . . .

꙰

PRAYER FOR THE CREATOR

Today, Creator, help me to create the story of my life as beautifully as you create the entire universe.

Beginning today, help me to recover my faith in the truth, in the silent voice of my integrity. I ask you, God, to manifest your love through me in every word I express, in every action I take. Help me to make every activity in my life a ritual of love and joy. Let me use love as the material for creating the most beautiful story about your creation.

Today, God, my heart is filled with gratitude for the gift of life. Thank you for the awareness that you only create perfection, and because you created me, I believe in my own perfection.

God, help me to love myself unconditionally so that I can share my love with other humans, with all forms of life on this beautiful planet. Help me to create my own dream of heaven, to the eternal happiness of humanity. Amen.

Prayer for an Angel

Today, Creator, help me to remember my real nature, which is love and happiness. Help me to become what I really am, and to express what I really am.

Beginning today, help me to recognize every human as your messenger with a message to deliver. Help me to see you in the soul of every human, behind the masks, behind the images we pretend to be. Today, help me to deliver the message of my integrity to that part of me that is always judging. Help me, God, to let go of all my judgments, to let go of all the false messages I deliver to myself and to everyone around me.

Today, help me to recover the awareness of my own creation as an angel, and let me use my awareness to deliver your message of life, your message of joy, your message of love. Let me express the beauty of my spirit, the beauty of my heart, in the supreme art of humans: the dream of my life. Amen.

About the Authors

DON MIGUEL RUIZ IS THE INTERNATIONAL BESTSELLING author of *The Four Agreements, The Four Agreements Companion Book, The Mastery of Love, The Voice of Knowledge, The Circle of Fire,* and *The Fifth Agreement* (with don Jose Ruiz). His books have sold over 10 million copies in the United States, and have been translated into 40 languages worldwide.

Ruiz has dedicated his life to imparting the wisdom of the ancient Toltec. Today, he continues to share his unique blend of ancient wisdom and modern-day awareness through lectures, workshops, and journeys to sacred sites around the world. For information about current programs offered by don Miguel Ruiz and his sons, don Miguel Ruiz, Jr. and don Jose Ruiz, please visit:

MiguelRuiz.com

JANET MILLS IS THE FOUNDER OF AMBER-ALLEN PUBLISHING. She is also the coauthor, with don Miguel Ruiz, of six books in *The Toltec Wisdom Series,* creator of *The Four Agreements for a Better Life* online course, and editor of Deepak Chopra's bestselling title, *The Seven Spiritual Laws of Success.* Her life's mission is to publish books of enduring beauty, integrity, and wisdom, and to inspire others to fulfill their most cherished dreams.

The Four Agreements*

Based on ancient Toltec wisdom, The Four Agreements offer a powerful code of conduct that can rapidly transform our lives to a new experience of freedom, true happiness, and love. Available in trade paperback, four-color illustrated edition, ebook, and audiobook.

The Four Agreements Companion Book*

Additional insights, practice ideas, questions and answers about applying The Four Agreements, and true stories from people who have already transformed their lives. Available in trade paperback and ebook.

The Mastery of Love*

Ruiz shows us how to heal our emotional wounds, recover the joy and freedom that are our birthright, and restore the spirit of playfulness that is vital to loving relationships. Available in trade paperback, ebook, and audiobook.

The Circle of Fire* (Formerly published as Prayers)

In this beautiful collection of essays, prayers, and guided meditations, Ruiz inspires us to enter into a new and loving relationship with ourselves, with others, and with all of creation. Available in trade paperback and ebook.

THE MASTERY OF
LOVE

A Practical Guide to the Art of Relationship

A
Toltec

THE MASTERY OF
LOVE

Wisdom
Book

DON MIGUEL RUIZ

WITH JANET MILLS

AMBER-ALLEN PUBLISHING
SAN RAFAEL, CALIFORNIA

Copyright © 1999 by Miguel Angel Ruiz, M.D. and Janet Mills

Published by Amber-Allen Publishing, Inc.
P.O. Box 6657
San Rafael, California 94903

Cover Illustration: Nicholas Wilton
Cover Design: Michele Wetherbee
Author Photo: Ellen Denuto

Library of Congress Cataloging-in-Publication Data
Ruiz, Miguel, 1952– The mastery of love : a practical guide to the art of relationship / Miguel Ruiz. p. cm. — (A Toltec wisdom book)
I. Love — Religious aspects — Miscellanea.   I. Title.
II. Series: Ruiz, Miguel, 1952 – Toltec wisdom book.
BL626.4.R85 1999   299'.792 — dc21   99-18199 CIP

ISBN 978-1-878424-42-6
Printed in China
Distributed by Hay House, Inc.

18 17 16 15 14 13 12 11 10

To my parents, my children, my siblings,
and the rest of my family,
with whom I am bonded not only by love,
but by our blood and ancestral roots.

To my spiritual family,
with whom I am bonded by our decision
to create a family based on unconditional love,
mutual respect, and the practice
of the Mastery of Love.

And to my human family,
whose minds are fertile for the seeds
of love contained in this book.
May these seeds of love flourish in your life.

Contents

CONTENTS

Note

To avoid using the masculine gender exclusively when referring to both male and female readers, we have randomly used masculine and feminine pronouns throughout the book.

Acknowledgments

I WISH TO EXPRESS MY GRATITUDE TO JANET MILLS who, like a mother with her own child, gave form to this book with all her love and dedication.

I would also like to thank those people who gave of their time and their love, and helped us with the realization of this book.

Finally, I want to express my gratitude to our Creator for the inspiration and beauty that gave this book Life.

The Toltec

THOUSANDS OF YEARS AGO, THE TOLTEC WERE known throughout southern Mexico as "women and men of knowledge." Anthropologists have spoken of the Toltec as a nation or a race, but, in fact, the Toltec were scientists and artists who formed a society to explore and conserve the spiritual knowledge and practices of the ancient ones. They came together as masters *(naguals)* and students at Teotihuacan, the ancient city of pyramids outside Mexico City known as the place where "Man Becomes God."

Over the millennia, the *naguals* were forced to conceal the ancestral wisdom and maintain its existence in obscurity. European conquest, coupled with rampant misuse of personal power by a few of the apprentices, made it necessary to shield the knowledge from those who were not prepared to use it wisely or who might intentionally misuse it for personal gain.

Fortunately, the esoteric Toltec knowledge was embodied and passed on through generations by different lineages of *naguals*. Though it remained veiled in secrecy for hundreds of years, ancient prophecies foretold the coming of an age when it would be necessary to return the wisdom to the people. Now, don Miguel Ruiz, a *nagual* from the Eagle Knight lineage, has been guided to share with us the powerful teachings of the Toltec.

Toltec knowledge arises from the same essential unity of truth as all the sacred esoteric traditions found around the world. Though it is not a religion, it honors all the spiritual masters who have taught on the earth. While it does embrace spirit, it is most accurately described as a way of life, distinguished by the ready accessibility of happiness and love.

A Toltec is an artist of Love,
an artist of the Spirit,
someone who is creating every moment,
every second, the most beautiful art —
the Art of Dreaming.

Life is nothing but a dream,
and if we are artists,
then we can create our life with Love,
and our dream becomes
a masterpiece of art.

INTRODUCTION

The Master

ONCE UPON A TIME, A MASTER WAS TALKING TO A crowd of people, and his message was so wonderful that everyone felt touched by his words of love. In the crowd there was a man who had listened to every word the Master said. This man was very humble, and he had a great heart. He was so touched by the Master's words that he felt the need to invite the Master to his home.

When the Master finished speaking, the man walked through the crowd, looked into the eyes of the Master, and told him, "I know you are busy and everyone wants your attention. I know you hardly have time to even listen to my words. But my heart is so open and I feel so much love for you that I have the need to invite you to my home. I want to prepare the best meal for you. I don't expect you will accept, but I just had to let you know."

The Master looked into the man's eyes, and with the most beautiful smile he said, "Prepare everything. I will be there." Then the Master walked away.

At these words, the joy in the man's heart was strong. He could hardly wait to serve the Master and to express his love for him. This would be the most important day of his life: The Master was going to be with him. He bought the best food and wine, and found the most beautiful clothes to offer as a gift to the Master. Then he ran home to prepare everything to receive the Master. He cleaned his entire house, prepared the most wonderful meal, and made the table look beautiful. His heart was full of joy because the Master would soon be there.

The man was waiting anxiously when someone knocked at the door. Eagerly, he opened the door, but instead of the Master, he found an old woman. She looked into his eyes and said, "I am starving. Can you give me a piece of bread?"

The man was a little disappointed because it was not the Master. He looked at the woman and said, "Please, come into my house." He sat her in the place he had prepared for the Master, and gave her the food he had made for the Master. But he was anxious and could hardly wait for her to finish eating. The old woman was touched by the generosity of this man. She thanked him and left.

The man had barely finished preparing the table for the Master again when someone knocked at the door. This time it was another stranger who had traveled across the desert. The stranger looked into the man's face and said, "I am thirsty. Can you give me something to drink?"

The man was a little disappointed again because it was not the Master. He invited the stranger into his home, and sat him in the place he had prepared for the Master. He served the wine he had intended to give the Master. When the stranger left, the man again prepared everything for the Master.

Someone knocked at the door again. When the man opened the door, there stood a child. The child looked up at the man and said, "I am freezing. Can you give me a blanket to cover my body?"

The man was a little disappointed because it was not the Master, but he looked into the eyes of the child and felt love in his heart. Quickly he gathered the clothes he had intended to give the Master, and he covered the child with the clothes. The child thanked him and left.

The man prepared everything again for the Master, and then he waited until it was very late. When he realized the Master was not coming, he was disappointed, but right away he forgave the Master. He said to himself, "I knew I could not expect the Master to come to this humble home. Although he said he would come, something more important must have taken him elsewhere. The Master did not come, but at least he told me he would, and that is enough for my heart to be happy."

Slowly he put the food away, he put the wine away, and he went to bed. That night he dreamed the Master came to his home. The man was happy to see him, but he didn't know that he was dreaming. "Master you came! You kept your word."

The Master replied, "Yes, I am here, but I was here before. I was hungry, and you fulfilled my need for food. I was thirsty, and you gave me the wine. I was cold, and you covered me with clothes. Whatever you do for others, you do for me."

The man woke up, and his heart was filled with happiness, because he understood what the Master had taught him. The Master loved him so much that he had sent three people to give him the greatest lesson: The Master lives within everyone. When you give food to the one who is starving, when you give water to the one who is thirsty, when you cover the one who is cold, you give your love to the Master.

1

The Wounded Mind

PERHAPS YOU HAVE NEVER THOUGHT ABOUT IT, but on one level or another, all of us are masters. We are masters because we have the power to create and to rule our own lives.

Just as societies and religions around the world create incredible mythologies, we create our own. Our personal mythology is populated by heroes and villains, angels and demons, kings and commoners. We create an entire population in our mind, including multiple personalities for ourselves. Then we master the image we are going to use in certain circumstances. We become artists of pretending and projecting our images, and we master whatever we believe we are. When we meet other people, we classify them right away, and assign them a role in our lives. We create an image for others, according to what we believe they are. And we do the same thing with everyone and everything around us.

You have the power to create. Your power is so strong that whatever you believe comes true. You create yourself, whatever you believe you are. You are the way you are because that is what you believe about yourself. Your whole reality, everything you believe, is your creation. You have the same power as any other human in the world. The main difference between you and someone else is how you apply your power, what you create with your power. You may be similar to others in many ways, but no one in the whole world lives her life the way you do.

You have practiced all of your life to be what you are, and you do it so well that you master what you believe you are. You master your own personality, your own beliefs; you master every action, every reaction. You practice for years and years, and you achieve the level of mastery to be what you believe you are. Once we can see that all of us are masters, we can see what kind of mastery we have.

When we are children, and we have a problem with someone, we get angry. For whatever reason, that anger pushes the problem away; we get the result we want. It happens a second time — we react with anger — and now we know if we get angry we push the problem away. Then we practice and practice, until we become masters of anger.

In the same way, we become masters of jealousy, masters of sadness, masters of self-rejection. All of our drama and suffering is by practice. We make an agreement with ourselves, and we practice that agreement until it becomes a whole mastery. The way we think, the way we feel, and the way we act become so routine that we no longer need to put our attention on what we are doing. It is just by action-reaction that we behave a certain way.

To become masters of love, we have to practice love. The art of relationship is also a whole mastery, and the only way to reach mastery is with practice. To master a relationship is therefore about action. It is not about concepts or attaining knowledge. It *is* about action. Of course, to have action, we need to have some knowledge, or at least a little more awareness of the way humans operate.

I want you to imagine that you live on a planet where everyone has a skin disease. For two or three thousand years, the people on your planet have suffered the same disease: Their entire bodies are covered by wounds that are infected, and those wounds really hurt when you touch them. Of course, they believe this is a normal physiology of the skin. Even the medical books describe this disease as a normal condition.

When the people are born, their skin is healthy, but around three or four years of age, the first wounds start to appear. By the time they are teenagers, there are wounds all over their bodies.

Can you imagine how these people are going to treat each other? In order to relate with one another, they have to protect their wounds. They hardly ever touch each other's skin because it is too painful. If by accident you touch someone's skin, it is so painful that right away she gets angry and touches your skin, just to get even. Still, the instinct to love is so strong that you pay a high price to have relationships with others.

Well, imagine that a miracle occurs one day. You awake and your skin is completely healed. There are no wounds anymore, and it doesn't hurt to be touched. Healthy skin you can touch feels wonderful because the skin is made for perception. Can you imagine yourself with healthy skin in a world where everyone has a skin disease? You cannot touch others because it hurts them, and no one touches you because they make the assumption that it will hurt you.

If you can imagine this, perhaps you can understand that someone from another planet who came to visit us would have a similar experience with humans. But it isn't our skin that is full of wounds. What the visitor would discover is that the human mind is sick with a disease called fear. Just like the description of the infected skin, the emotional body is full of wounds, and these wounds are infected with emotional poison. The manifestation of the disease of fear is anger, hate, sadness, envy, and hypocrisy; the result of the disease is all the emotions that make humans suffer.

All humans are mentally sick with the same disease. We can even say that this world is a mental hospital. But this mental disease has been in this world for thousands of years, and the medical books, the psychiatric books, and the psychology books describe the disease as normal. They consider it normal, but I can tell you it is not normal.

When the fear becomes too great, the reasoning mind starts to fail and can no longer take all those wounds with all the poison. In the psychology books we call this a mental illness. We call it schizophrenia, paranoia, psychosis, but these diseases are created when the reasoning mind is so frightened and the wounds so painful, that it becomes better to break contact with the outside world.

Humans live in continuous fear of being hurt, and this creates a big drama wherever we go. The way humans relate to each other is so emotionally painful that for no apparent reason we get angry, jealous, envious, sad. To even say "I love you" can be frightening. But even if it's painful and fearful to have an emotional interaction, still we keep going, we enter into a relationship, we get married, and we have children.

In order to protect our emotional wounds, and because of our fear of being hurt, humans create something very sophisticated in the mind: a big denial system. In that denial system we become the perfect liars. We lie so perfectly that we lie to ourselves and we even *believe* our own lies. We don't notice we are lying, and sometimes even when we know we are lying, we justify the lie and excuse the lie to protect ourselves from the pain of our wounds.

The denial system is like a wall of fog in front of our eyes that blinds us from seeing the truth. We wear a social mask because it's too painful to see ourselves or to let others see us as we really are. And the denial system lets us pretend that everyone believes what we want them to believe about us. We put up these barriers for protection, to keep other people away, but those barriers also keep us inside, restricting our freedom. Humans cover themselves, and protect themselves, and when someone says, "You are pushing my buttons," it is not exactly true. What is true is that you are touching a wound in his mind, and he reacts because it hurts.

When you are aware that everyone around you has emotional wounds with emotional poison, you can easily understand the relationship of humans in what the Toltecs call the *dream of hell.* From the Toltec perspective, everything we believe about ourselves, and everything we know about our world, is a dream. If you look at any religious description of *hell*, it is the same as human society, the way we dream. Hell is a place of suffering, a place of fear, a place of war and violence, a place of judgment and no justice, a place of punishment that never ends. There are humans versus humans in a jungle of predators; humans full of judgment, full of blame, full of guilt, full of emotional poison — envy, anger, hate, sadness, suffering. We create all these little demons in our mind because we have learned to dream hell in our own life.

Each of us creates a personal dream for our own self, but the humans before us created a big outside dream, the dream of human society. The outside Dream, or the Dream of the Planet, is the collective Dream of billions of dreamers. The big Dream includes all the rules of society, its laws, its religions, its different cultures, and ways to be. All of this information stored inside our mind is like a thousand voices talking to us at once. The Toltecs call this the *mitote*.

The real us is pure love; we are *Life*. The real us has nothing to do with the Dream, but the mitote keeps us from seeing what we really are. When you see the Dream from this perspective, and if you have the awareness of what you are, you see the nonsense behavior of humans, and it becomes amusing. What for everyone else is a big drama, for you becomes a comedy. You can see humans suffering over something that is not important, that is not even real. But we have no choice. We are born in this society, we grow up in this society, and we learn to be like everyone else, playing nonsense all the time, competing with mere nonsense.

Imagine that you could visit a planet where everyone has a different kind of emotional mind. The way they relate to each other is always in happiness, always in love, always in peace. Now imagine that one day you awake on *this* planet, and you no longer have wounds in your emotional body. You are no longer afraid to be who you are. Whatever someone says about you, whatever they do, you don't take it personally, and it doesn't hurt anymore. You no longer need to protect yourself. You are not afraid to love, to share, to open your heart. But no one else is like you. How can you relate with people who are emotionally wounded and sick with fear?

When a human is born, the emotional mind, the emotional body, is completely healthy. Maybe around three or four years of age, the first wounds in the emotional body start to appear and get infected with emotional poison. But if you observe children who are two or three years old, if you see how they behave, they are playing all the time. You see them laughing all the time. Their imagination is so powerful, and the way they dream is an adventure of exploration. When something is wrong they react and defend themselves, but then they just let go and turn their attention to the moment again, to play again, to explore and have fun again. They are living in the moment. They are not ashamed of the past; they are not worried about the future. Little children express what they feel, and they are not afraid to love.

The happiest moments in our lives are when we are playing just like children, when we are singing and dancing, when we are exploring and creating just for fun. It is wonderful when we behave like a child because this is the normal human mind, the normal human tendency. As children, we are innocent and it is natural for us to express love. But what has happened to us? What has happened to the whole world?

What has happened is that when we are children, the adults already have that mental disease, and they are highly contagious. How do they pass this disease to us? They "hook our attention," and they teach us to be like them. That is how we pass our disease to our children, and that is how our parents, our teachers, our older siblings, the whole society of sick people infected us with that disease. They hooked our attention and put information into our mind through repetition. This is the way we learned. This is the way we program a human mind.

The problem is the program, the information we have stored in our mind. By hooking the attention, we teach children a language, how to read, how to behave, how to dream. We domesticate humans the same way we domesticate a dog or any other animal: with punishment and reward. This is perfectly normal. What we call education is nothing but domestication of the human being.

We are afraid to be punished, but later we are also afraid of not getting the reward, of not being good enough for Mom or Dad, sibling or teacher. The need to be accepted is born. Before that, we don't care whether we are accepted or not. People's opinions are not important. They are not important because we just want to play and we live in the present.

The fear of not getting the reward becomes the fear of rejection. The fear of not being good enough for someone else is what makes us try to change, what makes us create an image. Then we try to project that image according to what they want us to be, just to be accepted, just to have the reward. We learn to pretend to be what we are not, and we practice trying to be someone else, just to be good enough for Mom, for Dad, for the teacher, for our religion, for whatever. We practice and practice, and we master how to be what we are not.

Soon we forget who we really are, and we start to live our images. We create not just one image, but many different images according to the different groups of people we associate with. We create an image at home, an image at school, and when we grow up we create even more images.

This is also true for a simple relationship between a man and a woman. The woman has an outer image that she tries to project to others, but when she is alone, she has another image of herself. The man also has an outer image and an inner image. By the time they are adults, the inner image and outer image are so different that they hardly match anymore. In the relationship between a man and woman, there are four images at least. How can they really know each other? They don't. They can only try to understand the image. But there are more images to consider.

When a man meets a woman, he makes an image of her from his point of view, and the woman makes an image of the man from her point of view. Then he tries to make her fit the image he makes for her, and she tries to make him fit the image she makes for him. Now there are six images between them. Of course, they are lying to each other, even if they don't know they are lying. Their relationship is based on fear; it is based on lies. It is not based on truth, because they cannot see through all that fog.

In the period when we are little children, there is no conflict with the images we pretend to be. Our images are not really challenged until we begin to interact with the outside world and no longer have our parents' protection. This is why being a teenager is particularly difficult. Even if we are prepared to support and defend our images, as soon as we try to project our images to the outside world, the world fights back. The outside world starts proving to us, not just privately but publicly, that we are not what we pretend to be.

Let's take the example of a teenage boy who pretends to be very intelligent. He goes to a debate at school, and in that debate someone who is more intelligent and more prepared wins the debate and makes him look ridiculous in front of everyone. He will try to explain and excuse and justify his image in front of his peers. He will be so kind to everyone and will try to save his image in front of them, but he knows he is lying. Of course, he tries his best not to break in front of his peers, but as soon as he is alone and sees himself in a mirror, he goes and breaks the mirror. He hates himself; he feels that he is so stupid, that he is the worst. There is a big discrepancy between the inner image and the image he tries to project to the outside world. The bigger the discrepancy, the more difficult the adaptation to the society Dream, and the less love he will have for himself.

Between the image he pretends to be and the inner image when he is alone are lies and more lies. Both images are completely out of touch with reality; they are false, but he doesn't see that. Maybe someone else can see that, but he is completely blind. His denial system tries to protect the wounds, but the wounds are real, and he is hurting because he is trying so hard to defend an image.

When we are children, we learn that everyone's opinions are important, and we rule our lives according to those opinions. A simple opinion from someone can put us deeper into hell, an opinion that is not even true: "You look ugly. You are wrong. You are stupid." Opinions have a lot of power over the nonsense behavior of people who live in hell. That is why we need to hear that we are good, that we are doing well, that we are beautiful. "How do I look? How was what I said? How am I doing?"

We need to hear the opinions of others because we are domesticated and we can be manipulated by those opinions. That is why we seek recognition from other people; we need emotional support from other people; we need to be accepted by the outside Dream, via other people. That is why teenagers drink alcohol, take drugs, or start smoking. It is just to be accepted by other people who have all those opinions; it is just to be considered "cool."

So many humans are suffering because of all the false images we try to project. Humans pretend to be something very important, but at the same time we believe we are nothing. We work so hard to be someone in that society Dream, to be recognized and approved by others. We try so hard to be important, to be a winner, to be powerful, to be rich, to be famous, to express our personal dream, and to impose our dream onto other people around us. Why? Because humans believe the Dream is real, and we take it very seriously.

2

The Loss of Innocence

HUMANS BY NATURE ARE VERY SENSITIVE BEINGS. We are so emotional because we perceive everything with the emotional body. The emotional body is like a radio that can be tuned to perceive certain frequencies or to react to certain frequencies. The normal frequency of humans before domestication is to explore and to enjoy life; we are tuned to love. As children, we don't have any definition of love as an abstract concept; we just live love. It's the way we are.

The emotional body has a component like an alarm system to let us know when something is wrong. It is the same with the physical body; it has an alarm system to let us know something is wrong with our body. We call this pain. When we feel pain it is because there is something wrong with the body that we have to look at and fix. The alarm system for the emotional body is fear. When we feel fear, it's because there is something wrong. Perhaps we are in danger of losing our life.

The emotional body perceives emotions, but not through the eyes. We perceive emotions through our emotional body. Children just *feel* emotions and their reasoning mind doesn't interpret or question them. This is why children accept certain people and reject other people. When they don't feel confident around someone, they reject that person because they can feel the emotions that person is projecting. Children can easily perceive when someone is angry and their alarm

system generates a little fear that says, "Stay away."
And they follow their instinct — they stay away.

We learn to be emotional according to the emotional energy in our home, and our personal reaction to that energy. That is why every brother and sister will react differently according to how they learn to defend themselves and adapt to different circumstances. When our parents are constantly fighting, when there is disharmony, disrespect, and lies, we learn the emotional way of being like them. Even if they tell us not to be that way and not to lie, the emotional energy of our parents, of our entire family, will make us perceive the world in a similar way.

The emotional energy that lives in our home is going to tune our emotional body to that frequency. The emotional body starts to change its tune, and it is no longer the normal tune of the human being. We play the game of the adults, we play the game of the outside Dream, and we lose. We lose our innocence, we lose our freedom, we lose our happiness, and we lose our tendency to love. We are forced to change and we start perceiving another world, another reality: the reality of injustice, the reality of emotional pain, the reality of emotional poison. Welcome to hell — the hell that humans create, which is the Dream of the Planet. We are welcomed into that hell, but we don't invent it personally. It was here before we were born.

You can see how real love and freedom are destroyed by looking at children. Imagine a child two or three years old running and having fun in the park. Mom is there watching the little guy, and she's afraid he might fall and hurt himself. At a certain point she wants to stop him, and the child thinks Mom is playing with him, so he tries to run faster from her. Cars are passing in the street nearby, which makes Mom even more afraid, and finally she catches him. The child is expecting her to play, but she spanks him. Boom! It's a shock. The child's happiness was the expression of love coming out of him and he does not understand why she is acting this way. This is a shock that stops love little by little over time. The child does not understand words, but even so, he can question, "Why?"

Running and playing is an expression of love, but it's no longer safe because your parents punish you when you express your love. They send you to your room, and you cannot do what you want to do. They tell you that you are being a bad boy, or a bad girl, and that puts you down, that means punishment.

In that system of reward and punishment there is a sense of justice and injustice, what is fair and what is not fair. The sense of injustice is like a knife that opens an emotional wound in the mind. Then, according to our reaction to the injustice, the wound may get infected with emotional poison. Why do some wounds get infected? Let's look at another example.

Imagine that you are two or three years old. You are happy, you are playing, you are exploring. You aren't conscious of what is good, what is bad, what is right, what is wrong, what you should be doing, what you shouldn't be doing, because you are not yet domesticated. You are playing in the living room with whatever is around you. You don't have any bad intention, you don't try to hurt anything, but you are

THE MASTERY OF LOVE

playing with your Daddy's guitar. For you, it's just a toy; you don't try to hurt your Daddy at all. But your father is having one of those days when he doesn't feel right. He has problems in his business, and he goes into the living room and finds you playing with his things. He gets mad right away, and he grabs you and spanks you.

This is injustice from your point of view. Your father just comes, and with anger he hurts you. This was someone you trusted completely because he is your Daddy, someone who usually protects you and allows you to play and allows you to be you. Now there is something that doesn't quite fit. That sense of injustice is like a pain in your heart. You feel sensitive; it hurts and makes you cry. But you cry not just because he spanks you. It's not the physical aggression that hurts you; it's the emotional aggression you feel is not fair. *You didn't do anything.*

That sense of injustice opens a wound in your mind. Your emotional body is wounded, and in that moment you lose a little part of your innocence. You learn that you cannot always trust your father. Even if your mind doesn't know that yet, because your mind doesn't analyze, it still understands, "I cannot trust." Your emotional body tells you there is something that you cannot trust, and that something can be repeated.

Your reaction might be fear; your reaction might be anger or being shy or just crying. But that reaction is already emotional poison, because the normal reaction before domestication is that your Daddy spanks you and you want to hit him back. You hit him back, or just intend to put your hand up, and that makes your father even madder at you. The reaction of your father for just putting your hand up against him creates a worse punishment. Now you know he will destroy you. Now you are afraid of him, and you no longer defend yourself because you know it will only make things worse.

You still don't understand why, but you know your father can even kill you. This opens a fierce wound in your mind. Before this, your mind was completely healthy; you were completely innocent. After this, the reasoning mind tries to do something with the experience. You learn to react in a certain way, your personal way. You keep that emotion with you, and it changes your way of life. This experience will repeat itself more often now. The injustice will come from Mom and Dad, from brothers and sisters, from aunts and uncles, from the school, from society, from everyone. With each fear, you learn to defend yourself, but not the way you did before domestication, when you would defend yourself and just keep playing.

Now there is something inside the wound that at first is not a big problem: emotional poison. The emotional poison accumulates, and the mind begins to play with that poison. Now we start to worry a little about the future because we have the memory of the poison and we don't want that to happen again. We also have memories of being accepted; we remember Mom and Dad being good to us and living in harmony. We want the harmony, but we don't know how to create it. And because we are inside the bubble of our own perception, whatever happens around us now seems as if it is *because of us.* We believe Mom and Dad fight because of us, even if it doesn't have anything to do with us.

Little by little we lose our innocence; we start to feel resentment, then we no longer forgive. Over time, these incidents and interactions let us know it's not safe to be who we really are. Of course this will vary in intensity with each human according to his intelligence and his education. It will depend on many things. If you are lucky, the domestication is not that strong. But if you are not so lucky, the domestication can be so strong and the wounds so deep, that you can even be afraid to speak. The result is, "Oh, I am shy." Shyness is the fear of expressing yourself. You may believe you don't know how to dance or how to sing, but this is just repression of the normal human instinct to express love.

Humans use fear to domesticate humans, and our fear increases with each experience of injustice. The sense of injustice is the knife that opens a wound in our emotional body. Emotional poison is created by our *reaction* to what we consider injustice. Some wounds will heal, others will become infected with more and more poison. Once we are full of emotional poison, we have the need to release it, and we practice releasing the poison by sending it to someone else. How do we do this? By hooking that person's attention.

Let's take an example of an ordinary couple. For whatever reason, the wife is mad. She has a lot of emotional poison from an injustice that comes from her husband. The husband is not home, but she remembers that injustice and the poison is growing inside. When the husband comes home, the first thing she wants to do is hook his attention because once she hooks his attention, all the poison can go to her husband and she can feel the relief. As soon as she tells him how bad he is, how stupid or how unfair he is, that poison she has inside her is transferred to the husband.

She keeps talking and talking until she gets his attention. The husband finally reacts and gets mad, and she feels better. But now the poison is going through him, and he has to get even. He has to hook her attention and release the poison, but it's not just her poison — it's her poison plus his poison. If you look at this interaction, you will see that they are touching each other's wounds and playing ping-pong with emotional poison. The poison keeps growing and growing, until someday one of them is going to explode. This is often how humans relate with each other.

By hooking the attention, the energy goes from one person to another person. The attention is something very powerful in the human mind. Everyone around the world is hunting the attention of others all the time. When we capture the attention, we create channels of communication. The Dream is transferred, power is transferred, but emotional poison is transferred also.

Usually we release the poison with the person we think is responsible for the injustice, but if that person is so powerful that we cannot send it to him, we don't care who we send it to. We send it to the little ones who have no defense against us, and that is how abusive relationships are formed. The people of power abuse the people who have less power because they need to release their emotional poison. We have the need to release the poison, and sometimes we don't want justice; we just want to release, we want peace. That is why humans are hunting power all the time, because the more powerful we are, the easier it is to release the poison to the ones who cannot defend themselves.

Of course, we are talking about relationships in hell. We are talking about the mental disease that exists on this planet. There is no one to blame for this disease; it is not good or bad or right or wrong; it is simply the normal pathology of this disease. No one is guilty for being abusive. Just as people on that imaginary planet are not guilty because their skin is sick, you are not guilty because you have wounds infected with poison. When you are physically sick or injured, you don't blame yourself or feel guilty. Then why feel bad or feel guilty because your emotional body is sick?

What is important is to have the awareness that we have this problem. If we have the awareness, we have the opportunity to heal our emotional body, our emotional mind, and stop the suffering. Without the awareness, there is nothing we can do. The only thing we can do is to keep suffering from the interaction with other humans, but not just with other humans, the interaction with our own self, because we also touch our own wounds just to be punished.

In our mind we create that part of us that is always judging. The Judge is judging everything we do, everything we don't do, everything we feel, everything we don't feel. We are judging ourselves all the time, and we are judging everyone else all the time, based on what we believe and based on the sense of justice and injustice. Of course, we find ourselves guilty and we need to be punished. The other part of our mind that receives the judgment and has the need to be punished is the Victim. That part of us says, "Poor me. I'm not good enough, I'm not strong enough, I'm not intelligent enough. Why should I try?"

When you were a child, you could not choose what to believe and what not to believe. The Judge

THE MASTERY OF LOVE

and the Victim are based on all those false beliefs you didn't choose. When that information went into your mind, you were innocent. You believed everything. The Belief System was put inside you like a program by the outside Dream. The Toltecs call this program the *Parasite.* The human mind is sick because it has a Parasite that steals its vital energy and robs it of joy. The Parasite is all those beliefs that make you suffer. Those beliefs are so strong that years later when you learn new concepts and try to make your own decisions, you find those beliefs still control your life.

Sometimes the little child inside you comes out — the real you that stays at the age of two or three years old. You are living in the moment and having fun, but there is something pulling you back; something inside feels unworthy of having too much fun. An inner voice tells you that your happiness is too good to be true; it isn't right to be too happy. All the guilt, all the blame, all the emotional poison in your emotional body keeps pulling you back into the world of drama.

The Parasite spreads like a disease from our grand-parents, to our parents, to ourselves, and then we give it to our own children. We put all those programs inside our children the same way we train a dog. Humans are domesticated animals, and this domesti-cation leads us into the dream of hell where we live in fear. The food for the Parasite is the emotions that come from fear. Before we get the Parasite, we enjoy life, we play, we are happy like little children. But after all that garbage is put into our minds, we are no longer happy. We learn to be right and to make everyone else wrong. The need to be "right" is the result of trying to protect the image we want to project to the outside. We have to impose our way of thinking, not just onto other humans, but even upon ourselves.

With awareness we can easily understand why relationships don't work — with our parents, with our children, with our friends, with our partner, and even with ourselves. Why doesn't the relationship with our-selves work? Because we are wounded and we have all that emotional poison that we can hardly handle. We are full of poison because we grew up with an *image of perfection* that is not true, which does not exist, and in our mind it isn't fair.

We have seen how we create that image of perfection to please other people, even though they create their own dream that has nothing to do with us. We try to please Mom and Dad, we try to please our teacher, our minister, our religion, and God. But the truth is that from their point of view, we are never going to be perfect. That image of perfection tells us how we should be in order to acknowledge that we are good, in order to accept ourselves. But guess what? This is the biggest lie we believe about ourselves, because we are *never* going to be perfect. And there is no way that we can forgive ourselves for not being perfect.

That image of perfection changes the way we dream. We learn to deny ourselves and reject ourselves. We are never good enough, or right enough, or clean enough, or healthy enough, according to all those beliefs we have. There is always *something* the Judge can never accept or forgive. That is why we reject our own humanity; that is why we never deserve to be happy; that is why we are searching for someone who abuses us, someone who will punish us. We have a very high level of self-abuse because of that image of perfection.

When we reject ourselves, and judge ourselves, and find ourselves guilty and punish ourselves so much, it looks like there is no love. It looks like there is only punishment, only suffering, only judgment in this world. Hell has many different levels. Some people are very deep in hell and other people are hardly in hell, but still they are in hell. There are very abusive relationships in hell and relationships with hardly any abuse.

You are no longer a child, and if you have an abusive relationship, it is because you accept that abuse, because you believe you deserve it. You have a limit to the amount of abuse you will accept, but no one in the whole world abuses you more than you abuse yourself. The limit of your self-abuse is the limit you will tolerate from other people. If someone abuses you more than you abuse yourself, you walk away, you run, you escape. But if someone abuses you a little less than you abuse yourself, perhaps you stay longer. You still deserve that abuse.

Usually in a normal relationship in hell, it's about payment for an injustice; it's about getting even. I abuse you the way you need to be abused, and you abuse me the way I need to be abused. We have a good equilibrium; it works. Of course, energy attracts the same kind of energy, the same vibration. If someone comes to you and says, "Oh, I am so abused," and you ask, "Well, why do you stay there?," he doesn't even know why. The truth is he needs that abuse because that is the way he punishes himself.

Life brings to you exactly what you need. There is perfect justice in hell. There is nothing to blame. We can even say that our suffering is a gift. If you just open your eyes and see what is around you, it's exactly what you need to clean your poison, to heal your wounds, to accept yourself, and to get out of hell.

3

The Man Who Didn't
Believe in Love

I WANT TO TELL YOU A VERY OLD STORY ABOUT
the man who didn't believe in love. This was an ordinary man just like you and me, but what made this
man special was his way of thinking: He thought *love
doesn't exist.* Of course, he had a lot of experience trying
to find love, and he had observed the people around

him. Much of his life had been spent searching for love, only to find that love didn't exist.

Wherever this man went, he used to tell people that love is nothing but an invention of the poets, an invention of religions just to manipulate the weak mind of humans, to have control over humans, to make them believe. He said that love is not real, and that's why no human could ever find love even though he might look for it.

This man was highly intelligent, and he was very convincing. He read a lot of books, he went to the best universities, and he became a respected scholar. He could stand in any public place, in front of any kind of people, and his logic was very strong. What he said was that love is just like a drug; it makes you very high, but it creates a strong need. You can become highly addicted to love, but what happens when you don't receive your daily doses of love? Just like a drug, you need your everyday doses.

He used to say that most relationships between lovers are just like a relationship between a drug addict and the one who provides the drugs. The one who has the biggest need is like the drug addict; the one who has a little need is like the provider. The one who has the little need is the one who controls the whole relationship. You can see this dynamic so clearly because usually in every relationship there is one who loves the most and the other who doesn't love, who only takes advantage of the one who gives his or her heart. You can see the way they manipulate each other, their actions and reactions, and they are just like the provider and the drug addict.

The drug addict, the one who has the biggest need, lives in constant fear that perhaps he will not be able to get the next dosage of love, or the drug. The drug addict thinks, "What am I going to do if she leaves me?" That fear makes the drug addict very possessive. "That's mine!" The addict becomes jealous and demanding, because the fear of not having the next dosage. The provider can control and manipulate the one who needs the drug by giving more doses, fewer doses, or no doses at all. The one who has the biggest need completely surrenders and will do whatever he can to avoid being abandoned.

The man went on explaining to everyone why love doesn't exist. "What humans call 'love' is nothing but a fear relationship based on control. Where is the respect? Where is the love they claim to have? There is no love. Young couples, in front of the representation of God, in front of their family and friends, make a lot of promises to each other: to live together forever, to love and respect each other, to be there for each other, through the good times and the bad times. They promise to love and honor each other, and make promises and more promises. What is amazing, is that they really believe these promises. But after the marriage — one week later, a month later, a few months later — you can see that none of these promises are kept.

"What you find is a war of control to see who will manipulate whom. Who will be the provider, and who will have the addiction? You find that a few months later, the respect they swear to have for each other is gone. You can see the resentment, the emotional poison, how they hurt each other, little by little, and it grows and grows, until they don't know when the love stops. They stay together because they are afraid to be alone, afraid of the opinions and judgments of others, and also afraid of their own judgments and opinions. But where is the love?"

He used to claim that he saw many old couples that had lived together thirty years, forty years, fifty years, and they were so proud to have lived together all those years. But when they talked about their relationship, what they said was, "We survived the matrimony." That means one of them surrendered to the other; at a certain time, she gave up and decided to endure the suffering. The one with the strongest will and less need won the war, but where is that flame they call love? They treat each other like a possession: "She is mine." "He is mine."

The man went on and on about all the reasons why he believed love doesn't exist, and he told others, "I have done all that already. I will no longer allow anyone to manipulate my mind and control my life in the name of love." His arguments were quite logical, and he convinced many people by all his words. *Love doesn't exist.*

Then one day this man was walking in a park, and there on a bench was a beautiful lady who was crying. When he saw her crying, he felt curiosity. Sitting beside her, he asked if he could help her. He asked why she was crying. You can imagine his surprise when she told him she was crying because love doesn't exist. He said, "This is amazing — a woman who believes that love doesn't exist!" Of course, he wanted to know more about her.

"Why do you say that love doesn't exist?" he asked.

"Well, it's a long story," she replied. "I married when I was very young, with all the love, all these illusions, full of hope that I would share my life with this man. We swore to each other our loyalty, respect, and honor, and we created a family. But soon everything changed. I was the devoted wife who took care of the children and the home. My husband continued to develop his career, and his success and image outside of home was more important to him than our family. He lost respect for me, and I lost respect for him. We hurt each other, and at a certain point I discovered that I didn't love him and he didn't love me either.

"But the children needed a father, and that was my excuse to stay and to do whatever I could to support him. Now the children are grown and they have left. I no longer have any excuse to stay with him. There's no respect, there's no kindness. I know that even if I find someone else, it's going to be the same, because love doesn't exist. There is no sense to look around for something that doesn't exist. That is why I am crying."

Understanding her very well, he embraced her and said, "You are right; love doesn't exist. We look for love, we open our heart and we become vulnerable, just to find selfishness. That hurts us even if we don't think we will be hurt. It doesn't matter how many relationships we have; the same thing happens again and again. Why even search for love any longer?"

They were so much alike, and they became the best friends ever. It was a wonderful relationship.

They respected each other, and they never put each other down. With every step they took together, they were happy. There was no envy or jealousy, there was no control, there was no possessiveness. The relationship kept growing and growing. They loved to be together, because when they were together they had a lot of fun. When they were not together, they missed each other.

One day when the man was out of town, he had the weirdest idea. He was thinking, "Hmm, maybe what I feel for her is love. But this is so different from what I have ever felt before. It's not what the poets say it is, it's not what religion says, because I am not responsible for her. I don't take anything from her; I don't have the need for her to take care of me; I don't need to blame her for my difficulties or to take my dramas to her. We have the best time together; we enjoy each other. I respect the way she thinks, the way she feels. She doesn't embarrass me; she doesn't bother me at all. I don't feel jealous when she's with other people; I don't feel envy when she is successful.

Perhaps love *does* exist, but it's not what everyone thinks love is."

He could hardly wait to go back home and talk to her, to let her know about his weird idea. As soon as he started talking, she said, "I know exactly what you are talking about. I had the same idea long ago, but I didn't want to share it with you because I know you don't believe in love. Perhaps love does exist, but it isn't what we thought it was." They decided to become lovers and to live together, and it was amazing that things didn't change. They still respected each other, they were still supportive of each other, and the love grew more and more. Even the simplest things made their hearts sing with love because they were so happy.

The man's heart was so full with all the love he felt that one night a great miracle happened. He was looking at the stars and he found the most beautiful one, and his love was so big that the star started coming down from the sky and soon that star was in his hands. Then a second miracle happened, and his soul merged with that star. He was intensely happy, and he could hardly wait to go to the woman and put that star in her hands to prove his love to her. As soon as he put the star in her hands, she felt a moment of doubt. This love was overwhelming, and in that moment, the star fell from her hands and broke in a million little pieces.

Now there is an old man walking around the world swearing that love doesn't exist. And there is a beautiful old woman at home waiting for a man, shedding a tear for a paradise that once she had in her hands, but for one moment of doubt, she let it go. This is the story about the man who didn't believe in love.

Who made the mistake? Do you want to guess what went wrong? The mistake was on the man's part in thinking he could give the woman his happiness. The star was his happiness, and his mistake was to put his happiness in her hands. Happiness never comes from outside of us. He was happy because of the love coming out of him; she was happy because of the love coming out of her. But as soon as he made her responsible for his happiness, she broke the star because she could not be responsible for his happiness.

No matter how much the woman loved him, she could never make him happy because she could never know what he had in his mind. She could never know what his expectations were, because she could not know his dreams.

If you take your happiness and put it in someone's hands, sooner or later, she is going to break it. If you give your happiness to someone else, she can always take it away. Then if happiness can only come from inside of you and is the result of your love, you are responsible for your happiness. We can never make anyone responsible for our own happiness, but when we go to the church to get married, the first thing we do is exchange rings. We put our star in each other's hands, expecting that she is going to make you happy, and you are going to make her happy. It doesn't matter how much you love someone, you are never going to be what that person wants you to be.

That is the mistake most of us make right from the beginning. We base our happiness on our partner, and it doesn't work that way. We make all those promises that we cannot keep, and we set ourselves up to fail.

4

The Track of Love, The Track of Fear

YOUR WHOLE LIFE IS NOTHING BUT A DREAM. YOU live in a fantasy where everything you know about yourself is only true for you. Your truth is not the truth for anyone else, and that includes your own children or your own parents. Just consider what you believe about yourself and what your Mother believes about you. She can say she knows you very well, but she has no idea who you really are. You know that she doesn't. You can believe that you know your Mother very well, but you don't have any idea who she really is. She has all those fantasies in her mind that she never shared with anyone else. You have no idea what is inside her mind.

If you look at your own life and try to remember what you did when you were eleven or twelve years old, you will hardly remember more than 5 percent of your own life. Of course you will remember the most important things, like your own name, because you repeat these all the time. But sometimes you forget the name of your own children or your friends. That's because your life is made by dreams — many little dreams that are changing all the time. Dreams have a tendency to dissolve, and that is why we forget so easily.

Every human being has a personal dream of life, and that dream is completely different from anyone else's dream. We dream according to all the beliefs that we have, and we modify our dream according to the way we judge, according to the way we are victimized. That is why dreams are never the same for any two people. In a relationship, we can pretend to be the same, to think the same, to feel the same, to dream the same, but there is no way that can happen. There are two dreamers with two dreams. Every dreamer is going to dream in his own way. That is why we need to accept the differences that exist between two dreamers; we need to *respect* each other's dream.

We can have thousands of relationships at the same time, but every relationship is between two persons and no more than two. I have a relationship with each one of my friends, and it is just between two.

I have a relationship with each one of my children, and each relationship is completely different from the others. According to the way the two people dream, they create the direction of that dream we call *relationship*. Every relationship we have — with Mom, with Dad, with brothers, with sisters, with friends — is unique because we dream a small dream together.

Every relationship becomes a living being made by two dreamers.

Just as your body is made by cells, your dreams are made by emotions. There are two main sources of those emotions: One is fear, and all the emotions that come from fear; the other is love, and all the emotions that come from love. We experience both emotions, but the one that predominates in everyday people is fear. We can say that the normal kind of relationship in this world is based 95 percent on fear and 5 percent on love. Of course, this will change depending upon the people, but even if fear is 60 percent and love is 40 percent, still it is based on fear.

In order to understand these emotions, we can describe certain characteristics about love and fear that I call the "track of love" and "the track of fear." These two tracks are merely points of reference to see how we are living our life. These divisions are for the logical mind to understand and to try to have some control of the choices we make. Let's look at some of the characteristics of love and of fear.

Love has no obligations. Fear is full of obligations. In the track of fear, whatever we do is because we *have* to do it, and we expect other people to do something because they *have* to do it. We have the obligation, and as soon we *have* to, we resist it. The more resistance we have, the more we suffer. Sooner or later, we try to escape our obligations. On the other hand, love has no resistance. Whatever we do is because we *want* to do it. It becomes a pleasure; it's like a game, and we have fun with it.

Love has no expectations. Fear is full of expectations. With fear we do things because we expect that we have to, and we expect that others are going to do the same. That is why fear hurts and love doesn't hurt. We expect something and if it doesn't happen, we feel hurt — it isn't fair. We blame others for not fulfilling our expectations. When we love, we don't have expectations; we do it because we want to, and if other people do it or not, it's because they want to or not and it's nothing personal. When we don't expect something to happen, if nothing happens, it's not important. We don't feel hurt, because whatever happens is okay. That is why hardly anything hurts us when we are in love; we aren't *expecting* that our lover will do something, and we have no obligations.

Love is based on respect. Fear doesn't respect anything, including itself. If I feel sorry for you, it means I don't respect you. You cannot make your own choices. When I have to make the choices for you, at that point I don't respect you. If I don't respect you, then I try to control you. Most of the time when we tell our children how to live their lives, it's because we don't respect them. We feel sorry for them, and we try to do for them what they should do for themselves. When I don't respect myself, I feel sorry for myself, I feel I'm not good enough to make it in this world. How do you know when you don't respect yourself? When you say, "Poor me, I'm not strong enough, I'm not intelligent enough, I'm not beautiful enough, I cannot make it." Self-pity comes from disrespect.

Love is ruthless; it doesn't feel sorry for anyone, but it does have compassion. Fear is full of pity; it feels sorry for everyone. You feel sorry for me when you don't respect me, when you don't think I am strong enough to make it. On the other hand, love respects. I love you; I know you can make it. I know you are strong enough, intelligent enough, good enough that you can make your own choices. I don't have to make your choices for you. You can make it. If you fall, I can give you my hand, I can help you to stand up. I can say, "You can do it, go ahead." That is compassion, but it is not the same as feeling sorry. Compassion comes from respect and from love; feeling sorry comes from a lack of respect and from fear.

Love is completely responsible. Fear avoids responsibility, but this doesn't mean that it's not responsible. Trying to avoid responsibility is one of the biggest mistakes we make because every action has a consequence. Everything we think, everything we do, has a consequence. If we make a choice, we have an outcome or a reaction. If we don't make a choice, we have an outcome or a reaction. We are going to experience the consequence of our actions in one way or another.

That is why every human is completely responsible for his actions, even if he doesn't want to be. Other people can try to pay for your mistakes, but you will pay for your mistakes anyway, and then you pay double. When others try to be responsible for you, it only creates a bigger drama.

Love is always kind. Fear is always unkind. With fear we are full of obligations, full of expectations, with no respect, avoiding responsibility, and feeling sorry. How can we feel good when we are suffering from so much fear? We feel victimized by everything; we feel angry or sad or jealous or betrayed.

Anger is nothing but fear with a mask. Sadness is fear with a mask. Jealousy is fear with a mask. With all those emotions that come from fear and create suffering, we can only pretend to be kind. We are not kind because we don't feel good, we are not happy. If you are in the track of love, you have no obligations, no expectations. You don't feel sorry for yourself or for your partner. Everything is going well for you, and that is why that smile is always on your face. You

THE TRACK OF LOVE, THE TRACK OF FEAR

are feeling good about yourself, and because you are
happy, you are kind. Love is always kind, and that
kindness makes you generous and opens all the doors.
Love is generous. Fear is selfish; it is only about me.
Selfishness closes all the doors.

Love is unconditional. Fear is full of conditions.
In the track of fear, I love you *if* you let me control
you, *if* you are good to me, *if* you fit into the image I
make for you. I create an image of the way you should
be, and because you are not and never will be the
image, I judge you because of that, and find you guilty.
Many times I even feel ashamed of you because you
are not what I want you to be. If you don't fit that
image I create, you embarrass me, you annoy me, I
have no patience at all with you. I am just pretending
kindness. In the track of love, there is no *if*; there are
no conditions. I love you for no reason, with no justification. I love you the way you are, and you are free to
be the way you are. If I don't like the way you are, then
I'd better be with someone who is the way I like her
to be. We don't have the right to change anyone else,

and no one else has the right to change us. If we are going to change, it is because we want to change, because we don't want to suffer any longer.

Most people live their entire lives in the track of fear. They are in a relationship because they feel they *have* to be. They are in a relationship where they have all those expectations about their partner and about themselves. All that drama and suffering is because we are using the channels of communication that existed before we were born. People judge and are victimized, they gossip about each other, they gossip with their friends, they gossip in a bar. They make their family members hate each other. They accumulate emotional poison, and they send it to their children. "Look at your father, what he did to me. Don't be like your father. All men are like this; all women are like that." This is what we do with the people we love so much — with our own children, with our own friends, with our partners.

In the track of fear we have so many conditions, expectations, and obligations that we create a lot of rules just to protect ourselves against emotional pain, when the truth is that there shouldn't be any rules. These rules affect the quality of the channels of communication between us, because when we are afraid, we lie. If you have the expectation that I have to be a certain way, then I feel the obligation to be that way. The truth is I am not what you want me to be. When I am honest and I am what I am, you are already hurt, you are mad. Then I lie to you, because I am afraid of your judgment. I am afraid you are going to blame me, find me guilty, and punish me. And every time you remember, you punish me again and again and again for the same mistake.

In the track of love, there is justice. If you make a mistake, you pay only once for that mistake, and if you truly love yourself, you learn from that mistake. In the track of fear, there is no justice. You make yourself pay a thousand times for the same mistake. You make your partner or your friend pay a thousand times for the same mistake. This creates a sense of injustice and opens many emotional wounds. Then, of course, you set yourself up to fail. Humans have dramas for everything, even for something so simple and so little. We see these dramas in normal relationships in hell because couples are in the track of fear.

In every relationship there are two halves of that relationship. One half is you, and the other half is your son, your daughter, your father, your mother, your friends, your partner. Of those halves, you are only responsible for your half; you are not responsible for the other half. It doesn't matter how close you think you are, or how strongly you think you love, there is no way you can be responsible for what is inside another person's head. You can never know what that person feels, what that person believes, all the assumptions she makes. You don't know anything about that person. That is the truth, but what do we do? We try to be responsible for the other half, and that is why relationships in hell are based on fear, drama, and the war of control.

If we are in a war of control, it is because we have no respect. The truth is that we don't love. It is self-ishness, not love; it is just to have the little doses that make us feel good. When we have no respect there is a war of control because each person feels responsible for the other. I have to control you because I don't respect you. I have to be responsible for you, because whatever happens to you is going to hurt me, and I want to avoid pain. Then, if I see that you are not being responsible, I am going to knock you all the time to try to make you be responsible, but "responsible" from my personal point of view. It doesn't mean that I am right.

This is what happens when we come from the track of fear. Because there is no respect, I act as though you are not good enough or intelligent enough to see what is good or not good for you. I make the assumption that you are not strong enough to go into certain situations and take care of yourself. I have to take control and say, "Let me do it for you," or "Don't do that." I try to suppress your half of the relationship and take control of the whole thing.

If I take control of our whole relationship, where is your part? It doesn't work.

With the other half we can share, we can enjoy, we can create the most wonderful dream together. But the other half always has its own dream, its own will, and we can never control that dream no matter how hard we try. Then we have a choice: We can create a conflict and a war of control, or we can become a playmate and a team player. Playmates and team players play together, but not against each other.

If you are playing tennis, you have a partner, you are a team, and you never go against each other — never. Even if you both play tennis differently, you have the same goal: to have fun together, to play together, to be playmates. If you have a partner who wants to control your game, and she says, "No, don't play like that; play like this. No, you are doing it wrong," you are not going to have any fun. Eventually, you won't want to play with that partner anymore. Instead of being a team, your partner wants to control how you play. And without the concept of a team, you are always going to have conflict. If you see your partnership, your romantic relationship, as a team, everything will start to improve. In a relationship, as in a game, it's not about winning or losing. You are playing because you want to have fun.

In the track of love, you are giving more than taking. And of course, you love yourself so much that you don't allow selfish people to take advantage of you. You are not going for revenge, but you are clear in your communication. You can say, "I don't like it when you try to take advantage of me, when you disrespect me, when you are unkind to me. I don't need someone to abuse me verbally, emotionally, physically. I don't need to hear you cursing all the time. It's not that I am better than you; it's because I love beauty. I love to laugh; I love to have fun; I love to love. It's not that I am selfish, I just don't need a big victim near me. It doesn't mean that I don't love you, but I cannot take responsibility for your dream. If you are in a relationship with me, it will be so hard for your Parasite, because I will not react to your garbage at all." This is not selfishness; this is self-love. Selfishness, control, and fear will break almost any relationship. Generosity, freedom, and love will create the most beautiful relationship: an ongoing romance.

To master a relationship is all about you. The first step is to become aware, to know that everyone dreams his own dream. Once you know this, you can be responsible for your half of the relationship, which is you. If you know that you are only responsible for half of the relationship, you can easily control your half. It is not up to us to control the other half. If we respect, we know that our partner, or friend, or son, or mother, is completely responsible for his or her own half. If we respect the other half, there is always going to be peace in that relationship. There is no war.

Next, if you know what is love and what is fear, you become aware of the way you communicate your dream to others. The quality of your communication depends upon the choices you make in each moment, whether you tune your emotional body to love or to fear. If you catch yourself in the track of fear, just by having that awareness, you can shift your attention into the track of love. Just by seeing where you are, just by changing your attention, everything around you will change.

Finally, if you are aware that no one else can make you happy, and that happiness is the result of love coming out of you, this becomes the greatest mastery of the Toltecs, the Mastery of Love.

We can talk about love and write a thousand books about it, but love will be completely different for each of us because we have to experience love. Love is not about concepts; love is about action. Love in action can only produce happiness. Fear in action can only produce suffering.

The only way to master love is to practice love. You don't need to justify your love, you don't need to explain your love; you just need to practice your love. Practice creates the master.

5

The Perfect Relationship

IMAGINE A PERFECT RELATIONSHIP. YOU ARE ALWAYS intensely happy with your partner because you live with the perfect woman or man for you. How would you describe your life with this person?

Well, the way you relate with this person will be exactly the way you relate with a dog. A dog is a dog. It doesn't matter what you do, it's going to be a dog.

You are not going to change a dog for a cat or a dog for a horse; it is what it is.

Just accepting this fact in your relations with other humans is very important. You cannot change other people. You love them the way they are or you don't. You accept them the way they are or you don't. To try to change them to fit what you want them to be is like trying to change a dog for a cat, or a cat for a horse. That is a fact. They are what they are; you are what you are. You dance or you don't dance. You need to be completely honest with yourself — to say what you want, and see if you are willing to dance or not. You must understand this point, because it is very important. When you truly understand, you are likely to see what is true about others, and not just what you want to see.

If you own a dog or a cat, think about how you relate to your pet. Let's consider your relationship with a dog, for example. The animal knows how to have a perfect relationship with you. When your dog does something wrong, what do you do with your dog? A dog doesn't care what you do; it just loves you.

It doesn't have any expectations. Isn't that wonderful? But what about your girlfriend, your boyfriend, your husband, or your wife? They have so many expectations, and they are changing all the time.

The dog is responsible for its half of the relationship with you. One half of the relationship is completely normal — the dog's half. When you come home, it barks at you, it wags his tail, it pants because it is so happy to see you. It does its part very well, and you know it is the perfect dog. Your part is almost perfect also. You handle your responsibility; you feed your dog; you take care of your dog; you play with your dog. You love your dog unconditionally; you will do almost anything for your dog. You do your part perfectly, and your dog does its part perfectly.

Most people can easily imagine this kind of relationship with their dog, but why not with a woman or with a man? Do you know any woman or any man who is not perfect? The dog is a dog, and that is okay with you. You don't need to be responsible for your dog, to make it be a dog. The dog doesn't try to make you be a good human, a good master. Then why can't we allow a woman to be a woman or a man to be a man and love that human just the way he or she is without trying to change that person?

Perhaps you are thinking, "But what if I am not with the right woman or the right man?" That is a very important question. Of course, you have to choose the right woman or the right man. And what is the right woman, the right man? Someone who wants to go in the same direction as you do, someone who is compatible with your views and your values — emotionally, physically, economically, spiritually.

How do you know if your partner is right for you? Let's imagine that you are a man and a woman is going to choose you. If there are a hundred women looking for a man, and each will look at you as a possibility, for how many of these women will you be the right man? The answer is: *You don't know.* That is why you need to explore and take the risk. But I can tell you that the right woman for you is the woman you love just the way she is, the woman you don't have the need to change at all. That's the right woman for you. You are lucky if you find the right woman for you and at the same time you are the right man for her.

You are going to be the right man for her if she loves you just the way you are and she doesn't want to change you. She doesn't have to be responsible for you; she can trust that you are going to be what you claim you are, what you project you are. She can be as honest as possible and project to you what she is. She will not come to you pretending to be something that you later discover she is not. The one who loves you, *loves you just the way you are.* Because if someone wants to change you, it means you are not what that person wants. Then why is she with you?

You know, it's easy to love your dog because your dog doesn't have opinions about you. The dog loves you unconditionally. This is important. Then if your partner loves you just the way you are, it is just like the dog loves you. You can be yourself with your partner; you can be a man, or you can be a woman, just the way the dog can be a dog with you.

When you meet a person, just after the "hello," she starts sending you information right away. She can hardly wait to share her dream with you. She opens herself even if she doesn't know she is doing it. It is so easy for you to see every person just the way she is. You don't need to lie to yourself. You can see what it is you are buying, and you either want it or you don't. But you cannot blame the other person for being a dog, or a cat, or a horse. If you want a dog, then why are you getting a cat? If you want a cat, why would you get a horse or a chicken?

You know the kind of man or woman that you want? The one who makes your heart sing, the one who is aligned with the way you are, the one who loves you just as you are. Why set yourself up for something else? Why not get what you want? Why pretend to make someone fit what she is not? It doesn't mean you don't love her. It means you make a choice and say yes or no, because you love yourself also. You make a choice, and you are responsible for your choices. Then if the choices are not working well, you do not blame yourself. You simply make another choice.

But let's imagine that you get a dog and you love cats. You want your dog to behave like a cat, and you try to change the dog because it never says, "Meow." What are you doing with a dog? Get a cat! This is the only way to begin a great relationship. First you have to know what you want, how you want it, when you want it. You have to know exactly what the needs of your body are, what the needs of your mind are, and what fits well with you.

There are millions of men and women, and each one is unique. Some will make a good match for you, and some won't make a good match at all. You can love everyone; but to deal with a person on an every-day basis, you will need someone more closely aligned to you. That person doesn't need to be exactly like you; the two of you only need to be like a key in the lock — a match that works.

You need to be honest with yourself, and honest with everyone else. Project what you feel you really are, and don't pretend to be what you are not. It's as if you are in a market: You are going to sell yourself, and you are also going to buy. In order to buy, you want to see the quality of what you are going to get. But in order to sell, you need to show others what you are. It isn't about being better or worse than someone else; it's about being what you are.

If you see what you want, why not take a risk? But if you see it is not what you want, you know you are going to pay for it. Don't go around crying, "My lover abuses me," when it was so clear for you to see. Don't lie to yourself. Don't invent in people what is not there. This is the message. If you know what you want, you will find it is just like your relationship with your dog, but better.

See what is in front of you; don't be blind or pretend to see what is not there. Don't deny what you see just to get the merchandise when that merchandise will not fit your needs. When you buy something you don't need, it ends up in the garage. It's the same in a relationship. Of course, it can take years for us to learn this painful lesson, but this is a good beginning. If you make a good beginning, the rest is going to be easier because you can be yourself.

Perhaps you already have a certain amount of time invested in a relationship. If you choose to keep going, you can still have a new beginning by accepting and loving your partner just as she is. But first you will need to take a step back. You have to accept yourself and love yourself just the way you are. Only by loving and accepting yourself the way you are can you truly be and express what you are. You are what you are, and that is all you are. You don't need to pretend to be something else. When you pretend to be what you are not, you are always going to fail.

Once you accept yourself just the way you are, the next step is to accept your partner. If you decide to be with a person, don't try to change anything about her. Just like your dog or your cat, let her be who she is. She has the right to be who she is; she has a right to be free. When you inhibit your partner's freedom, you inhibit your own because you have to be there to see what your partner is doing or not doing. And if you love yourself so much, you are never going to give up your personal freedom.

Can you see the possibilities a relationship offers? Explore the possibilities. Be yourself. Find a person who matches with you. Take the risk, but be honest. If it works, keep going. If it doesn't work, then do yourself and your partner a favor: Walk away; let her go. Don't be selfish. Give your partner the opportunity to find what she really wants, and at the same time give yourself the opportunity. If it's not going to work, it is better to look in a different direction. If you cannot love your partner the way she is, someone else can love her just as she is. Don't waste your time, and don't waste your partner's time. This is respect.

If you are the provider and your partner is the addict, and this is not what you want, perhaps you would be happier with someone else. But if you decide to be in that relationship, do your best. Do your best because you are the one who is going to reap the reward. If you can love your partner the way she is, if you can open your heart completely to your partner, you can reach heaven through your love.

If you already have a cat and you want a dog, what

can you do? You can start practicing from this point forward. You have to aim for a new beginning by cutting your ties with the past and starting all over again. You don't have to have attachments to the past. All of us can change, and it can be for better. This is a new beginning for you to forgive whatever happened between you and your partner. Let it go because it was nothing but personal importance. It was nothing but misunderstanding. It was nothing but someone being hurt and trying to get even. It's not worth whatever happened in the past to spoil the possibility that you can reach heaven in a relationship. Have the courage to go for it 100 percent or let it go. Let go of the past and begin every day at a higher level of love. This will keep the fire alive and make your love grow even more.

Of course, you need to look at what it means to have the good moments and the bad moments. If being emotionally or physically abused is a bad moment, I don't know if a couple should keep going. If a bad moment is that someone loses her job, something is wrong at work, or someone has an accident, that is another kind of bad moment. If the bad moments come from fear, if they come from a lack of respect, humiliation, or hatred, I don't know how many bad moments a couple can survive.

In the relationship with your dog, you can have a bad moment. For whatever reason, it happens — an accident, a bad day at work, or whatever. You come home, and the dog is there barking at you, tail wagging, looking for your attention. You don't feel like playing with the dog, but the dog is there. The dog will not feel hurt that you don't want to play, because it doesn't take it personally. Once the dog celebrates your arrival and finds out you don't want to play, the dog goes and plays by itself. The dog doesn't stay there and insist that you be happy.

Sometimes you can feel more support from your dog than from a partner who wants to make you happy. If you don't feel like being happy, and you only want to be quiet, it's nothing personal. It has nothing to do with your partner. Perhaps you have a problem and you need to be quiet. But that silence can cause your partner to make a lot of assumptions: "What did I do now? It's because of me." It has nothing to do with your partner; it's nothing personal. Left alone, the tension will go away, and you will return to happiness.

That is why the key in the lock has to be a match, because if one of you has a bad moment or an emotional crisis, your agreement is to allow each other to be what you are. Then the relationship is another story; it's another way of being, and the whole thing can be very beautiful.

Relationship is an art. The dream that two create is more difficult to master than one. To keep the two of you happy, you have to keep your half perfect. You are responsible for your half, and your half has a certain amount of garbage. Your garbage is your garbage. The one who has to deal with that garbage is you, not your partner. If your partner tries to clean your garbage, she is going to end up with a broken nose. We have to learn not to put our nose where no one wants it.

And it's the same with your partner's half. Your partner has a certain amount of garbage. Knowing your partner has garbage, you allow her to deal with her own garbage. You are going to love her and accept her with all of her garbage. You are going to respect her garbage. You are not in the relationship to clean your partner's garbage; she is going to clean her own.

Even if your partner asks for your help, you have the choice to say no. Saying no doesn't mean you don't love or accept your partner; it means you are not able or you don't want to play that game. For example, if your partner gets angry, you can say, "You have the right to be mad, but I don't have to be mad because you are mad. I didn't do anything to cause your anger." You don't have to accept your partner's anger at all, but you can allow her to be angry. There is no need to argue; just allow her to be what she is, allow her to heal without intervening. And you can also agree not to interfere with your own healing process.

Let's say that you are a man and you are happy, and for whatever reason, your partner cannot be happy. She has personal problems; she is dealing with her garbage, and she is unhappy. Because you love her you will support her, but supporting her doesn't mean you are going to be unhappy because she's unhappy. This is not support at all. If she's unhappy and you get unhappy, both of you sink. If you are happy, your happiness can bring her happiness back.

In the same way, if you are down and she is happy, her happiness is your support. For your own sake, let her be happy; don't even try to take her happiness away. Whatever happens in your work, don't come home and throw your poison at her. Be silent and let her know it's nothing personal, you're just dealing with yourself. You can say, "Keep being happy, keep playing, and I will join you when I can enjoy your happiness. Right now, I need to be alone."

If you understand the concept of the wounded mind, you will understand the reason why romantic relationships are so difficult. The emotional body is sick. It has wounds; it has poison. If we are not aware that we are sick or that our partner is sick, we become selfish. The wounds hurt, and we have to protect our wounds, even from the one we love. But if we have the awareness, we can have different agreements. When we are aware that our partner has emotional wounds, and we love our partner, we certainly don't want to touch her wounds. We don't want to push her to heal her wounds, and we don't want her to push us to heal our wounds.

Take the risk and take the responsibility to make a new agreement with your partner — not an agreement that you read in a book, but an agreement that works for you. If it doesn't work, change that agreement and create a new one. Use your imagination to explore new possibilities, to create new agreements based on respect and love. Communication through respect and love is the whole key to keeping the love alive and never getting bored in your relationship. It's about finding your voice and stating your needs. It's about trusting yourself and trusting your partner.

What you are going to share with your partner is not the garbage, but your love, your romance, your understanding. The goal is for the two of you to be happier and happier, and that calls for more and more love. You are the perfect man or woman, and your partner is the perfect human, just as the dog is the perfect dog. If you treat your partner with love and respect, who is going to get the benefit? No one else but you.

Heal your half, and you are going to be happy. If you can heal that part of you, then you are going to be ready for a relationship without fear, without need. But remember, you can only heal your half. If you are in a relationship and you work with your half, and your partner works with the other half, you will see how quickly progress is made. Love is what makes you happy, and if you become the servant of love, and your partner becomes the servant of love, you can just imagine all the possibilities. The day will come when you can be with your partner with no guilt and no blame, no anger and no sadness. That day will be wonderful when you can be completely open, only to share, only to serve, only to give your love.

Once you decide to be a couple, you are there to serve the one you love, the one you choose. You are there to serve your love to your lover, to be each other's servant. In every kiss, in every touch, you feel you are each there to please the one you love, without expecting anything back. More than sex, it's about being together. The sex becomes wonderful also, but it's completely different. Sex becomes a communion; sex becomes a complete surrendering, a dance, an art, a supreme expression of beauty.

You can make an agreement that says, "I like you; you are wonderful and you make me feel so good. I'll bring the flowers, you bring the soft music. We'll dance, and we'll both go to the clouds." It's beautiful, it's wonderful, it's romantic. It's no longer a war of control; it's about service. But you can only do that when the love you have for yourself is very strong.

6

The Magical Kitchen

IMAGINE THAT YOU HAVE A MAGICAL KITCHEN IN your home. In that magical kitchen, you can have any food you want from any place in the world in any quantity. You never worry about what to eat; whatever you wish for, you can have at your table. You are very generous with your food; you give your food unconditionally to others, not because you want something in return from them. Whoever comes to your home, you feed just for the pleasure of sharing your food, and your house is always full of people who come to eat the food from your magical kitchen.

Then one day someone knocks at your door, and it's a person with a pizza. You open the door, and the person looks at you and says, "Hey, do you see this pizza? I'll give you this pizza if you let me control your life, if you just do whatever I want you to do. You are never going to starve because I can bring pizza every day. You just have to be good to me."

Can you imagine your reaction? In your kitchen you can have the same pizza — even better. Yet this person comes to you and offers you food, *if* you just do whatever he wants you to do. You are going to laugh and say, "No, thank you! I don't need your food; I have plenty of food. You can come into my house and eat whatever you want, and you don't have to do anything. Don't believe I'm going to do whatever you want me to do. No one will manipulate me with food."

Now imagine exactly the opposite. Several weeks

have gone by, and you haven't eaten. You are starving, and you have no money in your pocket to buy food. The person comes with the pizza and says, "Hey, there's food here. You can have this food if you just do what I want you to do." You can smell the food, and you are starving. You decide to accept the food and do whatever that person asks of you. You eat some food, and he says, "If you want more, you can have more, but you have to keep doing what I want you to do."

You have food today, but tomorrow you may not have food, so you agree to do whatever you can for food. You can become a slave because of food, because you need food, because you don't have it. Then after a certain time you have doubts. You say, "What am I going to do without my pizza? I cannot live without my pizza. What if my partner decides to give the pizza to someone else — *my* pizza?"

Now imagine that instead of food, we are talking about love. You have an abundance of love in your heart. You have love not just for yourself, but for the whole world. You love so much that you don't need anyone's love. You share your love without condition; you don't love *if*. You are a millionaire in love, and someone knocks on your door and says, "Hey, I have love for you here. You can have my love, if you just do whatever I want you to do."

When you are full of love, what is going to be your reaction? You will laugh and say, "Thank you, but I don't need your love. I have the same love here in my heart, even bigger and better, and I share my love without condition."

But what is going to happen if you are starving for love, if you don't have that love in your heart, and someone comes and says, "You want a little love? You can have my love if you just do what I want you to do." If you are starving for love, and you taste that love, you are going to do whatever you can for that love. You can even be so needy that you give your whole soul just for a little attention.

Your heart is like that magical kitchen. If you open your heart, you already have all the love you need. There's no need to go around the world begging for love: "Please, someone love me. I'm so lonely, I'm not good enough for love; I need someone to love me, to prove that I'm worthy of love." We have love right here inside us, but we don't see this love.

Can you see the drama humans create when they believe they don't have love? They are starving for love, and when they taste a little love from someone else, that creates a big need. They become needy and obsessive about that love. Then comes the big drama: "What am I going to do if he leaves me?" "How can I live without her?" They cannot live without the provider, the one who provides them with the every-day doses. And for that little piece of love, because they are starving, they allow other people to control their lives. They let others tell them what to do, what not to do, how to dress, how not to dress, how to behave, how not to behave, what to believe, what not to believe. "I love you if you behave in this way. I love you if you let me control your life. I love you only if you are good to me. If not, then forget it."

The problem with humans is that they don't know they have a magical kitchen in their heart. All this suffering begins because long ago we closed our hearts and we no longer feel the love that is there. At some point in our life, we became afraid to love, because we believed love isn't fair. Love hurts. We tried to be good enough for someone else, we tried to be accepted by someone else, and we failed. We have already had two or three lovers and a few broken hearts. To love again is to risk too much.

Of course, we have so many self-judgments that we can't possibly have any self-love. And if there's no love for ourselves, how can we even pretend that we share love with someone else?

When we go into a relationship, we become selfish because we are needy. It's all about me. We are so self-ish that we want the person with whom we are sharing our life to be as needy as we are. We want "someone who needs me" in order to justify our existence, in order to feel that we have a reason to be alive. We think we are searching for love, but we are searching for "someone who needs me," someone we can control and manipulate.

There is a war of control in human relationships because we were domesticated to compete for the control of the attention. What we call love — someone who needs me, someone who cares about me — isn't love; it is selfishness. How can that work? Selfishness doesn't work because there is no love there. Both people are starving for love. In the sex they have, they taste a little love and it becomes addictive because they are starving for love. But then all the judgments are there. All the fear. All the blame. All the drama.

Then we search for advice on love and sex. So many books are written about it, and just about all these books could be called "How to Be Sexually Selfish." The intent is good, but where is love? They are not about learning to love; there is nothing to learn about love. Everything is already there in our genes, in our nature. We don't have to learn anything, except what we invent in this world of illusion. We search for love outside ourselves when love is all around us. Love is everywhere, but we don't have the eyes to see. Our emotional body is no longer tuned to love.

We are so afraid to love because it isn't safe to love. The fear of rejection frightens us. We have to pretend to be what we are not; we try to be accepted by our partner when we don't accept ourselves. But the problem is not that our partner rejects us. The problem is that we reject ourselves, because we are not good enough, because that is what we *believe*.

Self-rejection is the main problem. You are never going to be good enough for yourself when the idea of perfection is completely wrong. It's a false concept; it's not even real. But you believe it. Not being perfect, you reject yourself, and the level of self-rejection depends upon how strong the adults were in breaking your integrity.

After domestication, it is no longer about being good enough for anyone else. You are no longer good enough for yourself, because the big Judge is always there, reminding you that you are not perfect. As I said before, you can never forgive yourself for not being what you wish to be, and that's the real problem. If you can change that, you take care of your half of the relationship. The other half is not your problem.

If you tell someone you love him, and that person says, "Well, I don't love you," is that a reason for you to suffer? Just because someone rejects you doesn't mean you have to reject yourself. If one person doesn't love you, someone else will love you. There is always someone else. And it's better to be with someone who *wants* to be with you than to be with someone who *has* to be with you.

You have to focus on the most wonderful relationship you can have: the relationship with yourself. It is not about being selfish; it is about self-love. These are not the same. You are selfish with yourself because there is no love there. You need to love yourself, and the love will grow more and more. Then, when you enter a relationship, you don't go into it because you need to be loved. It becomes a choice. You can choose someone if you want to, and you can see who he really is. When you don't need his love, you don't have to lie to yourself.

You are complete. When love is coming out of you, you are not searching for love because you are afraid to be alone. When you have all that love for yourself, you can be alone and there's no problem. You are happy to be alone, and to share is also fun.

If I like you and we go out together, is it because we want to be jealous, because I have a need to control you, or you have a need to control me? If it's going to be that way, it isn't fun. If I'm going to be criticized or judged, if I am going to feel bad, then no thank you. If I am going to suffer, maybe it's better to be alone. Do people get together to have a drama, to possess each other, to punish each other, to be saved? Is that really why they get together? Of course, we have all those choices. But what are we really looking for?

When we are children — five, six, or seven years old — we are attracted to other children because we want to play, we want to have fun. We don't spend time with another child because we want to fight or have a big drama. That can happen, but it's going to be short-lived. We just keep playing and playing. When we get bored, we change the game, we change the rules, but we are exploring all the time.

If you go into a partnership to have drama, because you want to be jealous, because you want to be possessive, because you want to control your partner's life, you are not looking for fun, you are looking for pain, and that is what you are going to find. If you go into a relationship with selfishness, expecting that your partner is going to make you happy, it will not happen. And it's not that person's fault; it's your own.

When we go into a relationship of any kind, it is because we want to share, we want to enjoy, we want to have fun, we don't want to be bored. If we look for a partner, it is because we want to play, we want to be happy and enjoy what we are. We don't choose a partner just to give that person we claim to love all our garbage, to put all our jealousy, all our anger, all our selfishness onto that person. How can someone tell you, "I love you," and then mistreat you and abuse you, humiliate you, and disrespect you? That person may claim to love you, but is it really love? If we love, we want the best for those we love. Why put our garbage onto our own children? Why abuse them because we are full of fear and emotional poison? Why blame our parents for our own garbage?

People learn to become selfish and to close their hearts so tightly. They are starving for love, not knowing that the heart is a magical kitchen. *Your* heart is a magical kitchen. Open your heart. Open your magical kitchen, and refuse to walk around the world begging for love. In your heart is all the love you need. Your heart can create any amount of love, not just for yourself, but for the whole world. You can give your love with no conditions; you can be generous with your love because you have a magical kitchen in your heart. Then all those starving people who believe the heart is closed will always want to be near you for your love.

What makes you happy is love coming out of you. And if you are generous with your love, everyone is going to love you. You are never going to be alone if you are generous. If you are selfish, you are always going to be alone, and there is no one to blame but you. Your generosity will open all the doors, not your selfishness.

Selfishness comes from poverty in the heart, from the belief that love is not abundant. We become selfish when we believe that maybe tomorrow we won't have any pizza. But when we know that our heart is a magical kitchen, we are always generous, and our love is completely unconditional.

7

The Dream Master

EVERY RELATIONSHIP IN YOUR LIFE CAN BE HEALED, every relationship can be wonderful, but it's always going to begin with you. You need to have the courage to use the truth, to talk to yourself with the truth, to be completely honest with yourself. Perhaps you don't have to be honest with the whole world, but you can be honest with yourself. Perhaps you cannot control what is going to happen around you, but you can control your own reactions. Those reactions are going to guide the dream of your life, your personal dream. It's your reactions that make you so unhappy or make you so happy.

Your reactions are the key to having a wonderful life. If you can learn to control your own reactions, then you can change your routines, and you can change your life.

You are responsible for the consequences of whatever you do, think, say, and feel. Perhaps it's hard for you to see what actions caused the consequence — what emotions, what thoughts — but you can see the consequence because you are suffering the consequence or enjoying the consequence. You control your personal dream by making choices. You have to see if you like the consequence of your choices or not. If it's a consequence you enjoy, then keep doing what you are doing. Perfect. But if you don't like what is happening in your life, if you aren't enjoying your dream, then try to find out what is causing the consequences you don't like. This is the way to transform your dream.

Your life is the manifestation of your personal dream. If you can transform the program of your personal dream, you can become a dream master. A dream master creates a masterpiece of life. But to master the dream is a big challenge because humans become slaves of their own dreams. The way we learn to dream is a setup. With all the beliefs we have that nothing is possible, it's hard to escape the Dream of Fear. In order to awake from the Dream, you need to master the Dream.

That is why the Toltecs created the Mastery of Transformation, to break free of the old Dream and to create a new dream where everything is possible, including escaping from the Dream. In the Mastery of Transformation, the Toltecs divide people into Dreamers and Stalkers. The Dreamers know that the dream is an illusion, and they play in that world of illusion, knowing it's an illusion. The Stalkers are like a tiger or a jaguar, stalking every action and reaction.

You have to stalk your own reactions; you have to work with yourself every moment. It takes a lot of time and courage, because it's easier to take things personally and react the way you always react. And that leads you to a lot of mistakes, to a lot of suffering and pain, because your reactions only generate more emotional poison and increase the drama.

If you can control your reactions, you will find that soon you are going to *see*, meaning to perceive things as they really are. The mind normally perceives things as they are, but because of all the programming, all the beliefs we have, we make interpretations of what we perceive, of what we hear, and mainly of what we see.

There's a big difference between seeing the way people see in the Dream, and seeing without judgment, as it is. The difference is in the way your emotional body reacts to what you perceive. For example, if you are walking on the street and someone who doesn't know you says, "You are so stupid" and walks away, you can perceive and react to that in many ways. You can accept what that person said and think, "Yes, I must be stupid." You can get mad, or feel humiliated, or simply ignore it.

The truth is that this person is dealing with his own emotional poison, and he said that to you because you were the first person to cross his path. It has nothing to do with you. There is nothing personal there. If you can see that truth, the way it is, you don't react.

You can say, "Look at that person who is suffering so much," but you don't take it personally. This is just one example, but it applies to almost everything that happens in every moment. We have a little ego that takes everything personally, that makes us overreact. We don't see what is really happening because we react right away and make it part of our dream.

Your reaction comes from a belief that is deep inside you. The way you react has been repeated thousands of times, and it becomes a routine for you. You are conditioned to be a certain way. And that is the challenge: to change your normal reactions, to change your routine, to take a risk and make different choices. If the consequence is not what you want, change it again and again until you finally get the result you want.

I have said that we never chose to have the Parasite, which is the Judge, the Victim, and the Belief System. If we know we didn't have a choice, and we have the awareness that it's nothing but a dream, we recover something very important that we lost — something that religions call "free will." Religions say that when humans were created, God gave us free will. This is true, but the Dream took it away from us and kept it, because the Dream controls the will of most humans.

There are people who say, "I want to change, I *really* want to change. There is no reason for me to be so poor. I am intelligent. I deserve to live a good life, to earn much more money than I earn." They know this, but that is what their mind is telling them. What do these people do? They go and turn the television on and spend hours and hours watching it. Then how strong is their will?

Once we have awareness, we have a choice. If we could have that awareness all the time, we could change our routines, change our reactions, and change our entire life. Once we have the awareness, we recover free will. When we recover free will, in any moment we can choose to remember who we are. Then, if we forget, we can choose again, *if* we have the awareness. But if we don't have the awareness, we have no choice.

Becoming aware is about being responsible for your own life. You are not responsible for what is happening in the world. You are responsible for yourself. You didn't make the world the way it is; the world was already the way it is before you were born. You didn't come here with a great mission to save the world, to change society, but surely you come with a big mission, an important mission. The real mission you have in life is to make yourself happy, and in order to be happy, you have to look at what you believe, the way you judge yourself, the way you victimize yourself.

Be completely honest about your happiness. Don't project a false sense of happiness by telling everyone, "Look at me. I'm a success in life, I have everything I want, I am so happy," when you don't like yourself.

Everything is there for us, but first we need to have the courage to open our eyes, to use the truth, and to see what really is. Humans are so blind, and they are blind because they don't want to see. Let's look at an example.

A young woman meets a man and she feels a strong attraction for him right away. Her hormones go all the way up, and she just wants the man. All her girlfriends can see what this man is. He's on drugs, he's not working, he's got all those traits that make a woman suffer so much. But she sees him, and what does she see? She only sees what she wants to see. She sees that he's tall, he's handsome, he's strong, he's charming. She creates an image of the man and tries to deny what she doesn't want to see. She lies to herself. She really wants to believe the relationship will work. The girlfriends say, "But he's on drugs, he's an alcoholic, he's not working." She says, "Yes, but my love is going to change him."

Of course, her mother hates the man, and the father does, too. Her parents are worried about her because they can see where she is going. They say, "This is not a good man for you." The young woman says, "You are telling me what to do." She goes against Mom and against Dad to follow her hormones, and she lies to herself trying to justify her choices. "It's my life, and I'm going to do whatever I want to do."

Months later, the relationship brings her back to reality. The truth starts coming out, and she blames the man for what she didn't want to see before. There's no respect, there's a lot of abuse, but now her pride is more important. How can she go back home when Mom and Dad were right? That will only give them satisfaction. How long will it take for this woman to learn the lesson? How much does she love herself? What is the limit of her self-abuse?

All that suffering occurs because we don't want to see, when it is so clear before our eyes. Even when we meet someone and he tries to pretend to be the best he can, even with that false mask, he cannot avoid presenting the lack of love, the lack of respect he has. But we don't want to see it and we don't want to hear.

That is why an ancient prophet once said, "There is no worse blind man than the one who doesn't want to see. There is no worse deaf man than the one who doesn't want to hear. And there is no worse madman than the one who doesn't want to understand."

We are so blind, we really are, and we pay for that. But if we open our eyes and see life as it is, we can avoid a lot of emotional pain. It doesn't mean we don't take a risk. We are alive and we need to take risks, and if we fail, so what? Who cares? It doesn't matter. We learn and we move on without judgment.

We don't need to judge; we don't need to blame or feel guilt. We just need to accept our truth and intend a new beginning. If we can see ourselves the way we are, that is the first step toward self-acceptance — toward stopping the self-rejection. Once we are able to accept ourselves just the way we are, everything can start changing from that point forward.

Everyone has a price, and Life respects that price. But that price is not measured in dollars or in gold; it is measured in love. More than that, it is measured in self-love. How much you love yourself — that is your price — and Life respects the price. When you love yourself, your price is very high, which means your tolerance for self-abuse is very low. It's very low because you respect yourself. You like yourself the way you are, and this makes your price higher. If you don't like things about yourself, the price is a little lower.

Sometimes the self-judgment is so strong that people need to be numb just to be with themselves. If you don't like a person, you can walk away from that person. If you don't like a group of people, you can walk away from those people. But if you don't like yourself, it doesn't matter where you go, you are right there. To avoid being with yourself, you need to take something to numb you, to take your mind away from yourself. Perhaps some alcohol is going to help. Perhaps some drugs will help. Perhaps eating — just eat, eat, eat. The self-abuse can get much worse. There are people who really feel self-hatred. They are self-destructive, killing themselves little by little, because they don't have the courage to kill themselves fast.

If you observe self-destructive people, you will see they attract people just like them. What do we do if we don't like ourselves? We try to get numb with alcohol to forget our suffering. That's the excuse we use. Where are we going to get alcohol? We go to a bar to drink, and guess who's going to be there? People just like us, who try to avoid themselves also, who also try to get numb. We get numb together, we start talking about our suffering, and we understand each other very well. We even start to enjoy it. We understand each other perfectly because we vibrate in the same frequency. We are both being self-destructive. Then I hurt you, you hurt me — a perfect relationship in hell.

What happens when you change? For whatever reason, you no longer need the alcohol. It's okay now to be with yourself, and you really enjoy it. You no longer drink, but you have the same friends, and everyone's drinking. They get numb, they start getting happier, but you can clearly see that their happiness is not real. What they call happiness is a rebellion against their own emotional pain. In that "happiness" they are so hurt that they have fun hurting other people and hurting themselves.

You no longer fit in, and of course they resent you because you are no longer like them. "Hey, you are rejecting me because you no longer drink with me, because you don't get high with me." Now you have to make a choice: You can step back, or you can go to another level of frequency and meet people who finally accept themselves like you do. You find there is another realm of reality, a new way of relationship, and you no longer accept certain kinds of abuse.

8

Sex: The Biggest Demon in Hell

IF WE COULD TAKE HUMANS OUT OF THE CREATION of the universe, we would see that the whole creation — the stars, the moon, the plants, the animals, everything — is perfect just the way it is. Life doesn't need to be justified or judged; without us, it keeps going the way it is. If you put humans in that creation, but take away the ability to judge, you will find we are exactly

THE MASTERY OF LOVE

like the rest of nature. We are not good or bad or right or wrong; we are just the way we are.

In the Dream of the Planet, we have the need to justify everything — to make everything good or bad or right or wrong, when it is just the way it is, period. Humans accumulate a lot of knowledge; we learn all those beliefs, morals, and rules from our family, society, religion. And we base most of our behavior, most of our feelings, on that knowledge. We create angels and demons, and of course, sex becomes the biggest demon in hell. Sex is the biggest sin of the humans, when the human body is made for sex.

You are a biological, sexual being, and that is just the way it is. Your body is so wise. All that intelligence is in the genes, in the DNA. The DNA doesn't need to understand or justify everything; it just knows. The problem is not with sex. The problem is the way we manipulate the knowledge and our judgments, when there is really nothing to justify. It's so hard for the mind to surrender, to accept that it's just the way it is. We have a whole set of beliefs about what sex should be, about how relationships should be, and these beliefs are completely distorted.

In hell, we pay a high price for a sexual encounter, but the instinct is so strong that we do it anyway. Then we have all that guilt, all that shame; we hear all that gossip about sex. "Look at what this woman is doing, ooh! Look at that man." We have a whole definition of what a woman is, what a man is, how a woman should behave sexually, how a man should behave sexually. Men are always too macho or too wimpy depending on who is judging. Women are always too thin or too fat. We have all these beliefs about how a woman should be in order to be beautiful. You have to buy the right clothes, create the right image, so you can be seductive and fit that image. If you don't fit that image of beauty, you grow up believing that you're not worthy, that no one will like you.

We believe so many lies about sex that we don't enjoy sex. Sex is for animals. Sex is evil. We should be ashamed to have sexual feelings. These rules about sex go completely against nature, and it's just a dream, but we believe it. Your true nature comes out and it doesn't fit with all those rules. You are guilty. You are not what you should be. You are judged; you are victimized. You punish yourself, and it's not fair. This creates wounds that become infected with emotional poison.

The mind plays this game, but the body doesn't care what the mind believes; the body just feels the sexual need. At a certain time in our lives, we cannot avoid feeling sexual attraction. This is completely normal; it is not a problem at all. The body is going to feel sexual when it's excited, when it's touched, when it's visually stimulated, when it sees the possibility of sex. The body can feel sexual, and a few minutes later, stop feeling sexual. If the stimulation ends, the body stops feeling the need for sex, but the mind is another story.

Let's say that you are married and were raised as a Catholic. You have all those ideas about how sex should be — about what is good or bad or right or wrong, about what is a sin and what is acceptable. You need to sign a contract to make sex okay; if you don't sign the contract, sex is a sin. You have given your word to be loyal, but one day you are walking on the street and a man crosses in front of you. You feel a strong attraction; the *body* feels the attraction. There is no problem, it doesn't mean you will take any action, but you cannot avoid the feeling because it's completely normal. When the stimulation is gone, the body lets go, but the mind needs to justify what the body feels.

The mind *knows,* and that's the problem. Your mind knows, *you* know, but what is it that you know? You know what you believe. It doesn't matter if it's good or bad, right or wrong, correct or incorrect. You are raised to believe this is bad, and right away you make that judgment. Now the drama and conflict begin.

Later you think of that man, and just thinking of him makes your hormones go up again. Because of the powerful memory that's in the mind, it's as if your body is seeing him again. The body reacts because the mind thinks about it. If the mind would leave the body alone, that reaction would go away as if it never happened. But the mind remembers it, and because you know it's not okay, you start to judge yourself. The mind says it's not okay and tries to repress what it feels. When you try to repress your mind, guess what? You think about it more. Then you see that man, and even if it's in a different situation, your body reacts more strongly.

If the first time you had just let go of the judgment, perhaps you would see him the second time and you would have no reaction at all. Now you see the man, you have sexual feelings, and you judge these feelings and think, "Oh my God, it's not okay. I'm a terrible woman." You need to be punished; you are guilty; you are going in a downward spiral, and for nothing, because it's all in the mind. Perhaps that man doesn't even notice that you exist. You start imagining the whole thing, you make assumptions, and you start to want him more. For whatever reason you meet the man, you talk to him, and it's beautiful for you. It becomes an obsession, it's very attractive, but you are afraid.

Then you make love to him, and it's the greatest thing and the worst thing at the same time. Now you really need to be punished. "What kind of woman would allow her sexual desire to be greater than her morals?" Who knows what games the mind is going to play. You hurt, but you try to deny your feelings; you try to justify your actions to avoid the emotional pain. "Well, my husband is probably the same way."

The attraction becomes stronger, but it's not because of your body; it's because the mind is playing a game. The fear becomes an obsession, and all that fear you have about your sexual attraction is building up. When you make love with this man, you have a great experience, but not because he is great, and not because the sex was great, but because all the tension, all the fear, is released. To build it up again, the mind plays the game that it's because of that man, but it isn't true.

The drama keeps growing, and it's nothing but a simple mental game. It's not even real. It's not love either, because this kind of relationship becomes very destructive. It is self-destructive, because you are hurting yourself, and the place that hurts most is what you believe. It doesn't matter if your belief is right or wrong or good or bad, you are breaking your beliefs, which is something that we wish to do, but in the way of the spiritual warrior, not the way of the victim. Now you are going to use that experience to go deeper into hell, not to get out of hell.

Your mind and your body have completely different needs, but your mind has control of your body. Your body has needs that you cannot avoid; you have to fulfill the need for food, the need for water, shelter, sleep, sex. All those needs of your body are completely normal, and it's so easy to satisfy the needs of the body. The problem is that the mind says these are *my* needs.

In the mind we create a whole picture in this bubble of illusion, and the mind takes responsibility for everything. The mind thinks it has the need for food, for water, for shelter, for clothing, for sex. But the mind has no needs at all, no physical needs. The mind doesn't need food, doesn't need oxygen, doesn't need water, doesn't need sex at all. How do we know this is true? When your mind says, "I need food," you eat, and the body is completely satisfied, but your mind still thinks it needs food. You keep eating and eating and eating, and you cannot satisfy your mind with food, because that need is not real.

The need to cover your body is another example. Yes, your body needs to be covered because the wind is too cold or because the sun is too hot, but it's your body that has the need and it's so easy to satisfy the need. When the need is in the mind, you can have tons of clothes and the mind still needs clothes. You open the closet and it's full of clothes, but your mind isn't satisfied. What does it say? "I have nothing to wear."

The mind needs another car, another vacation, a guest house for your friends — all those needs that you never can fully satisfy are in the mind. Well, it's the same with sex. When the need is in the mind, you cannot satisfy the need. When the need is in the mind, the whole judgment, the whole knowledge, is also there. This makes sex so difficult to deal with. The mind doesn't need sex. What the mind really needs is love, not sex. More than the mind, it's your soul that needs love, because your mind can survive with fear. Fear is energy also, and it's food for the mind — not exactly the food you want, but it works.

We need to give the body the freedom from the tyrant that is the mind. If we no longer have the need for food in our mind, the need for sex in our mind, everything becomes so easy. The first step is to split the needs into two categories: These are the needs of the body; these are the needs of the mind.

The mind confuses the needs of the body with its own needs because the mind needs to know: *What am I?* We live in this world of illusion, and we have no idea what we are. The mind creates all these questions. *What am I?* becomes the biggest mystery, and any answer satisfies the need to feel safe. The mind says, "I am the body. I am what I see; I am what I think; I am what I feel. I am hurting; I am bleeding."

The affinity between the mind and the body is so close that the mind believes, "I am the body." The body has a need, and the mind says, "I need." The mind takes everything about the body personally because it tries to understand *What am I?* So it is completely normal that the mind starts to gain control of the body at a certain point. And you live your life until something happens that shakes you and allows you to see what you are not.

You start to become aware when you see what you are not, when your mind starts to realize that it is not the body. Your mind says, "Then what am I? Am I the hand? If I cut off my hand, I am still me. Then I am not the hand." You take away what is not you, until in the end the only thing that remains is what you really are. It's a long process of the mind finding its own identity. In the process, you let go of the personal story, what makes you feel safe, until finally you understand what you really are.

You find out that you are not what you believe you are, because you never chose your beliefs. These beliefs were there when you were born. You find out that you are also not the body, because you start to function without your body. You start to notice that you are not the dream, that you are not the mind. If you go deeper, you start noticing that you are not the soul either. Then what you find out is so incredible. You find out that what you are is a *force* — a force that makes it possible for your body to live, a force that makes it possible for your whole mind to dream.

Without you, without this force, your body would collapse on the floor. Without you, your whole dream just dissolves into nothing. What you really are is that force that is *Life*. If you look into the eyes of someone near you, you will see the self-awareness, the manifestation of Life, shining in his eyes. Life is not the body; it is not the mind; it is not the soul. It is a force. Through this force, a newborn baby becomes a child, a teenager, an adult; it reproduces and grows old. When Life leaves the body, the body decomposes and turns to dust.

You are Life passing through your body, passing through your mind, passing through your soul. Once you find that out, not with the logic, not with the intellect, but because you can *feel* that Life — you find out that you are the force that makes the flowers open and close, that makes the hummingbird fly from flower to flower. You find out that you are in every tree, you are in every animal, vegetable, and rock. You are that force that moves the wind and breathes through your body. The whole universe is a living being that is moved by that force, and that is what you are. *You are Life.*

9

The Divine Huntress

IN GREEK MYTHOLOGY THERE IS A STORY ABOUT Artemis, the divine huntress. Artemis was the supreme huntress because the way she hunted was effortless. She fulfilled her needs so easily and lived in perfect harmony with the forest. Everything in the forest loved Artemis, and to be hunted by her was an honor. It never seemed like Artemis was hunting; whatever she needed came to her. That is why she was the best hunter, but this also made her the most difficult prey. Her animal form was a magical deer that was almost impossible to hunt.

Artemis lived in perfect harmony in the forest, until one day a king gave an order to Hercules, the son of Zeus, who was searching for his own transcendence. The order was that Hercules had to hunt the magical deer of Artemis. Hercules, being the undefeated son of Zeus, did not refuse; he went to the forest to hunt the deer. The deer saw Hercules, and she wasn't afraid of him. She let Hercules come close, but when Hercules tried to capture her, she ran. There was no way Hercules could get this deer unless he became a better hunter than Artemis.

Hercules called upon Hermes, the messenger of the Gods, the fastest one, to lend him his wings. Now Hercules was as fast as Hermes, and soon the most valuable prey was in the hands of Hercules. You can imagine the reaction of Artemis. She was hunted by Hercules, and of course she wanted to get even. She wanted to hunt Hercules, and she did her best to capture him, but Hercules was now the most difficult prey. Hercules was so free and although she tried and tried, Artemis could not capture him.

Artemis didn't need Hercules at all. She felt a strong need to have him, but of course it was only an illusion. She believed she was in love with Hercules, and she wanted him for herself. The one thing on her mind was to get Hercules, and it became an obsession until she was no longer happy. Artemis started to change. She was no longer in harmony with the forest because now she hunted just for the pleasure of getting the prey. Artemis broke her own rules and became a predator. The animals were afraid, and the forest started to reject her, but Artemis didn't care. She didn't see the truth; she only had Hercules on her mind.

Hercules had many works to do, but sometimes he would go to the forest to visit Artemis. Every time he did, Artemis did her best to hunt him. When she was with Hercules, she felt so happy to be with him, but she knew he would leave, and she became jealous and possessive. Every time Hercules left, she suffered and she cried. She hated Hercules, but she loved him also.

Hercules had no idea what was going on in the mind of Artemis; he didn't notice she was hunting him. In his mind, he was never the prey. Hercules loved and respected Artemis, but this is not what she wanted. Artemis wanted to own him; she wanted to hunt him and be the predator with him. Of course everyone in the forest noticed the difference in Artemis except her. In her mind she was still the divine huntress. She didn't have the awareness that she had fallen. She wasn't aware that the heaven that was the forest had become hell, because after her fall, the rest of the hunters fell with her; they all became predators.

One day Hermes took an animal form, and just as Artemis was ready to destroy Hermes, he became a God and she rediscovered the wisdom she had lost. He let her know she had fallen, and with this aware-ness Artemis went to Hercules to ask for his forgive-ness. It was nothing but her personal importance that brought her to that fall. In talking to Hercules she realized she had never offended him because he didn't know what was going on in her mind. Then she looked around the forest and she saw what she had done to the forest. She apologized to every flower and to every animal until she recovered love. Once again, Artemis became the divine huntress.

I tell this story to let you know that all of us are hunters, and all of us are prey. Everything that exists is both hunter and prey. What is it that we hunt? We hunt to fulfill our needs. I have talked about the needs of the body versus the needs of the mind. When the mind believes it is the body, the needs are only illusions, and they cannot be fulfilled. When we hunt those needs that are unreal in the mind, we become the predators — we are hunting for what we don't need.

Humans hunt for love. We feel that we need that love because we believe we don't have love, because we don't love ourselves. We hunt for love in other humans just like us, expecting to get love from them when these humans are in the same condition as we are. They don't love themselves either, so how much love can we get from them? We merely create a bigger need that isn't real; we keep hunting and hunting, but in the wrong place, because other humans don't have the love we need.

When Artemis became aware of her fall, she went back to herself, because everything she needed was inside herself. It is the same for all of us, because all of us are like Artemis after she fell and before her redemption. We are hunting for love. We are hunting for justice and happiness. We are hunting for God, but God is inside us.

The hunting of the magical deer teaches you that you have to hunt inside yourself. This is a great story to keep in mind. If you remember the story of Artemis, you will always find the love inside you. Humans who hunt each other for love will never be satisfied; they will never find the love they need in other humans. The mind feels the need, but we cannot fulfill it, because it isn't there. *It's never there.*

The love we need to hunt is inside ourselves, but that love is difficult prey. It is so difficult to hunt inside yourself, to get that love from inside you. You have to be very fast, as fast as Hermes, because anything can distract you from your goal. Whatever traps your attention distracts you from reaching your goal, from getting the prey that is the love inside. If you can capture the prey, you will see that your love can grow strong inside you, and it can fulfill all your needs. This is so important for your happiness.

Usually humans go into relationships as the hunter. They look for what they feel they need, hoping to find what they need in the other person, only to find that it's not there. When you enter a relationship without this need, it's a different story.

How do you hunt inside yourself? To capture the love inside yourself, you have to surrender to yourself as the hunter and the prey. Inside your own mind, there is the hunter and there is also the prey. Who is the hunter, who is the prey? In ordinary people the hunter is the Parasite. The Parasite knows everything about you, and what the Parasite wants are the emotions that come from fear. The Parasite is a garbage eater. It loves fear and drama; it loves anger, jealousy, and envy; it loves any emotion that makes you suffer. The Parasite wants to get even, and it wants to be in control.

Your self-abuse, as the Parasite, is hunting you twenty-four hours a day; it is always after you. So we become the prey of the Parasite, a very easy prey. The Parasite is the one who abuses you. It is more than a hunter; it is a predator, and it is eating you alive. The prey, the emotional body, is that part of us that suffers and suffers; it's that part of us that wants to be redeemed.

In Greek mythology, there is also the story of Prometheus, who is chained to a rock. During the day an eagle comes and eats his innards; during the night he recovers. Every day the eagle comes and eats his insides again. What does this mean? When Prometheus is awake, he has a physical and emotional body. The eagle is the Parasite that is eating his insides. During the night, he doesn't have the emotional body, and he recovers. He is born again to be the food for that eagle, until Hercules comes to release him. Hercules is like the Christ, Buddha, or Moses who breaks the chain of suffering and gives you your freedom.

To hunt inside yourself, you start by hunting every reaction you have. You are going to change one routine at a time. It is a war for freedom from the Dream that controls your life. It is a war between you and the predator with the Truth in the middle. In all the Western traditions from Canada to Argentina, we call ourselves warriors because a warrior is the hunter who hunts herself. It is a big war, because it's a war against the Parasite. To be a warrior doesn't mean you will win the war, but at least you rebel, and you no longer accept that the Parasite is eating you alive.

Becoming the hunter is the first step. When Hercules went into the forest in search of Artemis, there was no way he could capture the deer. Then he went to Hermes, the supreme teacher, and he learned to become a better hunter. He needed to be better than Artemis in order to hunt her. To hunt yourself, you also need to be a better hunter than the Parasite.

If the Parasite is working twenty-four hours a day, you also have to work twenty-four hours a day. The Parasite has an advantage: It knows you very well. There is no way you can hide. The Parasite is the most difficult prey. It's that part of you that tries to justify your behavior in front of other people, but when you are alone, it is the worst judge. It is always judging, blaming, and making you feel guilty.

In a normal relationship in hell, the Parasite of your partner allies with your Parasite against the real you. You have against yourself not just your own Parasite, but the Parasite of your partner, who aligns with your Parasite to make the suffering eternal. If you know that, you can make a difference. You can have more compassion for your partner and allow her to deal with her own Parasite. You can be happy every time your partner takes another step toward freedom. You can be aware that when your partner gets upset, gets sad or jealous, it's not the one you love that you are dealing with at that moment. It's a Parasite that is possessing your partner.

Knowing the Parasite is there, and knowing what is going on in your partner, you can give your partner the space to deal with it. Since you are only responsible for your half of the relationship, you can allow her to deal with her own personal dream. In that way, it will be easy not to take personally what your partner is doing. This will help your relationship a lot, because nothing that your partner does is personal. Your partner is dealing with her own garbage. If you don't take it personally, it will be so easy for you to have a wonderful relationship with your partner.

10

Seeing With Eyes of Love

IF YOU LOOK AT YOUR BODY, YOU WILL FIND billions of living beings who depend on you. Every cell in your body is a living being that depends on you. You are responsible for all of those beings. For all those living beings that are your cells, you are God. You can provide what they need; you can love all those living beings, or you can be so mean to them.

THE MASTERY OF LOVE

The cells in your body are completely loyal to you; they work for you in harmony. We can even say they pray to you. You are their God. That is absolutely the truth. Now what are you going to do with this knowledge?

Remember, the whole forest was in complete harmony with Artemis. When Artemis fell, she lost respect for the whole forest. When she recovered her awareness, Artemis went from flower to flower to say, "I am sorry; now I will take care of you again." And the relationship between Artemis and the forest became a love relationship again.

The whole forest is your body, and if you just acknowledge this truth, you will say to your body, "I am sorry; now I will take care of you again." The relationship between you and your body, between you and all those living cells that depend on you, can become the most beautiful relationship. Your body and all those living cells are perfect in their half of the relationship, just like the dog is perfect in its half. The other half is your mind. Your body takes care of its half of the relationship, but the mind is the one

SEEING WITH EYES OF LOVE

that abuses the body, that mistreats the body, that gets so mean with the body.

Just look at the way you treat your cat or your dog. If you can treat your body the same way you treat your pet, you will see that it's about love. Your body is willing to receive all the love from the mind, but the mind says, "No, I don't like this part of my body. Look at my nose; I don't like my nose. My ears — they are too large. My body is too fat. My legs are too short." The mind can imagine all kinds of things about the body.

Your body is perfect the way it is, but we have all those concepts about right and wrong, good and bad, beautiful and ugly. These are just concepts, but we believe them, and that's the problem. With the image of perfection we have in our mind, we expect our body to look a certain way, to act a certain way. We reject our own body when the body is completely loyal to us. Even when our body can't do something because of its limitations, we push our body and our body at least tries.

Look at what you do with your own body. If you reject your own body, what can other people expect from you? If you accept your own body, you can accept almost everyone, almost everything. This is a very important point when it comes to the art of relationship. The relationship you have with yourself is reflected in your relationships with others. If you reject your own body, when you are sharing your love with your partner, you become shy. You think, "Look at my body. How can he love me when I have a body like this?" Then you reject yourself and make the assumption that the other person will reject you for the same thing you reject in yourself. And when you reject someone else, you reject him for the same things you reject in yourself.

To create a relationship that takes you all the way to heaven, you have to accept your body completely. You have to love your body and allow your body to be free to just be, to be free to give, free to receive, without being shy, because "shy" is nothing but fear.

Imagine how you see your pet dog. You see the dog with eyes of love and you enjoy the beauty of that dog. It doesn't make any difference whether that dog is beautiful or ugly. You can go into ecstasy just seeing the beauty of that dog, because it's not about possessing beauty. Beauty is just a concept we learned.

Do you think a turtle or a frog is ugly? You can see a frog, and the frog is beautiful; it's gorgeous. You can see a turtle, and it's beautiful. Everything that exists is beautiful — everything. But you think, "Oh, that is ugly," because someone made you believe what is ugly and what is beautiful, just as someone made you believe what is good and what is bad.

There's no problem at all with being beautiful or ugly, short or tall, thin or heavy. There's no problem with being gorgeous. If you walk through a crowd of people, and they tell you, "Oh, you are beautiful," you can say, "Thank you, I know," and keep going. It doesn't make any difference to you. But it will make a difference to you if you don't believe you are beautiful and someone tells you that. Then you are going to say, "Am I really?" This opinion can impress you, and, of course, that makes you easy prey.

This opinion is what you think you need, because you believe you are not beautiful. Remember the story of the Magical Kitchen? If you have all the food you need, and someone asks you to let him control you for food, you say, "No, thank you." If you wish to be beautiful, but you don't believe you are, and someone says, "I will always tell you how beautiful you are if you just let me control you," you will say, "Oh yes, please tell me I'm beautiful." You are going to allow that to happen because you think you need that opinion.

What is important are not all those opinions from others, but your own opinions. You are beautiful no matter what your mind tells you. That is a fact. You don't have to do anything because you already have all the beauty you need. To be beautiful you don't have any obligation to anyone. Others are free to see whatever they want to see. If others see you and judge you beautiful or not, if you are aware of your own beauty and accept your own beauty, their opinion doesn't affect you at all.

Perhaps you grew up believing that you are unattractive and you envy beauty in others. Then to justify the envy, you tell yourself, "I don't want to be beautiful." You may even have a fear of being beautiful. This fear can come from many directions, and it's not the same for everyone, but often it is the fear of your own power. Women who are beautiful have power over men, and not just over men, but over women. Other women who are not as beautiful as you are, may envy you because you attract the attention of men. If you dress a certain way and all the men are crazy about you, what are the women going to say about you? "Oh, she's a loose woman." You become afraid of all those judgments people have about you. This is nothing but concepts again, nothing but false beliefs that open wounds in the emotional body. Then, of course we have to cover these wounds with lies and denial systems.

Envy is also a belief that can easily be broken with awareness. You can learn to deal with the envy of other women or other men because the truth is that each of you is beautiful. The only difference between the beauty of one person and the beauty of another is the concept of beauty that people have.

Beauty is nothing but a concept, nothing but a belief, but you can believe in that concept of beauty, and base all your power on that beauty. Time passes, and you see you are getting old. Perhaps you are not as beautiful as you were from your point of view, and a younger woman comes along who is now the one who is beautiful. Time for plastic surgery, to try to keep the power because we believe that our beauty is our power. Our own aging starts to hurt us. "Oh my god, my beauty is going away. Will my man still love me if I am not as attractive? Now he can see other women who are more attractive than me."

We resist aging; we believe that because someone is old, it means she is not beautiful. This belief is completely wrong. If you see a newborn baby, it is beautiful. Well, an old person is also beautiful. The problem is the emotion we have in our eyes to perceive what is and what is not beautiful. We have all these judgments, all these programs that put limits on our own happiness, that push us to self-rejection and to reject other people also. Can you see how we play the drama, how we set ourselves up to fail with all these beliefs?

Aging is something beautiful, just as growing up is beautiful. We grow from a child, to a teenager, to a young woman or a young man. It is beautiful. To become an old woman or an old man is also beautiful. In the life of humans, there are certain years when we actively reproduce. During those years, we may want to be sexually attractive, because nature makes us that way. After that, we don't have to be sexually attractive from that point of view, but it does not mean we are not beautiful.

You are what you believe you are. There is nothing to do except to be just what you are. You have the right to feel beautiful and enjoy it. You can honor your body and accept it as it is. You don't need anyone to love you. Love comes from the inside. It lives inside us and is always there, but with that wall of fog, we don't feel it. You can only perceive the beauty that lives outside you when you *feel* the beauty that lives inside you.

You have a belief about what is beautiful and what is ugly, and if you don't like yourself, you can change your belief and your life will change. It sounds simple, but it isn't easy. Whoever controls the belief, controls the dream. When the dreamer finally controls the dream, the dream can become a masterpiece of art.

You can begin by doing a *puja* for your body every day. In India, people perform pujas, or rituals, for the different Gods and Goddesses. In the puja, they bow to the idol, they put flowers near the idol, and they feed the idol with all their love, because these statues represent God. Every day, you can offer a devotional love to your own body. When you take a shower, when you take a bath, treat your body with all your love, treat your body with honor, with gratitude, with respect. When you eat, take a bite, close your eyes, and enjoy the food. That food is an offering to your own body, to the temple where God lives. Do this every day, and you will feel your love for your body growing stronger each day, and you will never again reject yourself.

Just imagine how you will feel the day you adore your own body. When you accept yourself completely, you will feel so good about your own body, and you are going to be so happy. Then when you relate with someone else, your limit of self-abuse is almost zero. This is self-love. This is not personal importance because you treat others with the same love, the same honor, the same respect, and the same gratitude you use with yourself. Can you see the perfection in a relationship like that? It's about honoring the God inside each other.

When you make it your goal to create the perfect relationship between you and your body, you are learning to have a perfect relationship with anyone you are with, including your mother, your friends, your lover, your children, your dog. When you have the perfect relationship between you and your body, in that moment your half of any relationship outside you is completely fulfilled. You no longer depend upon the success of a relationship from the outside.

When you do a puja with your own body, when you know how to have that devotion for your own body, and you touch your lover's body, you touch it with the same devotion, the same love, the same honor, the same gratitude. And when your lover touches your body, it's completely open; there is no fear, there is no need — it is full of love.

Imagine all the possibilities in sharing your love this way. You don't even need to touch. Just looking into each other's eyes is enough to fulfill the needs of the mind and the needs of the soul. The body is already satisfied because it has all your love. You are never lonely anymore, because you are fulfilled with your own love.

Wherever you turn your face, you will be fulfilled by love, but not from other humans. You can see a tree and feel all the love coming from the tree to you. You can see the sky, and it's going to fulfill the needs of your mind for love. You will see God everywhere, and it will no longer be just a theory. *God is everywhere. Life is everywhere.*

Everything is made by *Love*, by *Life*. Even fear is a reflection of love, but fear exists in the mind, and in humans, that fear controls the mind. Then we interpret everything according to what we have in our mind. If we have fear, what we perceive will be analyzed with fear. If we are mad, what we perceive will be perceived according to anger. Our emotions act like a filter through which we see the rest of the world.

You could say that the eyes are an expression of what you feel. You perceive the outside Dream according to your eyes. When you are angry, you see the world with eyes of anger. If you have eyes of jealousy, your reactions will be different, because the way you see the world is through jealousy. When you have the eyes of madness, everything will bother you. If you have the eyes of sadness, you are going to cry because it's raining, because there is noise, because of everything. Rain is rain. There is nothing to judge or interpret, but you are going to see the rain according to your emotional body. If you are sad, you see with the eyes of sadness, and everything you perceive will be sad.

But if you have the eyes of love, you just see love wherever you go. The trees are made with love. The animals are made with love. The water is made with love. When you perceive with the eyes of love, you can connect your will with the will of another dreamer, and the dream becomes one. When you perceive with love, you become one with the birds, with nature, with a person, with everything. Then you can see with the eyes of an eagle or transform into any kind of life. With your love you connect with the eagle and you become the wings, or you become the rain, or the clouds. But to do this, you need to clean the mind of fear and perceive with eyes of love. You have to develop your will until it is so strong that it can hook the other will and become one will. Then you have wings to fly. Or being the wind, you can come here, you can go there, you can push away the clouds and the sun is shining. This is the power of love.

When we fulfill the needs of our mind and our body, our eyes see with love. We see God everywhere. We even see God behind the Parasite of other people.

Inside every human is the Promised Land that Moses promised his people. That Promised Land is in the realm of the human mind, but only the mind that is fertile for Love, because that is where God lives. If you see the ordinary human mind, it is also a fertile land, but for the Parasite that grows the seeds of envy, anger, jealousy, and fear.

In the Christian tradition, you hear of Gabriel coming with the trumpet for the Resurrection, and everyone comes out of his grave to live the Eternal Life. That grave is the Parasite and the Resurrection is the return to *Life*, because you are alive only when your eyes can see *Life*, which is *Love*.

You can have a relationship that fulfills your dream of Heaven; you can create a Paradise, but you have to begin with you. Begin with complete acceptance of your body. Hunt the Parasite, and make it surrender. Then the mind will love your body and will no longer sabotage your love. It's up to you; it's not up to anyone else. But first, you are going to learn how to heal your emotional body.

11

Healing the Emotional Body

LET'S IMAGINE AGAIN THAT WE HAVE A SKIN disease with wounds that are infected. When we want to heal the skin, and we go to a doctor, the doctor is going to use a scalpel to open the wounds. Then the doctor is going to clean the wounds, apply medicine, and keep the wounds clean until they heal and no longer hurt us.

To heal the emotional body, we are going to do the same thing. We need to open the wounds and clean the wounds, use some medicine, and keep the wounds clean until they heal. How are we going to open the wounds? We are going to use the truth as a scalpel to open the wounds. Two thousand years ago, one of the greatest Masters told us, "And you will know the truth, and the truth will set you free."

The truth is like a scalpel because it is painful to open our wounds and uncover all of the lies. The wounds in our emotional body are covered by the denial system, the system of lies we have created to protect those wounds. When we look at our wounds with eyes of truth, we can finally heal these wounds.

You begin by practicing the truth with yourself. When you are truthful with yourself, you start to see everything as it is, not the way you want to see it. Let's use an example that is emotionally charged: rape.

Let's say that someone raped you ten years ago, and it is true that you were raped. Right now, it is no longer true. It was a dream, and in that dream someone abused you with violence. You didn't look for that. It was nothing personal. For whatever reason, it happened to you and can happen to anyone. But by being raped, will you condemn yourself to suffer in your sexuality for the rest of your life? The rapist is not condemning you to do that. You are the victim, and if you judge yourself and find yourself guilty, for how many years will you punish yourself by not enjoying something that is one of the most beautiful things in the world? Sometimes being raped can destroy your sexuality for the rest of your life. Where is the justice? You are not the rapist, so why should you suffer the rest of your life for something you didn't do? You are not guilty for being raped, but the Judge in your mind can make you suffer and live in shame for many years.

Of course, this injustice will create a strong emotional wound and a lot of emotional poison that could take years of therapy to be released. The truth is that, yes, you were raped, but it's no longer true that you must suffer this experience. That is a choice.

This is the first step in using the truth as a scalpel: You find that the injustice that created a wound is no longer true, right now, in this moment. You discover that perhaps what you *believe* hurt you so badly was never true. Even if it was true, it doesn't mean that *now* it is true. By using the truth, you open the wound and see the injustice from a new perspective.

The truth is relative in this world; it's changing all the time because we live in a world of illusions. What is true right now is not true later. Then it could be true again. The truth in hell could also be just another concept, another lie that can be used against you. Our own denial system is so powerful and strong that it becomes very complicated. There are truths covering lies, and lies covering truth. Like peeling an onion, you uncover the truth little by little until in the end, you open your eyes to find out that everyone around you, including yourself, is lying all the time.

Almost everything in this world of illusion is a lie. That is why I ask my apprentices to follow three rules for seeing what is true. The first rule is: *Don't believe me.*

You don't have to believe me, but think, and make choices. Believe what you want to believe according to what I say, but only if it makes sense for you, if it makes you happy. If it guides you into your awakening, then make the choice to believe it. I am responsible for what I say, but I am not responsible for what you understand. We live in a completely different dream. What I say, even if it is absolutely true for me, is not necessarily true for you. The first rule is very easy: *Don't believe me.*

Rule number two is more difficult: *Don't believe yourself.* Don't believe all the lies you tell yourself — all those lies that you never chose to believe, but were programmed to believe. Don't believe yourself when you say you are not good enough, you are not strong enough, you are not intelligent enough. Don't believe your own boundaries and limitations. Don't believe you are unworthy of happiness or love. Don't believe you are not beautiful. Don't believe whatever makes you suffer. Don't believe in your own drama. Don't believe in your own Judge or your own Victim. Don't believe the inner voice that tells you how stupid you are, that tells you to kill yourself. Don't believe it, because it isn't true. Open your ears, open your heart, and listen. When you hear your heart guiding you to your happiness, then make a choice and stick to it. But don't believe yourself just because you say so, because more than 80 percent of what you believe is a lie — it isn't *true*. The second rule is a difficult one: *Don't believe yourself.*

Rule number three is: *Don't believe anyone else.* Don't believe other people because they are lying all the time anyway. When you no longer have emotional wounds, when you don't have the need to believe other people just to be accepted, you see everything more clearly. You see if it is black or white, if it is or is not. What is right now, maybe in a few moments is not. What is not right now, maybe in a few moments will be. Everything is changing so fast, but if you are aware, you can see the change. Don't believe others because they will use your own stupidity to manipulate your mind. Don't believe anyone who says she comes from Pleiades and she wants to save the world. Bad news!

We don't need anyone to come and save the world. The world doesn't need the aliens to come from the outside to save us. The world is alive; it's a living being, and it's more intelligent than all of us together. If we believe the world needs to be saved, soon someone will come and say, "Okay, a comet is coming, we need to escape from the planet. Kill yourself and boom! You will reach the comet and go to heaven." Don't believe these mythologies. You create your own dream of heaven; no one can create it for you. Nothing but common sense will guide you to your own happiness, your own creation. Rule number three is difficult because we have the need to believe other people. *Don't believe them.*

Don't believe me, don't believe yourself, and don't believe anyone else. By not believing, whatever is untrue will disappear like smoke in this world of illusion. Everything is what it is. You don't need to justify what is true; you don't need to explain it. What is true doesn't need anyone's support. Your lies need your support. You need to create a lie to support the first lie, another lie to support that lie, and more lies to support all of those lies. You create a big structure of lies, and when the truth comes out, everything falls apart. But that's just the way it is. You don't need to feel guilty because you are lying.

Most of the lies we believe simply dissipate if we don't believe them. Whatever is not true will not survive skepticism, but the truth will always survive skepticism. What is truth is true, believe it or not. Your body is made of atoms. You don't have to believe it. Believe it or not, it is true. The universe is made of stars; this is true, believe it or not. Only what is true will survive, and that includes the concepts you have about yourself.

We have said that when we were children, we didn't have the opportunity to choose what to believe and what not to believe. Well, now it is different. Now that we are grown, we have the power to make a choice. We can believe or not believe. Even if something is not the truth, if we choose to believe it, we can believe it just because we *want* to believe it. You can choose how you want to live your life. And if you are honest with yourself, you will know you are always free to make new choices.

When we are willing to see with eyes of truth, we uncover some of the lies and open the wounds. Still, there is the poison inside the wounds.

Once we open the wounds, we are going to clean the wounds of all the poison. How are we going to do this? The same Master gave us the solution two thousand years ago: Forgiveness. There is no other way but forgiveness to clean the wounds of all the poison.

You must forgive those who hurt you, even if whatever they did to you is unforgivable in your mind. You will forgive them not because they deserve to be forgiven, but because you don't want to suffer and hurt yourself every time you remember what they did to you. It doesn't matter what others did to you, you are going to forgive them because you don't want to feel sick all the time. Forgiveness is for your own mental healing. You will forgive because you feel compassion for yourself. Forgiveness is an act of self-love.

Let's take an example of a divorced woman. Imagine you have been married for ten years, and for whatever reason you have a big fight with your husband over a big injustice. You get divorced, and you really hate your ex-husband. Just hearing his name, you feel a strong pain in your stomach and you want to throw up. The emotional poison is so strong that you can't stand it any longer. You need help, so you go to a therapist and say, "I am suffering so much. I am full of anger, jealousy, envy. What he did is unforgivable. I hate that man."

The therapist looks at you and says, "You need to release your emotions; you need to express your anger. What you should do is have a big tantrum. Get a pillow, bite the pillow, hit the pillow, and release your anger." You go and have the biggest tantrum, and you release all these emotions. It really seems to work. You pay your therapist $100 and say, "Thank you very much. I feel much better." Finally, you have a big smile on your face.

You walk out of the therapist's office, and guess who is driving through town? As soon as you see your ex-husband, the same anger comes up, but even worse. You have to run to the therapist again and pay another $100 for another tantrum. Releasing your emotions in this way is only a temporary solution. It may release some poison and make you feel better for a while, but it does not heal the wound.

The only way to heal your wounds is through forgiveness. You have to forgive your ex-husband for the injustice. You will know you have forgiven someone when you see him and you don't feel anything anymore. You will hear the name of the person and have no emotional reaction. When you can touch a wound and it doesn't hurt, then you know you have truly forgiven. Of course, a scar is going to be there, just as it is on your skin. You will have a memory of what happened, of how you used to be, but once the wound has healed, it won't hurt you any longer.

Perhaps you are thinking, "Well, it's easy to say we should forgive. I have tried, but I cannot do it."

You have all these reasons, all these justifications why you cannot forgive. But this is not the truth. The truth is that you cannot forgive because you learned not to forgive, because you practiced not to forgive, because you mastered not to forgive.

There was a time when we were children when forgiveness was our instinct. Before we caught the mental disease, it was effortless and natural to forgive. We used to forgive others almost right away. If you see two children playing together, and they start to fight and hit each other, the children cry and run to their mothers. "Hey, she hit me!" One mother goes to talk with the other mother. The two mothers have a big fight, and five minutes later the two children are playing together again as if nothing happened. Now the mothers hate each other for the rest of their lives.

It is not that we need to learn forgiveness, because we are born with the capacity for forgiveness. But guess what happened? We learned the opposite behavior, and we practiced the opposite behavior, and now forgiveness is very difficult. Whoever does something to us, forget it, that's it, she is out of our life. It becomes a war of pride. Why? Because our personal importance grows when we don't forgive. It makes our opinion more important when we can say, "Whatever she does, I will not forgive her. What she did is unforgivable."

The real problem is pride. Because of pride, because of honor, we add more fire to the injustice to remind ourselves that we cannot forgive. Guess who is going to suffer and accumulate more and more emotional poison? We are going to suffer for all kinds of things people do around us, even though they have nothing to do with us.

We also learn to suffer just to punish whoever abused us. We behave like a little child having a tantrum, just asking for attention. I'm hurting myself just to say, "Look at what I am doing because of you." It's a big joke, but that's exactly what we do. What we really want to say is, "God, forgive me," but we will not say a word until God comes and asks us for forgiveness first. Many times we don't even know why we are so upset with our parents, our friends, our mate.

We are upset, and if for some reason the other person asks us for forgiveness, right away we start to cry and say, "Oh no, you forgive me."

Go and find the little child in the corner having a tantrum. Take your pride and put it in the trash. You don't need it. Just let go of the personal importance and ask for forgiveness. Forgive others, and you will see miracles start to happen in your life.

First, make a list of everyone you believe you need to ask for forgiveness. Then ask them for forgiveness. Even if there is not enough time to call everyone, ask for their forgiveness in your prayers and through your dreams. Second, make a list of all the people who hurt you, all the people you need to forgive. Start with your parents, your brothers and sisters, your children, your spouse, your friends, your lover, your cat, your dog, your government, and God.

Now, you are going to forgive others by knowing that whatever anyone did to you had nothing to do with you. Everyone dreams her own dream, remember? The words and actions that hurt you are merely a reaction to the demons in that person's own mind. She is dreaming in hell, and you are a secondary character in her dream. Nothing anyone does is because of you. Once you have this awareness, and you do not take it personally, compassion and understanding will lead you to forgiveness.

Start working on forgiveness; start practicing forgiveness. It will be difficult at first, but then it just becomes a habit. The only way to recover forgiveness is to practice again. You practice and practice, until in the end you see if you can forgive yourself. At a certain point, you find that you must forgive yourself for all those wounds and all that poison you created for yourself in your own dream. When you forgive yourself, self-acceptance begins and self-love grows. That is the supreme forgiveness — when you finally forgive yourself.

Create an act of power and forgive yourself for everything you have done in your whole life. And if you believe in past lives, forgive everything you believe you did in all of your past lives. The concept of karma is true only because we believe it is true. Because of our beliefs about being good and bad, we feel ashamed about what we believe is bad. We find ourselves guilty, we believe we deserve to be punished, and we punish ourselves. We have the belief that what we create is so dirty that it needs to be cleaned. And just because you believe it, then, *"Thy will be done."* It is real for you. You create your karma, and you have to pay for it. That is how powerful you are. To break old karma is simple. You just stop that belief by refusing to believe it, and the karma is gone. You don't need to suffer, you don't need to pay anything; it is over. If you can forgive yourself, the karma is gone just like that. From this point on, you can start all over again. Then life becomes easy, because forgiveness is the only way to clean the emotional wounds. Forgiveness is the only way to heal them.

Once we have cleaned the wounds, we are going to use a powerful medicine to accelerate the process of healing. Of course, the medicine also comes from the same great Master: It is Love. Love is the medicine that accelerates the process of healing. There is no other medicine but unconditional love. Not: I love you *if*, or I love myself *if*. There is no *if*. There is no justification. There is no explanation. It is just to love. Love yourself, love your neighbor, and love your enemies. This is simple, common sense, but we cannot love others until we love ourselves. That is why we must begin with self-love.

There are millions of ways to express your happiness, but there is only one way to really be happy, and that is to love. There is no other way. You cannot be happy if you don't love yourself. That is a fact. If you don't love yourself, you don't have any opportunity to be happy. You cannot share what you do not have. If you do not love yourself, you cannot love anyone else either. But you can have a need for love, and if there's someone who needs you, that's what humans call love. That is not love. That is possessiveness, that is selfishness, that is control with no respect. Don't lie to yourself; that is not love.

Love coming out of you is the only way to be happy. Unconditional love for yourself. Complete surrender to that love for yourself. You no longer resist life. You no longer reject yourself. You no longer carry all that blame and guilt. You just accept who you are, and accept everyone else the way he or she is. You have the right to love, to smile, to be happy, to share your love, and to not be afraid to receive it also.

That is the healing. Three simple points: the truth, forgiveness, and self-love. With these three points, the whole world will heal and will no longer be a mental hospital.

These three keys to heal the mind were given to us by Jesus, but he is not the only one who taught us how to heal. Buddha did the same; Krishna did the same. Many other Masters came to the same conclusions and gave us these same lessons. All around the world, from Japan to Mexico to Peru to Egypt to Greece, there were humans who were healed. They saw that the disease is in the human mind, and they used these three methods: the truth, forgiveness, and self-love. If we can see our state of mind as a disease, we find there is a cure. We don't have to suffer any longer; if we are aware that our mind is sick, that our emotional body is wounded, we can also heal.

Just imagine if all humans could start being truthful with themselves, start forgiving everyone, and start loving everyone. If all humans loved in this way, they would no longer be selfish; they would be open to give and receive, and they would no longer judge each other. Gossiping would be over, and the emotional poison would simply dissolve.

Now we are talking about a completely different Dream of the Planet. It doesn't look like the planet Earth. This is what Jesus called "Heaven on Earth," Buddha called "Nirvana," and Moses called "The Promised Land." It is a place where all of us can live in love because we put our attention on love. We choose to love.

Whatever you call the new Dream, it is still a dream as real or as false as the dream of hell. But now you can choose which dream you want to live in. Now you have the tools in your hands to heal yourself. The question is: What are you going to do with them?

12

God Within You

YOU ARE THE FORCE THAT PLAYS WITH YOUR mind and uses your body as its favorite toy to play and have fun with. That is the reason you are here: to play and have fun. We are born with the right to be happy, with the right to enjoy life. We are not here to suffer. Whoever wants to suffer is welcome to suffer, but we don't have to suffer.

Then why do we suffer? Because the whole world suffers, and we make the assumption that suffering is normal. Then we create a belief system to support that "truth." Our religions tell us that we came here to suffer, that life is a valley of tears. Suffer today, have patience, and when you die you will have your reward. Sounds beautiful, but it isn't true.

We choose to suffer because we learned to suffer. If we continue to make the same choices, we will continue to suffer. The Dream of the Planet carries the story of humanity, the evolution of humans, and suffering is the result of human evolution. Humans suffer because we *know*: We know what we believe, we know all those lies, and because we can't fulfill all those lies, we suffer.

It's not true that you go to hell or to heaven after you die. You live in hell or you live in heaven, but now. Heaven and hell only exist in the level of the mind. If we suffer now, when we die we still suffer, because the mind doesn't die with the brain. The dream continues and when our dream is hell, our brain dies and we are still dreaming in the same hell. The only difference between being dead and being asleep is that when we are sleeping we can awake because we have a brain. When we are dead, we cannot awake because we don't have a brain, but the dream is there.

Heaven or hell is here and now. You don't need to wait to die. If you take responsibility for your own life, for your own actions, then your future is in your hands, and you can live in heaven while the body is alive.

The dream most humans create on this planet is obviously hell. This isn't right or wrong or good or bad, and there is no one to blame. Can we blame our parents? No. They did the best they could when they programmed you as a little child. Their own parents did the same with them: the best they could. If you have children, you couldn't know what else to do either. How can you blame yourself? To become aware doesn't mean you need to blame anyone, or carry guilt for what you have done. How can we carry guilt or blame for a mental disease that is seriously contagious?

You know, everything that exists is perfect. You are perfect just the way you are. That is the truth. You are a master. Even if you master anger and jealousy, your anger and jealousy are perfect. Even if you have a big drama going on in your life, it's perfect, it's beautiful. You can go to a movie like *Gone with the Wind* and cry for all that drama. Who says that hell is not beautiful? Hell can inspire you. Even hell is perfect, because only perfection exists. Even if you dream hell in your life, you are perfect just the way you are.

It is only knowledge that makes us believe we are not perfect. Knowledge is nothing more than a description of the Dream. The Dream is not real, so knowledge isn't real either. Wherever knowledge comes from, it is only real from one point of perception. Once you shift the perception, it is no longer real. We are never going to find ourselves with our knowledge. In the end that is what we are looking for: to find ourselves, to be ourselves, to live our own life, instead of the life of the Parasite — the life we were programmed to live.

It isn't knowledge that will lead us to ourselves; it is wisdom. We have to make a distinction between knowledge and wisdom, because they are not the same.

The main way to use knowledge is to communicate with each other, to agree on what we perceive. Knowledge is the only tool we have to communicate, because humans hardly communicate heart to heart. What is important is how we use our knowledge, because we become the slaves of knowledge and we are no longer free.

Wisdom has nothing to do with knowledge; it has to do with freedom. When you are wise, you are free to use your own mind and run your own life. A healthy mind is free of the Parasite; it is free again the way it was before domestication. When you heal your mind, when you break free of the Dream, you are no longer innocent, but wise. You become just like a child again in many ways, except for one big difference: A child is innocent, and that's why he can fall into suffering and unhappiness. The one who transcends the Dream is wise; that is why she doesn't fall anymore, because now she *knows* — she also has knowledge of the Dream.

You don't need to accumulate knowledge to become wise; anyone can become wise. Anyone. When you become wise, life becomes easy, because you become who you really are. It's difficult to try to be what you are not, to try to convince yourself and everyone else that you are what you are not. Trying to be what you are not expends all your energy. Being what you are doesn't require any effort.

When you become wise, you don't have to use all those images you created; you don't have to pretend to be something else. You accept yourself the way you are, and the complete acceptance of yourself becomes the complete acceptance of everyone else. You no longer try to change other people or impose your point of view. You respect other people's beliefs. You accept your body and your own humanity with all the instincts of your body. There is nothing wrong with being an animal. We are animals, and animals always follow their instinct. We are humans, and because we are so intelligent, we learn to repress our instincts; we don't listen to what comes from the heart. That's why we go against our own body and try to repress the needs of the body or deny they exist. This is not wise.

When you become wise, you respect your body, you respect your mind, you respect your soul. When you become wise, your life is controlled by your heart, not your head. You no longer sabotage yourself, your own happiness, or your own love. You no longer carry all that guilt and blame; you no longer have all those judgments against yourself, and you no longer judge anyone else. From that moment on, all the beliefs that make you unhappy, that push you to struggle in life, that make your life difficult, just vanish.

Surrender all those ideas about being what you are not, and become what you really are. When you surrender to your nature, to what you really are, you no longer suffer. When you surrender to the real you, you surrender to Life, you surrender to God. Once you surrender, there is no longer a struggle, there is no resistance, there is no suffering.

Being wise, you always go for the easy way, which is to be yourself, whatever you are. Suffering is nothing but resistance to God. The more you resist, the more you suffer. It is simple.

Imagine that from one day to another, you awake from the Dream and you are completely healthy. You no longer have wounds, you no longer have emotional poison. Imagine the freedom you are going to experience. Everything is going to make you happy just to be alive, wherever you go. Why? Because the healthy human being is not afraid to express love. You are not afraid to be alive, and you are not afraid to love. Imagine how you would live your life, how you would treat the people you are close to, if you no longer had those wounds and that poison in your emotional body.

In the mystery schools around the world, this is called the awakening. It is as if you awake one day, and you no longer have emotional wounds. When you no longer have those wounds in the emotional body, the boundaries disappear, and you start to see everything as it is, not according to your belief system.

When you open your eyes and you don't have those wounds, you become a skeptic — not to increase your personal importance by telling everyone how intelligent you are, or to make fun of other people who believe in all those lies. No, when you awake, you become a skeptic because it's clear in your eyes that the Dream is not true. You open your eyes, you are awake, and everything becomes obvious.

When you awake, you cross a line of no return, and you never see the world in the same way. You are still dreaming — because you cannot avoid dreaming, because dreaming is the function of the mind — but the difference is that you know it's a dream. Knowing that, you can enjoy the dream or suffer the dream. That depends on you.

The awakening is like being at a party where there are thousands of people and everyone is drunk except you. You are the only sober person in the party. That is the awakening, because the truth is that most humans see the world through their emotional wounds, through their emotional poison. They don't have the awareness that they are living in a dream of hell. They aren't aware that they are living in a dream just as fish swimming in water are not aware that they are living in water.

When we awake and we are the only sober person in the party where everyone is drunk, we can have compassion because we were drunk too. We don't need to judge, not even people in hell, because we, too, were in hell.

When you awake, your heart is an expression of the Spirit, an expression of Love, an expression of Life. The awakening is when you have the awareness that *you are Life.* When you are aware that you are the force that is Life, anything is possible. Miracles happen all the time, because those miracles are performed by the heart. The heart is in direct communion with the human soul, and when the heart speaks, even with the resistance of the head, something inside you changes; your heart opens another heart, and true love is possible.

There is a an old story from India about the God, Brahma, who was all alone. Nothing existed but Brahma, and he was completely bored. Brahma decided to play a game, but there was no one to play the game with.

So he created a beautiful goddess, Maya, just for the purpose of having fun. Once Maya existed and Brahma told her the purpose of her existence, she said, "Okay, let's play the most wonderful game, but you have to do what I tell you to do." Brahma agreed, and following Maya's instructions, he created the whole universe. Brahma created the sun and the stars, the moon and the planets. Then he created life on earth: the animals, the oceans, the atmosphere, everything.

Maya said, "How beautiful is this world of illusion you created. Now I want you to create a kind of animal that is so intelligent and aware that it can appreciate your creation." Finally Brahma created humans, and after he finished the creation, he asked Maya when the game was going to start.

"We will start right now," she said. She took Brahma and cut him into thousands of teeny, tiny pieces. She put a piece inside every human and said, "Now the game begins! I am going to make you forget what you are, and you are going to try to find yourself!" Maya created the Dream, and still, even today,

Brahma is trying to remember who he is. Brahma is there inside you, and Maya is stopping you from remembering what you are.

When you awake from the Dream, you become Brahma again, and reclaim your divinity. Then if Brahma inside you says, "Okay, I am awake; what about the rest of me?" you know the trick of Maya, and you can share the truth with others who are going to wake up too. Two people who are sober in the party can have more fun. Three people who are sober is even better. Begin with you. Then others will start to change, until the whole dream, the whole party, is sober.

The teachings that come from India, from the Toltecs, the Christians, the Greeks — from societies all over the world — come from the same truth. They talk about reclaiming your Divinity and finding God within you. They talk about having your heart completely open and becoming wise. Can you imagine what kind of world this would be if all humans opened their hearts and found the love inside? Of course we can do it. Everyone can do it in his own way. It's not about following any imposed idea; it's about finding yourself, and expressing yourself in your own particular way. That is why your life is an art. Toltec means "artist of the spirit." The Toltecs are the ones who can express with the heart, the ones who have unconditional love.

You are alive because of the power of God, which is the power of Life. You are the force that is Life, but because you are able to think at the level of the mind, you forget what you really are. Then it's easy to see someone else and say, "Oh, there is God. God will be responsible for everything. God will save me." No. God has just come to tell you — to tell the God in you — to be aware, to make a choice, to have the courage to work through all your fears and change them, so you are no longer afraid of love. The fear of love is one of the biggest fears that humans have. Why? Because in the Dream of the Planet, a broken heart means "Poor me."

Perhaps you wonder, "If we are truly Life or God, why don't we know it?" Because we are programmed not to know. We are taught: "You are a human; these are your limitations." Then we limit our possibilities by our own fears. You are what you believe you are. Humans are powerful magicians. When you believe you are what you are, then that is what you are. And you can do that because you are Life, God, Intent. You have the power to make yourself what you are right now. But it's not your reasoning mind that controls your power; it's what you believe.

You see, everything is about belief. Whatever we believe rules our existence, rules our life. The belief system we create is like a little box we put ourselves inside of; we cannot escape because we believe we cannot escape. That is our situation. Humans create their own boundaries, their own limitations. We say what is humanly possible, and what is not possible. Then just because we believe it, it becomes truth for us.

The prophecies of the Toltecs have foreseen the beginning of a new world, a new humanity where humans take responsibility for their own beliefs, for their own lives. The time is coming when you will become your own guru. You don't need other humans to tell you what the Will of God is. Now it's you and God face-to-face, without any intermediary. You were searching for God, and you found God within you. God is no longer there, outside you.

When you know that the power that is Life is inside you, you accept your own Divinity, and yet you are humble, because you see the same Divinity in everyone else. You see how easy it is to understand God, because everything is a manifestation of God. The body is going to die, the mind is going to dissolve also, but not you. You are immortal; you exist for billions of years in different manifestations, because you are Life, and Life cannot die. You are in the trees, the butterflies, the fish, the air, the moon, the sun. Wherever you go, you are there, waiting for yourself.

Your body is a temple, a living temple where God lives. Your mind is a living temple where God lives. God is living within you as Life. The proof that God lives within you is that you are alive. Your Life *is* the proof. Of course, in your mind there is garbage and emotional poison, but God is also there.

You don't have to do anything to reach God, to reach enlightenment, to awaken. There is no one who can take you to God. Whoever says they will take you to God is a liar, because you are already there. There's only one living being, and want it or not, resist it or not, effortlessly you are with God already.

The only thing left is to enjoy your life, to be alive, to heal your emotional body so you can create your life in such a way that you openly share all the love inside you.

The whole world can love you, but that love will not make you happy. What will make you happy is the love coming out of you. That is the love that will make a difference, not the love everyone has for you. Your love for everyone is your half; the other half can be a tree, it can be a dog, it can be a cloud. You are one half; the other half is what you perceive. You are the half as a dreamer, and the dream is the other half.

You are always free to love. If your choice is to be in a relationship, and your partner is playing the same game, what a gift! When your relationship is completely out of hell, you will love yourselves so much that you don't need each other at all. By your own will, you get together and create beauty. And what the two of you are going to create is a dream of heaven.

You have already mastered fear and self-rejection; now you are returning to self-love. You can be so strong and so powerful that with your self-love you transform your personal dream from fear to love, from suffering to happiness. Then just like the sun, you are giving light and giving love all the time, with no conditions. When you love with no conditions, you the human, and you the God, align with the Spirit of Life moving through you. Your life becomes the expression of the beauty of the Spirit. Life is nothing but a dream, and if you create your life with Love, your dream becomes a masterpiece of art.

Prayers

PLEASE TAKE A MOMENT TO CLOSE YOUR EYES, OPEN your heart, and feel all the love that is coming from your heart.

I want you to join me in a special prayer to experience a communion with our Creator.

Focus your attention on your lungs, as if only your lungs existed. Feel the pleasure when your lungs expand to fulfill the biggest need of the human body: to breathe.

Take a deep breath and feel the air as it fills your lungs. Feel how the air is made of love. Notice the connection between the air and the lungs, a connection of love. Expand your lungs with air until your body has the need to expel that air. Then exhale, and feel the pleasure again. When we fulfill any need of the human body, it gives us pleasure. To breathe gives us pleasure. Just to breathe is enough for us to always be happy, to enjoy life. Just to be alive is enough. Feel the pleasure of being alive, the pleasure of the feeling of love. . . .

PRAYER FOR AWARENESS

Today, Creator of the Universe, we ask that you open our heart and open our eyes so we can enjoy all of your creations and live in eternal love with you. Help us to see you in everything we perceive with our eyes, with our ears, with our heart, with all our senses. Let us perceive with eyes of love so that we find you wherever we go and see you in everything you create. Let us see you in every cell of our body, in every emotion of our mind, in every dream, in every flower, in every person we meet. You cannot hide from us because you are everywhere, and we are one with you. Let us be aware of this truth.

Let us be aware of our power to create a dream of heaven where everything is possible. Help us to use our imagination to guide the dream of our life, the magic of our creation, so we can live without fear, without anger, without jealousy, without envy. Give us a light to follow, and let today be the day that our search for love and happiness is over. Today let something extra-ordinary happen that will change our life forever: Let everything we do and say be an expression of the beauty in our heart, always based on love.

Help us to be the way you are, to love the way you love, to share the way you share, to create a masterpiece of beauty and love, the same way that all of your creations are masterpieces of beauty and love. Begin-ning today and gradually over time, help us to increase the power of our love so that we may create a master-piece of art — our own life. Today, Creator, we give you all of our gratitude and love because you have given us Life. Amen.

PRAYER FOR SELF-LOVE

Today, Creator of the Universe, we ask that you help us to accept ourselves just the way we are, without judgment. Help us to accept our mind the way it is, with all our emotions, our hopes and dreams, our personality, our unique way of being. Help us to accept our body just the way it is, with all its beauty and perfection. Let the love we have for ourselves be so strong that we never again reject ourselves or sabotage our happiness, freedom, and love.

From now on, let every action, every reaction, every thought, every emotion, be based on love. Help us, Creator, to increase our self-love until the entire dream of our life is transformed, from fear and drama to love and joy. Let the power of our self-love be strong enough to break all the lies we were pro-grammed to believe — all the lies that tell us we are not good enough, or strong enough, or intelligent enough, that we cannot make it. Let the power of our self-love be so strong that we no longer need to live our life according to other people's opinions. Let us trust ourselves completely to make the choices we must make. With our self-love, we are no longer afraid to face any responsibility in our life or face any problems and resolve them as they arise. Whatever we want to accomplish, let it be done with the power of our self-love.

Starting today, help us to love ourselves so much that we never set up any circumstances that go against us. We can live our life being ourselves and not pretending to be someone else just to be accepted by other people. We no longer need other people to accept us or tell us how good we are because we know what we are. With the power of our self-love, let us enjoy what we see every time we look in the mirror. Let there be a big smile on our face that enhances our inner and outer beauty. Help us to feel such intense self-love that we always enjoy our own presence.

Let us love ourselves without judgment, because when we judge, we carry blame and guilt, we have the need for punishment, and we lose the perspective of your love. Strengthen our will to forgive ourselves in this moment. Clean our minds of emotional poison and self-judgments so we can live in complete peace and love.

Let our self-love be the power that changes the dream of our life. With this new power in our hearts, the power of self-love, let us transform every relationship we have, beginning with the relationship we have with ourselves. Help us to be free of any conflict with others. Let us be happy to share our time with our loved ones and to forgive them for any injustice we feel in our mind. Help us to love ourselves so much that we forgive anyone who has ever hurt us in our life.

Give us the courage to love our family and friends unconditionally, and to change our relationships in the most positive and loving way. Help us to create new channels of communication in our relationships so there is no war of control, there is no winner or loser. Together let us work as a team for love, for joy, for harmony.

Let our relationships with our family and friends be based on respect and joy so we no longer have the need to tell them how to think or how to be. Let our romantic relationship be the most wonderful relationship; let us feel joy every time we share ourselves with our partner. Help us to accept others just the way they are, without judgment, because when we reject them, we reject ourselves. When we reject ourselves, we reject you.

Today is a new beginning. Help us to start our life over beginning today with the power of self-love. Help us to enjoy our life, to enjoy our relationships, to explore life, to take risks, to be alive, and to no longer live in fear of love. Let us open our heart to the love that is our birthright. Help us to become Masters of Gratitude, Generosity, and Love so that we can enjoy all of your creations forever and ever. Amen.

DON MIGUEL RUIZ IS THE INTERNATIONAL BESTSELLING author of *The Four Agreements, The Four Agreements Companion Book, The Mastery of Love, The Voice of Knowledge, The Circle of Fire,* and *The Fifth Agreement* (with don Jose Ruiz). His books have sold over 10 million copies in the United States and have been translated into 40 languages worldwide.

Ruiz has dedicated his life to imparting the wisdom of the ancient Toltec. Today, he continues to share his unique blend of ancient wisdom and modern-day aware- ness through lectures, workshops, and journeys to sacred sites around the world. For information about current programs offered by don Miguel Ruiz and his sons, don Miguel Ruiz, Jr. and don Jose Ruiz, please visit:

MiguelRuiz.com

JANET MILLS IS THE FOUNDER OF AMBER-ALLEN PUBLISHING. She is also the coauthor, with don Miguel Ruiz, of six books in *The Toltec Wisdom Series,* creator of *The Four Agreements for a Better Life* online course, and editor of Deepak Chopra's bestselling title, *The Seven Spiritual Laws of Success.* Her life's mission is to publish books of enduring beauty, integrity, and wisdom, and to inspire others to fulfill their most cherished dreams.

The Circle of Fire* (Formerly Published as *Prayers*)

A beautiful collection of essays, prayers, and guided meditations that will inspire and transform your life. (Available in Spanish as *Oraciones.*)

The Voice of Knowledge*

Ruiz reminds us of a profound and simple truth: The only way to end our emotional suffering and restore our joy in living is to stop believing in lies — mainly about ourselves.

The Voice of Knowledge Audiobook

In this abridged reading of *The Voice of Knowledge*, actor Peter Coyote brings to life Ruiz's profound teachings on how we can return to our authentic state of truth, love, and joy.

The Fifth Agreement*

Ruiz joins his son, don Jose Ruiz, to encourage us to see the truth, to recover our authenticity, and to change the message we deliver to ourselves and to everyone around us.

The Fifth Agreement Audiobook*

In this unabridged reading of *The Fifth Agreement*, actor Peter Coyote lends his powerful voice to the timeless wisdom of don Miguel Ruiz and his son, don Jose Ruiz.

Toltec Wisdom Card Decks
Each card deck contains 48 beautifully illustrated cards with pearls of wisdom from *The Four Agreements* and *The Fifth Agreement.*

The Four Agreements for a Better Life (Online Course)
Take the course and begin a journey of personal transformation unlike any other. Watch inspiring videos, deepen your understanding and practice of The Four Agreements, download a poster, read our blog, and become a member of a worldwide community of people who are dedicated to changing their lives for the better by practicing The Four Agreements. For information about the online course and other ways to support your practice of The Four Agreements, please visit TheFourAgreements.com.

⁎ Also Available in Spanish

For information about other bestselling titles from
Amber-Allen Publishing, please visit:
AmberAllen.com